"Let God Be True"

"'What if some did not believe? shall their unbelief make the faith of God without effect? God forbid: yea, let God be true, but every man a liar; as it is written, That thou mightest be justified in thy sayings."
—Romans 3:3, 4.

PUBLISHERS

WATCHTOWER BIBLE AND TRACT SOCIETY, INC.
INTERNATIONAL BIBLE STUDENTS ASSOCIATION
Brooklyn, New York, U. S. A.

First Edition
10,519,680 Copies
REVISED April 1, 1952
Second Edition
6,500,000 Copies
Printed in 50 languages

DEDICATED to the Most High,
"a God of truth," and in behalf of the "other sheep" of
His Right Shepherd.

—Deuteronomy 32:4
John 10:11, 14, 16, *NW*.

Abbreviations of Bible versions quoted or cited in this book

AS – American Standard Version, by the American Committee of Revision

AT – An American Translation, by J. M. P. Smith and E. J. Goodspeed

CB – The Holy Bible, translated by the Catholic Biblical Association of America

Dy – Translation of the Latin Vulgate made at Douay and Rheims

ED – The Emphatic Diaglott, by Benjamin Wilson (1864)

Le – The Twenty-four Books of the Holy Scriptures, by Isaac Leeser (1853)

Mo – A New Translation of The Bible, by James Moffatt

NW – New World Translation of the Christian Greek Scriptures, 2d edition

Ro – The Emphasised Bible, a New Translation, by J. B. Rotherham

Yg – The Holy Bible, translated by Robert Young

Any quotation not followed by any specific
abbreviation should be understood to be made
from the Authorized or King James Version.

CONTENTS

CHAPTER I

"LET GOD BE FOUND TRUE"

TO WIN the confidence of intelligent living creatures God must be true. He must be faithful to his promise, reliable regarding his prophecies, and harmonious with proved scientific facts. There is such a God of truth. But not only have those who are his outspoken enemies tried to discredit him, but also most of those who claim to be his servants, priests and ministers. These religious hypocrites have gone so far as to pit their word, their wisdom, philosophies, predictions and plans against God's word, law and purposes. So in this day when all unfounded theories and systems are being shaken from top to bottom, the issue has now become, Who is to be found true, God or man?

[2] The vast universe which we see is founded upon truth, and therefore it moves on orderly and undisturbed despite the waywardness of men on earth. Its Creator is the great God of truth. He is the One whom the peoples of Christendom have all claimed to worship in common, but their centuries-old religious differences, quarrels and errors have brought reproach upon both Him and the written Word which he has given mankind. Bewildered seekers for truth have in many cases

---

1. To win our confidence what must God be, and what has become the issue today?
2. (a) Why could not the Bible be subject to any old interpretation? (b) To what kind of Bible study are readers of this book invited and led?

7

said in hopelessness: "Oh, the Bible is an old fid-
dle upon which you can play any old tune." If
true, that would mean that the Bible's Author was
all mixed up and divided against himself. But this
could not be so of the God whose visible creation
of the universe is marvelously harmonious and at
unity with itself. Reasonably, then, his Book, the
Bible, could not be all mixed up and allowing any
interpretation to be made of it. The mix-up lies
with its would-be interpreters, the religious leaders of this so-called "Christendom", who disagree
among themselves, and violently so at times.
Hence, as the reader approaches the study of the
Bible with this book in hand, he is neither being
invited nor being led to study God's Word according to the perplexing, mysterious religious errors
of Christendom. He is asked to study according to
what God himself has to say in his own Word.
"For God is not a God of confusion, but of peace."*

³ To arrive at truth we must dismiss religious
prejudices from heart and mind. We must let God
speak for himself. Any other course would lead
only to further confusion. What if men, religious
and nonreligious, have discredited and belittled
the Bible and have placed men's opinions and traditions above it? What if religious leaders have rejected the Bible's straight testimony? What if the
highly esteemed clergy of Christendom have been
found false and misleading? Do these shocking and
disappointing facts change the Bible itself or its
message of truth? Sound thinking assures us that
the true and living God must have given searching

---

* Quoted from 1 Corinthians 14:33, AS.

3, 4. (a) To arrive at truth, what must we do? (b) In
view of the faithlessness of men, what stand should
we take?

mankind some inspired written revelation about himself. That being so, then let our stand be that of one of the Bible writers who said: "What, then, is the case? If some did not express faith, will their lack of faith perhaps make the faithfulness of God without effect? Never may that happen! But LET GOD BE FOUND TRUE, though every man be found a liar, even as it is written: 'That you might be vindicated in your words and might win when you are being judged.' "†

⁴ The writer just quoted was an honest man who was courageous enough to confess he was an erring sinner and to justify God as being true in every case. He said to God: "Against thee, thee only, have I sinned, and done that which is evil in thy sight. Inasmuch as thou art in the right when thou speakest, and pure when thou givest judgment."* If we let God be found true, he will instruct us in the truth by his recorded Word.

⁵ To let God be found true means to let God have the say as to what is the truth that sets men free. It means to accept his Word, the Bible, as the truth. Hence, in this book, our appeal is to the Bible for truth. Our obligation is to back up what is said herein by quotations from the Bible for proof of truthfulness and reliability. That is the course the inspired writers and faithful characters of the Bible took and recommended. Isaiah, a major prophet, asked God's chosen people: When spiritualists advise you to inquire of mediums and wizards who whisper and mutter mysteriously,

---

† Quoted from Romans 3:3, 4, *NW*.

* Quoted from Psalm 51:4, *AT*.

---

5. (a) What does it mean to let God be found true? (b) Why is the study course of this book in harmony with Isaiah 8:20?

ought you not as God's people inquire rather of him? Should you try to inquire of the dead in behalf of the living? Then Isaiah gave the safe advice: "(Hold) to the law and to the testimony: if they are not to speak according to this word, in which there is no light." (Isaiah 8:19, 20, *Le*) "To the law rather, and to the testimony. And if they speak not according to this word, they shall not have the morning light." (Isaias 8:20, *Dy*) There is no light of truth in the teachings of worldly men who are under the influence of superhuman invisible demons, wicked spirits who are primarily responsible for the darkness of this world. Unless we seek direct to the law and testimony of God's written Word, we shall never attain to the light the beams of which show that the morning of a new world of righteousness is at hand.

[6] Malachi, the very last of the old Hebrew prophets, pointed in the same direction that Isaiah did, to God's written Word. As an inspired spokesman for God Malachi said: "Remember ye the law of Moses my servant, whom I commanded on Horeb for all Israel, statutes and ordinances." (Malachi 3:22, *Le*) The writings of the prophet Moses make up the first five books of the present-day Bible; and thus the last of the old Hebrew prophets declares himself in agreement with the very first Bible writer, although Moses preceded him by more than a thousand years. All Bible writers in between Moses and Malachi take the same position; and in his record Moses himself preserved the inspired utterances of prophets of God who preceded him.

---

6. How do the first and the last of the writers of the old Hebrew Scriptures, as well as the writers in between, stand as to teaching?

⁷ None of the Bible writers, from Malachi back to Moses, make any mention of an oral law or traditional law as existing alongside the written Word of God. Nowhere do they declare that the oral traditions of religious men are on an equality with the recorded Word of God or that the written Word is incomplete without such oral traditions. The prophet Moses earnestly declared against adding the oral traditions of uninspired men to God's given law and testimony. Moses said: "Ye shall not add unto the word which I command you, nor shall ye diminish aught from it; that ye may keep the commandments of the LORD your God which I command you." (Deuteronomy 4:2, Le) God's written Word is pure without such man-made traditions; and those who teach and hold to such traditions and who value them as equal to the written Word or even higher than it make liars of themselves. "Every saying of God is purified: he is a shield unto those that put their trust in him. Do not add aught unto his words: lest he reprove thee, and thou be found a liar."—Proverbs 30:5, 6, Le.

⁸ God inspired his prophet Isaiah to speak out in strong words against those who claim to be God's people but who practice hypocrisy by following the precepts and traditions of men rather than the inspired Scriptures. "And the Lord said, Forasmuch as this people draw near with their mouth, and with their lips do honour me, but have removed their heart far from me, and their fear toward me is but the acquired precept of men: therefore, behold, I will do yet farther a marvel-

7. What do Moses and the Proverbs show as to the so-called "oral law" or traditional law?

8. With what strong words did Isaiah speak against those following human traditions and precepts?

lous work with this people, doing wonder on wonder; so that the wisdom of their wise men shall be lost, and the understanding of their prudent men shall be hidden."—Isaiah 29:13, 14, *Le*.

WRITTEN WORD VERSUS TRADITION

[9] Because of this very controversy over the traditions and precepts of religious leaders the great Teacher from Nazareth came into conflict with the rabbis of the first century of the Christian era. About this we read the following record: "Then Scribes and Pharisees from Jerusalem came to him, saying, 'Why do thy disciples transgress the tradition of the ancients? For they do not wash their hands when they take food.' But he answered and said to them, 'Why do you too transgress the commandment of God because of your tradition? For God said, "Honor thy father and thy mother"; and, "Let him who curses father or mother be put to death." But you say, "Whoever shall say to his father or mother, 'Any support thou mightest have had from me is dedicated to God,' does not have to honor his father or his mother." So you have made void the commandment of God by your tradition. Hypocrites, well did Isaias prophesy of you, saying, "This people honors me with their lips, but their heart is far from me; but in vain do they worship me, teaching for doctrines precepts of men."'" (Matthew 15:1-9, *CB*) Thus the religious traditionalists were proved to be liars and breakers of God's written law; whereas the honest Teacher from Nazareth was letting God be found true because he appealed to God's written Word and followed it.

---

9. What controversy over tradition is recorded at Matthew 15:1-9, and who were proved true and who liars?

[10] This is certain: The old Hebrew Scriptures do not teach us to put faith in the oral traditions of religionists. Such traditions men have since recorded and published as being equal to the inspired Scriptures or even superior to the Scriptures where there is a conflict between the two. During our first century the inspired Christian Scriptures were written in Greek, but neither do these teach us to accept and rely upon the traditions and moral precepts of men who claim to be Christian clergy. Hundreds of times those Christian Greek Scriptures quote and refer to God's written Word contained in the Hebrew Scriptures. Those Scriptures were the only ones Jesus of Nazareth had in those days, and referring to them in prayer to God for his disciples he said: "Sanctify them by means of the truth; your word is truth." (John 17:17, *NW*) When he was tempted by the great adversary during his forty days of isolation in the wilderness, he resisted the enemy's attacks by using the written Word of God. He used it to show the adversary to be a liar. In meeting the first temptation he said: "*It is written,* 'Man must live, not on bread alone, but on every utterance coming forth through Jehovah's mouth.'" In foiling the second temptation he

"It is written"

10. (a) What is certain concerning the position of all the Holy Scriptures toward human traditions? (b) How did Jesus, in prayer and in temptation, show regard for the written Word?

said: "Again *it is written,* 'You must not put Jehovah your God to the test.'" In turning back the third temptation he said: "Go away, Satan! For *it is written,* 'It is Jehovah your God you must worship, and it is to him alone you must render sacred service.'" In each case Jesus quoted God's Word as written down by the prophet Moses.—Matthew 4:4, 7, 10, *NW;* Deuteronomy 8:3; 6:16; 6:13.

¹¹ In declaring his mission on earth Jesus, while at the synagogue in Nazareth, called for the Scripture roll of the prophecy of Isaiah and read from its sixty-first chapter, verses one and two. (Luke 4:16-21) He later said: "Do not think I came to destroy the Law or the Prophets. I came, not to destroy, but to fulfill; for truly I say to you that sooner would heaven and earth pass away than for the smallest letter or one particle of a letter to pass away from the Law by any means and not all things take place." To the religionists who did not believe in him he gave the advice to believe God's written Word: "You are searching the Scriptures, because you think that by means of them you will have everlasting life; and these are the very ones that bear witness about me. In fact, if you believed Moses you would believe me, for that one wrote about me. But if you do not believe the writings of that one, how will you believe my sayings?"—Matthew 5:17, 18 and John 5:39, 46, 47, *NW.*

¹² Finally, by the aid of a traitor, his religious enemies were able to take him under illegal arrest.

---

11. How did Jesus further show regard for the Scriptures in preaching and in advising the unbelieving religionists?
12. Why did he not resist when his enemies arrested him? and how some days later did he magnify God's Word to his disciples?

Why did he refuse to resist them? Because he gave the truth to God's Word. He said to his disciples in support of God's Word: "I tell you that this which is written must be accomplished in me, namely, 'And he was reckoned with lawless ones.' For that which concerns me is having an accomplishment." (Luke 22:37, *NW*) Some days later, when explaining his strange experiences to his astonished followers, he again magnified God's written Word as true by pointing out how it had been fulfilled in him. Of his conversation with two of his disciples we read: "Commencing at Moses and all the Prophets he interpreted to them things pertaining to himself in all the Scriptures." Later, in conversation with a larger group of disciples, he said: "These are my words which I spoke to you while I was yet with you, that all the things written in the law of Moses and in the Prophets and Psalms about me must be fulfilled." "Then he opened up their minds fully to grasp the meaning of the Scriptures, and he said to them: 'In this way it is written.' " (Luke 24:27, 44-46, *NW*) In no case did he appeal to the rabbinic schools of teaching with their traditions and precepts of men. He faithfully referred his disciples to God's Word, thereby to glorify God as true, though at the same time it proved the publicly respected religious leaders liars.

[13] The case of Jesus of Nazareth is an example. It makes certain that men who follow the interpretations of religionists and who put human traditions before the sacred written Word will surely oppose and persecute his faithful followers who

---

13. What does Jesus' case make certain as to followers of traditions? and how does his disciple Paul use himself as an example?

proclaim God's pure Word. One of Jesus' own followers uses himself as an illustration to show how
a blind adherence to religious traditions and systems leads a person into opposition to those who
hold to God's Word as true. Paul, a follower of
Jesus, makes this confession: "You, of course,
heard about my conduct formerly in Judaism, that
to the point of excess I kept on persecuting the
congregation of God and devastating it, and I was
making greater progress in Judaism than many
of my own age in my race, as I was far more zeal-
ous for the traditions of my fathers."—Galatians
1:13, 14, *NW*.

¹⁴ Paul knew how the religious traditions had
for a time blinded him to the truth in the writings
of Moses and of the other prophets and the Psalms.
He also foreknew that men pretending to be Christian clergymen would develop a system of religious
traditions and precepts and would thereby hide the
truth from the members of the religious organizations. So he wrote: "Beware lest any man cheat
you by philosophy and vain deceit; according to
the tradition of men, according to the elements
of the world and not according to Christ." (Colossians 2:8, *Dy*) Paul knew that such traditions
would be lies and would offer a way of salvation
different from what is contained in the inspired
written Word of God. The people of today whom
religious traditions have misled away from the
good news as recorded in the sacred Bible do well
to consider Paul's counsel, namely: "There are
some who trouble you, and wish to pervert the
gospel of Christ. But even if we or an angel from
heaven should preach a gospel to you other than

14. What warnings did Paul write concerning the setting up of a system of religious traditions?

that which we have preached to you, let him be anathema! As we have said before, so now I say again: If anyone preach a gospel to you other than that which you have received, let him be anathema!"—Galatians 1:7-9, *CB*.

¹⁵ Therefore Paul stuck close to God's written Word when he taught and preached. He also allowed his hearers to check up on him with their copies of the Scriptures. In fact, Paul's personal physician, Luke, pronounced those persons noble who did so, rather than denouncing them for reading the Bible to test the truthfulness of an *apostle*. Luke writes: "The brethren immediately sent away Paul and Silas by night unto Berea. Who, when they were come thither, went into the synagogue of the Jews. Now these were more noble than those in Thessalonica, who received the word with all eagerness, daily searching the scriptures, whether these things were so." (Acts 17:10, 11, *Dy*) Hence, when a religious organization forbids its members to read the Bible and requires its members to accept what its clergymen teach without comparing their teachings with the Holy Scriptures, such religious organization belies its claim that it is apostolic.

PETER'S POSITION TOWARD THE WORD

¹⁶ Paul's fellow apostle, Peter, was of the same mind on the matter of giving first place to the Holy Scriptures. Peter quoted again and again from the Hebrew Scriptures and wrote: "But *the*

---

15. Therefore what course did Paul pursue toward God's Word? and what is the noble course toward those who preach?

16. How did Peter show the same mind as Paul on the matter?

word of the Lord endureth for ever. And this is the word which by the gospel hath been preached unto you."—1 Peter 1:25, *Dy.*

[17] Nowhere in Peter's writings or in his recorded utterances does he claim infallibility or assume any high-sounding religious titles or ask for worshipful honors to be rendered him. Always he turns his hearers or readers to the changeless Word of God as their shining guide until the day of God's kingdom dawns. Peter writes: "We have the word of prophecy, surer still, to which you do well to attend, as to a lamp shining in a dark place, until the day dawns and the morning star rises in your hearts. This, then, you must understand first of all, that no prophecy of Scripture is made by private interpretation. For not by will of man was prophecy brought at any time; but holy men of God spoke as they were moved by the Holy Spirit. But there were false prophets also among the people, just as among you there will be lying teachers who will bring in destructive sects. They even disown the Lord who bought them, thus bringing upon themselves swift destruction. . . . be mindful of what I formerly preached of the words of the holy prophets and of your apostles, which are the precepts of the Lord and Savior."—2 Peter 1:19 to 2:1; 3:2, *CB.*

[18] Therefore in this book in the hands of the reader we choose to follow the apostolic course. We shall let God be found true by turning our readers to his imperishable written Word. Knowing that God by his holy spirit inspired the Holy Scriptures, thus making them reliable, we choose

---

17. Does Peter seek to exalt himself? and why does he urge Christians to take heed to God's written Word?
18. How does this book follow the apostolic course?

to let him do the interpreting. How? By his records of fulfilled prophecy and by the things he has caused to occur in modern history to fulfill prophecies due to come to pass in our day. "Doth not interpretation belong to God?" (Genesis 40:8, *Dy*) Yes, and his interpretation is the true one. Accordingly this book will be found filled with Scripture quotations and references, and we suggest that our readers look up in their Bibles all the unquoted references and read them therefrom.

[19] Our readers will quickly observe in this book that quotations are made from various editions of the Bible, Jewish, Roman Catholic and others, according as each best makes clear the sense of the original Hebrew and Greek text. Turn back and see the list of the Bible versions quoted or cited, on page 5 of this book. The questions at the bottom of the pages are for the reader's self-examination on what he has read in the paragraphs, or for use in Bible study classes with others. The chapters following this one are devoted to a progressive investigation of the primary or essential teachings of the divine Word.

---

19. How about the quotations, printed questions, and chapter contents of this book?

CHAPTER II

"WHO IS JEHOVAH?"

"WHO is Jehovah?" That is an old question. When it was first asked in that tone, by Pharaoh of Egypt in the sixteenth century B.C., it was asked defiantly and with contempt, and the questioner added: "that I should hearken unto his voice to let Israel go? I know not Jehovah, and moreover I will not let Israel go." This challenge called forth the following words of comfort to the prophet Moses: "Pharaoh will not hearken unto you, and I will lay my hand upon Egypt, and bring forth my hosts, my people the children of Israel, out of the land of Egypt by great judgments. And the Egyptians shall know that I am Jehovah, when I stretch forth my hand upon Egypt, and bring out the children of Israel from among them."—Exodus 5:2 and 7:4, 5, *AS*.

[2] In the Bible Egypt is used as a small-scale pattern of this entire world of today. Hence in those words concerning Egypt a prophetic notice is served that shortly all the world will learn and know that the only living and true God is He who is named Jehovah, but in a manner that they will not enjoy. It is therefore well to learn now who and what he is, that we may act now with benefit to ourselves.

1, 2. When was "Who is Jehovah?" first asked, and with what importance?

[3] When Moses stood before Egypt's Pharaoh and made God's demands upon him, Moses uttered the name of the God who sent him. Moses did not say, '*The Lord* says so and so'; because Pharaoh and the Egyptians worshiped and acknowledged their own false gods as *lords*. Even when addressing his own people in Egypt to explain his return to them, Moses spoke the name of God to identify the particular One sending him back to Egypt. We read: "God said unto Moses, I AM THAT I AM: and he said, Thus shalt thou say unto the children of Israel, I AM [Hebrew: *Ehyeh*] hath sent me unto you. And God said moreover unto Moses, Thus shalt thou say unto the children of Israel, Jehovah, the God of your fathers, the God of Abraham, the God of Isaac, and the God of Jacob, hath sent me unto you: this is my name for ever, and this is my memorial unto all generations." (Exodus 3:14, 15, *AS*) After Moses and his brother Aaron had appeared before Pharaoh for the first time, we read, "God spake unto Moses, and said unto him, I am Jehovah: and I appeared unto Abraham, unto Isaac, and unto Jacob, as God Almighty; but by my name Jehovah I was not known to them." —Exodus 6:2, 3, *AS*.

[4] We cannot escape it. If we read his written Word, we are faced with the name of God. Nothing is gained by arguing that the name is not correctly pronounced as *Jehovah*. The Scriptures written before the Christian era were written practically all in Hebrew, a portion in Aramaic; and

---

3. By what term did Moses refer to God before Pharaoh and Israel?

4. How does God's name appear in the Hebrew Scriptures, and did his name appear in the Greek *Septuagint Version?*

in those Scriptures the alphabetic letters for God's name occur, namely, Yod He Waw He (יהוה, or YHWH), from the first book to the last. The name, symbolized by these four Hebrew consonants, occurs, all together, 6,823 times* in the Hebrew Scriptures. The Hebrew Scriptures began to be translated into Greek about 280 B.C. But some time before that superstitious Hebrews began to leave off pronouncing the name, out of a fear of taking it in vain. So whenever they read and came to the name, they pronounced instead the word *Adonay* (Lord) or *Elohim* (God). However, in making that first translation into Greek known as the *Septuagint Version* (*LXX*) the translators did not follow this custom but put the four Hebrew letters (יהוה) for God's name into their Greek version.

⁵ The writers of the Christian Greek Scriptures used that *Septuagint Version* and they quoted its Greek text which contained the literal name of Almighty God. But later copyists of the *Septuagint* began to omit the divine name in Hebrew letters and to substitute for it the Greek words meaning "Lord" or "God". Then Bible translators began to follow this rabbinic custom, which partly explains why the name does not occur by itself in most translations of the Christian Greek Scriptures. Jerome, in making the Latin *Vulgate* translation, followed the same practice, and at Exodus 6:3 he used the title *Adonai* instead of *Jehovah,* all of which explains why the name does not occur in the English Roman Catholic *Douay Version*. In the

* Page 39 ¶ 2 of *The Biblical Text in the Making,* by Robt. Gordis. Also *Lexicon in Veteris Testamenti Libros,* by Koehler-Baumgartner.

5. Why does the name "Jehovah" not occur in most translations of the Christian Greek Scriptures? But why is use of the name helpful?

Authorized or *King James Version* we find the name "Jehovah" by itself at Exodus 6:3; Psalm 83:18; and Isaiah 12:2 and 26:4. *The Emphasised Bible* by J. B. Rotherham renders the name in its 6,823 occurrences as "Yahweh"; but the *American Standard Version* renders it every time as "Jehovah". Even if neither of these pronunciations may be just as God pronounced his name to Moses, yet it helps us to identify instantly who is meant by that name. In like manner the name "Jesus" is not the original way this one's name was pronounced in the Hebrew or Aramaic; nevertheless this near pronunciation helps us to identify at once who is meant and it does not do any dishonor or blasphemy to him.

[6] To illustrate: The Catholic *Douay Version* reads, at Psalm 109:1, 2: "The Lord said to my Lord: Sit thou at my right hand: until I make thy enemies thy footstool. The Lord will send forth the sceptre of thy power out of Sion: rule thou in the midst of thy enemies." But the *American Standard Version,* at this same psalm of King David (Psalm 110:1, 2), reads: "Jehovah saith unto my Lord, Sit thou at my right hand, until I make thine enemies thy footstool. Jehovah will send forth the rod of thy strength out of Zion: Rule thou in the midst of thine enemies." Thus this latter translation, by honestly giving due value to God's name, does away with all confusion of mind; it shows that the one whom David called "My Lord" is the Messiah, whom Jehovah makes a King and Priest after the likeness of Melchizedek. When the *Authorized* or *King James Version* translates God's name by the title "Lord" or

6. What is a good illustration of the helpfulness of this name?

"God", it always puts this title in all capital letters, as "LORD", "GOD," to distinguish it from the common words "Lord" and "God".—Note this at Psalm 110:1.

WHO HE IS

[7] By looking up the verses where the name occurs in the Hebrew Bible we are enabled to find the answer to the question, Who is Jehovah? At Psalm 90 the prophet Moses writes: "Lord, thou hast been our dwelling-place in all generations. Before the mountains were brought forth, or ever thou hadst formed the earth and the world, even from everlasting to everlasting, thou art God. Return, O Jehovah; how long? and let it repent thee concerning thy servants." (Psalm 90:1, 2, 13, *AS*) Who, then, is Jehovah? He is God and, as such, never had a beginning. His eternalness is declared also at Isaiah 57:15: "Thus saith the high and lofty One that inhabiteth eternity, whose name is Holy; I dwell in the high and holy place." In view of his eternity, it is outright blasphemy to speak of any woman as "the mother of God", for woman is merely a lowly creature whom God created for man as man's helper.

[8] Jehovah eternally reigns over all the universal space. He is worthy of all honor and glory, and one of his inspired writers well says: "Now to the King of eternity, incorruptible, invisible, the only God, be honor and glory for ever and ever." (1 Timothy 1:17, *NW*) He being eternal and incorruptible, he is the Source of all life. There are those who think his name *Jehovah* means "self-existing or eternal"; and the Bible translation by

---

7. Who is Jehovah, and for how long?
8. Why must he be the Source of all life?

the Jewish scholar I. Leeser and that also by J. Moffatt render the Hebrew name in English as "The Eternal" instead of *Jehovah*.

⁹ There was, therefore, a time when Jehovah was all alone in universal space. All life and energy and thought were contained in him alone. Yet he could not have been lonesome, for he is self-contained, which means he is complete in himself and lacks nothing. Then the time came when Jehovah began to create. First at that time he came to be *God* to all his creation. Hence in opening up the account of creation the very first verse of the Bible speaks of him as *God*. "In the beginning God created the heaven and the earth." (Genesis 1:1) Because Jehovah is God the Creator, the expression "Jehovah God" is fitting and is used. This expression occurs immediately after the account of creation. We read: "These are the generations of the heavens and of the earth when they were created, in the day that JEHOVAH GOD made earth and heaven." (Genesis 2:4, 5, 7-9, 15, 18, 19, 21, 22, *AS*) His first creatures were spirit creatures, spirits like himself. Jesus said: "God is a Spirit, and those worshiping him must worship with spirit and truth." (John 4:24, *NW*) Because he is a spirit, Jehovah is and will ever be invisible to human eyes. He said to Moses: "Thou canst not see my face: for there shall no man see me, and live." (Exodus 33:20) He is so glorious that no human creature could endure to see him.

¹⁰ Although he is the Great Spirit, the great in-

---

9. (a) Was he ever alone, and why is the expression "Jehovah God" appropriate? (b) Why will man never see God?

10. How did he make himself discernible to mankind? and what did he make his angels?

telligent active Personage invisible to man, yet he has made himself discernible to man by his wondrous works of creation. Hence those who deny his divinity or his being God the Creator are subject to condemnation. "For his invisible qualities are clearly seen from the world's creation onward, because they are understood by the things made, even his eternal power and Godship, so that they are inexcusable." (Romans 1:20, *NW*) Speaking of His glory as the Creator, the inspired psalmist sang out in faith: "Bless the LORD, O my soul. O LORD my God, thou art very great; thou art clothed with honour and majesty. Who coverest thyself with light as with a garment: who stretchest out the heavens like a curtain: who layeth the beams of his chambers in the waters: who maketh the clouds his chariot: who walketh upon the wings of the wind: who maketh his angels spirits; his ministers a flaming fire."—Psalm 104:1-4; Hebrews 1:7, 14.

[11] As the Creator, Jehovah is the Source of all existence and power and of every good quality, and his works are perfect. To him Moses sang this song: "I will proclaim the name of Jehovah: Ascribe ye greatness unto our God. The Rock, his work is perfect; for all his ways are justice: a God of faithfulness and without iniquity, just and right is he." He is therefore the One of whom it is written: "Every good gift and every perfect present is from above, for it comes down from the Father of the celestial lights, and with him there is not a variation of the turning of the shadow." (Deuteronomy 32:3, 4, *AS;* James 1:17, *NW*) So God never gave the universe a devil, for he

11. How are his works? and to whom is our salvation due?

never created such a wicked creature. Instead, he is the Author of all the provisions for saving humankind from the sin, bondage, sorrow and death which that wicked adversary has brought upon our race. For this reason it is said: "Salvation belongeth unto Jehovah: thy blessing be upon thy people."—Psalm 3:8, *AS*.

HIS UNIVERSAL ORGANIZATION

[12] Jehovah God arranged all his holy, intelligent creatures in the heavens into an orderly, harmonious, peaceful organization under himself to accomplish his will. All such angelic spirit creatures, being thus arranged, made up his universal organization which is above. All were sons of God, all having received life from him, the Fountain of life. When perfect man and woman were created on the earth and set to fulfilling God's mandate to them in the garden of Eden, they were made the visible part of His universal organization. They were his earthly children; for which reason Adam was then called "the son of God". (Luke 3:38) Adam and Eve lost their relationship as God's children in his universal organization when they joined in the rebellion against Jehovah's universal sovereignty.

[13] As the Creator and Head over his universal organization of holy faithful creatures, Jehovah rightfully exercises the universal domination. Yet today the great issue before all heaven and earth is, Who is supreme? Who in fact and in right exercises the sovereignty over all the universe? Jehovah's primary purpose is to settle this issue. To

---

12. How did he set up a universal organization?
13. What is the great issue today, and how will it be settled?

do so means the vindication of his universal sovereignty or domination. At Psalm 83:17, 18 a prayer is expressed for him to vindicate his supreme position and rulership against all his combined opposers, in these words: "Let them be confounded and troubled for ever; yea, let them be put to shame, and perish: that men may know that thou, whose name alone is JEHOVAH, art the most high over all the earth." His supremacy will be proved beyond all future denial.

¹⁴ When Jehovah thus vindicates his universal sovereignty by destroying all his foes in heaven and in earth, then he will be again the great Theocrat or theocratic Ruler over all creatures that live. His theocratic government will govern all inhabited parts of the universe. His theocratic law will be obeyed everywhere. Then no long-time rebellion such as has existed during man's six thousand years of history will again be permitted, for Jehovah God will once and for all time have vindicated his universal sovereignty and his holy name against all false charges, reproaches and challenges of his malicious enemies, demon and human. He is the Almighty and Supreme One. He and his heavenly Son, whom he makes theocratic King under Him in the theocratic government, constitute together "the Higher Powers", to whom all souls worthy of living must be subject. Jehovah God has ordained it to be so.—Romans 13:1, 2.

¹⁵ That heavenly Son taught his followers to pray: "Our Father in the heavens, let your name be sanctified. Let your kingdom come. Let your will come to pass, as in heaven, also upon earth." (Matthew 6:9, 10, NW) He was there referring to

14. How will his Theocracy again rule all the universe?
15. Whose name must be sanctified, and how?

the sacred name and kingdom of Jehovah God. God's name must eventually be sanctified by Jehovah's own stupendous act of vindicating himself at the universal war of Armageddon. The means by which his name will be proved to be holy and deserving to be held sacred is his kingdom by his Messiah, which will shortly fight this war of Armageddon to a successful finish against all enemies. No rebel or idolatrous thing or organization will take the glory from him. Says he: "I am Jehovah, that is my name; and my glory will I not give to another, neither my praise unto graven images."—Isaiah 42:8, AS.

[16] The name "Jehovah" is a Hebrew verb and is understood to mean "He causes to be", that is, for a purpose. When making known his name in a special way to his prophet Moses, he did so in connection with declaring his purpose regarding his chosen people, then in bondage to Egypt. Thus, aside from its literal meaning, his name "Jehovah" implies his purpose respecting his creatures. (Exodus 3:15-21; 6:2-8, AS) Many times throughout the Bible he declares his purpose to cause all the nations as well as his own favored people to know that he is Jehovah. In the prophetic book of Ezekiel alone this declaration of his purpose to have all such to know that he is Jehovah occurs more than sixty times. (Exodus 6:7; Ezekiel 6:7, 10, 13, 14, AS) Hence an important part of his great purpose is the vindication of his reproached and misrepresented name. His vindication is more important than the salvation of men.

---

16. What does his name mean and stand for? and what is his purpose concerning it?

¹⁷ Why has this Almighty God permitted his chief adversary and all that wicked one's servants to live and carry on their wickedness down till the final battle of Armageddon? In brief explanation Jehovah said to hardhearted Pharaoh of Egypt: "To teach you that there is no one like me in all the world. Otherwise, I would have exerted my force and struck you and your people with pestilence, till you were swept off the earth; but this is why I have kept you alive, to let you see my power and to publish my fame all over the world." (Exodus 9:14-16, *Mo;* also *AT; Le*) Here Jehovah discloses his purpose to raise up his witnesses to declare and publish his fame or name throughout all the earth before all the enemies are destroyed. His Chief Witness is the One whom he makes his Messiah or the Anointed King in his theocratic government. But more as to this Chief Witness and his fellow witnesses, concerning whom the Bible has much to say, we leave succeeding chapters herein to tell.

---

17. Why has Almighty God permitted the great adversary and his wicked agents to operate down till Armageddon?

CHAPTER III

"WHAT DO YOU SAY RESPECTING THE MESSIAH?"

THE Aramaic-speaking Jews of the first century of the Christian era called him "Ye·shu' Mshi'hha". The Greek-speaking Jews and Gentiles called him "Jesus Messias" or "Jesus Christ". In either language it means "Jesus the Anointed"; and the name *Jesus* or *Jeshua* is just the shortened form of the Hebrew name *Je·hóshua*, meaning *Jehovah is the Savior*. That a Jew bearing that name and title walked and taught in Palestine in the first half of the first century is so fully established by history that it needs no further proof here. Now we take the authentic records written by his personal companions and their friends to learn some details about him.

[2] This Jew's life and teachings have affected the course of all human history and are destined to affect it still further in the next thousand years. Before he appeared on earth he had already had a wonderful past. To get facts about this we turn to the words of a man formerly his bitter enemy but who became a faithful friend and who said as regards himself: "Circumcised the eighth day, out of the family stock of Israel, of the tribe of Benjamin, a Hebrew born from Hebrews; as respects law, a Pharisee; as respects zeal, persecuting the

---

1. What does the full name "Jesus Christ" mean?
2. What does a former enemy write as to Jesus' prehuman existence?

congregation." (Philippians 3:5, 6, *NW*) In this same letter to the Philippian believers this Hebrew writer tells something about the prehuman past of Jesus, saying: "Keep this mental attitude in you which was also in Christ Jesus, who, although he was existing in God's form, gave no consideration to a seizure, namely, that he should be equal to God. No, but he emptied himself and took a slave's form and came to be in the likeness of men. More than that, when he found himself in fashion as a man, he humbled himself and became obedient as far as death, yes, death on a torture stake. For this very reason also God exalted him to a superior position and kindly gave him the name that is above every other name, so that in the name of Jesus every knee should bend of those in heaven and those on earth and those under the ground, and every tongue should openly confess that Jesus Christ is Lord to the glory of God the Father." —2:5-11, *NW*.

[3] This One was not Jehovah God, but was "existing in God's form". How so? He was a spirit person, just as "God is a Spirit"; he was a mighty one, although not almighty as Jehovah God is; also he was before all others of God's creatures, for he was the first son that Jehovah God brought forth. Hence he is called "the only begotten Son" of God, for God had no partner in bringing forth his first-begotten Son. He was the first of Jehovah God's creations. He speaks so of himself, at Revelation (or Apocalypse) 3:14: "These are the things the Amen says, the faithful and true witness, the beginning of the creation by God." (*NW*) Also at Colossians 1:15 he is spoken of as "the image of

---

3. How was he "existing in God's form"?

the invisible God, the firstborn of all creation".
Thus he is ranked with God's creation, being first
among them and also most beloved and most favored among them. He is not the author of the
creation of God; but, after God had created him
as his firstborn Son, then God used him as his
working Partner in the creating of all the rest of
creation. It is so stated at Colossians 1:16-18 and
at John 1:1-3, *NW*.

[4] In John, chapter 1, he is spoken of as being
the *Word* of God, that is to say, the mouthpiece
or representative speaker for God. In the Greek
Bible text the *Word* is *Logos*. Hence he may be
called "the Word or Logos". Being a mighty one
and holding this high official capacity as Logos
and being before all other creatures, he was a
God, but not the Almighty God, who is Jehovah.
This distinction is shown in the *Emphatic Diaglott*
translation of John 1:1-3, as follows: "In the beginning was the LOGOS, and the LOGOS was with
GOD, and the LOGOS was God. This was in the beginning with GOD. Through it every thing was
done; and without it not even one thing was done,
which has been done." Here in our quotation the
typographical difference between GOD and God is
just as found in the *Diaglott*. The *Diaglott's* inter-
linear translation of the Greek, word for word,
makes the distinction between Jehovah as "GOD"
and the Logos as "God" still clearer, reading as
follows: "In a beginning was the Word, and the
Word was with the God, and a god was the Word.
This was in a beginning with the God." Happily
the *New World Translation of the Christian Greek
Scriptures* (published in 1950) renders John 1:1, 2:

---

4. What prehuman office did he exercise?

"Originally the Word was, and the Word was with God, and the Word was a god. This one was originally with God." Thus the Word or Logos came into existence long before one of God's later creatures made a devil out of himself and became, as he is called at 2 Corinthians 4:4 (*NW*), "the god of this system of things."

⁵ That Jesus Christ had a prehuman existence he himself testifies, saying: "What, therefore, if you behold the Son of man ascending to where he was before?" (John 6:62, *NW*) "You are from the realms below; I am from the realms above. . . . Before Abraham came into existence, I have been." (John 8:23, 58, *NW; Mo; AT*) In his last prayer with his disciples Jesus said to God: "I have glorified you on the earth, having finished the work you have given me to do. So now you, Father, glorify me alongside yourself with the glory which I had alongside you before the world was. . . . I am no longer in the world, but they are in the world and I am coming to you." (John 17:4-11, *NW*) Less than two months later his faithful disciples, as his witnesses, saw him ascend heavenward and then disappear from their sight. Ten days later they had the evidence by means of the outpouring of God's spirit through Jesus that he had reached the heavenly presence of his Father above.—Acts, chapters 1 and 2.

⁶ Prior to coming to earth, this only-begotten Son of God did not think himself to be co-equal with Jehovah God; he did not view himself as "equal in power and glory" with Almighty God; he did not follow the course of the Devil and plot

---

5. How did Jesus testify of his prehuman existence?
6. Regarding Jesus, what do the Scriptures show as to aspiring to be like God?

and scheme to make himself like or equal to the Most High God and to rob God or usurp God's place. On the contrary, he showed his subjection to God as his Superior by humbling himself under God's almighty hand, even to the most extreme degree, which means to a most disgraceful death on a torture stake. To quote the *Emphatic Diaglott* translation, at Philippians 2:5-8: "Christ Jesus, who, though being in God's form, yet did not meditate a usurpation to be like God, but divested himself, taking a bondman's form, having been made in the likeness of men; and being in condition as a man, he humbled himself, becoming obedient unto death, even the death of the cross."

[7] Jesus asked the Jews concerning the Messiah's descent, saying: "What do you say respecting the Messiah? whose son is he?" His foes admitted from whose ancestral line the Messiah should come, saying: "David's son." (Matthew 22:41, 42, Delitzsch's translation) Just so, the Son of God on coming to earth was born in David's line, for his virgin mother Mary was descended from David. Joseph, to whom the young woman was betrothed, was also a descendant of David, but before Mary was united to him, the angel from God announced her coming motherhood, saying: "You will conceive in your womb and give birth to a son, and you are to call his name Jesus. . . . Holy spirit will come upon you, and power of the Most High will overshadow you. For that reason also what is born will be called holy, God's Son."—Luke 1:30-35, *NW*.

[8] The angel said Mary's child should be called

---

7. How did Jesus meet the requirement as to Messiah's line of descent?
8. Why is it improper to call Mary the "mother of God"?

"God's Son". So it is blasphemously improper to call her "the mother of God". That title was borrowed by the Roman Catholic clergy from pagan Babylon, where Rhe'a (Semíramis) or Venus was worshiped as the "mother of the gods". Jesus did not address Mary as "Blessed Mother". In every case on Bible record he addressed her as "woman". (John 2:4; 19:26; Matthew 12:46-50) Also, his apostle Paul writes: "When the full limit of the time arrived, God sent forth his Son, who was produced out of a woman." (Galatians 4:4, *NW*) At the time that the young woman conceived by the miracle-working power of Almighty God then the life of the Son of God was transferred from his glorious position with God his Father in heaven to the embryo of a human.

⁹ Mary conceived at the city of Nazareth in Galilee, but, due to Caesar's registration decree, she transferred to Bethlehem in Judea, where King David had been born about eleven centuries previous. There Jesus was born, about October 1, B.C. 2. This was in fulfillment of the prophecy at Micah 5:2. To the Jewish shepherds out in the fields that fall night the angel announced: "There was born to you today a Savior, who is Christ the Lord, in David's city." Then a multitude of the heavenly army appeared also and said: "Glory in the heights above to God, and upon earth peace among men of good-will." (Luke 2:8-14, *NW; Dy*) On the eighth day he was circumcised like any normal Jewish boy, and then after the fortieth day Mary was permitted to enter the temple at Jerusalem and present him. Later the child was carried down into Egypt to escape King Herod's

---

9. Where was Jesus conceived, born, and brought up?

murderous soldiers, but was brought back after Herod's death and was taken up to Nazareth to live and grow up. This fulfilled another prophecy, at Hosea 11:1: "Out of Egypt I called my son." —Matthew 2:13-23, *NW*.

¹⁰ The cousin of Jesus' mother married a priest, Zechariah, to whom she bore a son, Jesus' cousin John. Six months before Jesus became thirty years old, John began to preach as a forerunner of Jesus and he also baptized in water in connection with his preaching. To the Jews exclusively he preached, saying: "Repent, for the kingdom of the heavens has drawn near." After this announcement of the Kingdom Jesus went to John, showing the primary purpose for which he came to earth, namely, to bear witness to God's kingdom which will vindicate the sovereignty and holy name of Jehovah God. When Jesus stood on trial before Governor Pontius Pilate three and a half years later, he said: "My kingdom is no part of this world. . . . my kingdom is not from this source." "Therefore Pilate said to him: 'Well, then, are you a king?' Jesus answered: 'It is for you to say that I am a king. For this purpose I have been born and for this purpose I have come into the world, that I should bear witness to the truth. Everyone that is on the side of the truth listens to my voice.'" (John 18:36, 37, *NW*) It was to this kingdom of God that Jesus was anointed to be the Messianic King. When?

¹¹ Jesus at thirty years of age went to John the Baptist to be immersed in water. After John had

---

10. How did Jesus show forth the primary purpose for which he came to earth?
11. What marked events took place at Jesus' baptism?

dipped him in the Jordan river and Jesus came out of the water, then "the heaven was opened up and the holy spirit in bodily shape like a dove came down upon him, and a voice came out of heaven: 'You are my Son, the beloved; I have approved you.'" (Luke 3:21-23, *NW*) By his water baptism Jesus showed his submitting of himself to do God's will; and now God consecrated him by his holy spirit. By acknowledging him as his beloved Son, God begot Jesus to be his spiritual Son once more instead of a human Son. By pouring out his holy spirit upon the baptized Jesus, God anointed him with the spirit to be the long-promised King in God's kingdom. By being thus anointed with the spirit Jesus became the Messiah, or Mashíahh or Christ, which words all mean "Anointed". Thus he became in fact Jesus *Christ*, or Jesus the *Anointed*. His Jewish disciple Peter declared: "Jesus who was from Nazareth, how God anointed him with holy spirit and power."—Acts 10:38, *NW*.

[12] After spending forty days in the wilderness, where he beat back the Devil's temptations, Jesus returned to John's locality, to get in touch with his first disciples. On seeing Jesus approaching, John said to his hearers: "See, the Lamb of God that takes away the sin of the world!" (John 1:29, 36, *NW*) Thus John showed the secondary purpose for which the Son of God came to earth, namely, to die as a holy sacrifice to Jehovah God in order to cancel the sins of believing men and to free them from death's condemnation, that they might gain eternal life in the righteous new world which God has promised to create. Jesus was suit-

---

12. As shown by John the Baptist, what secondary purpose did Jesus fulfill on coming to earth?

able to be such a ransom sacrifice. By having his perfect, sinless life transferred from heaven to the womb of a Jewish virgin, Jesus was born a perfect human and grew up to be a perfect man, absolutely sinless, guileless, undefiled. (Hebrews 7:26, *NW*) So, when he presented himself in full dedication to God's will, Jehovah God accepted him for sacrifice as mankind's Redeemer. Because Jesus was bound by this to lay aside his humanity forever as a sacrifice, God begot him by his spirit to become again a spirit Son of God. Hence Jesus said: "The Son of man came, not to be ministered to, but to minister and to give his soul a ransom in exchange for many." (Matthew 20:28, *NW*) So he laid down his human life forever.

[13] On his return visit to Nazareth the anointed Jesus spoke in its synagogue. There he applied to himself the prophecy of Isaiah 61: 1, 2. He confessed he had been anointed with God's spirit in order to preach the good news or gospel to meek persons seeking release from bondage to sin and religious error. (Luke 4:16-21) After that he preached "The kingdom of the heavens has drawn near" up and down the land of Judea and Galilee and Trans-Jordan. He gathered about him twelve apostles and other disciples, whom he trained to preach the heavenly kingdom to which he had been anointed. He exposed religious traditions and errors and preached the truth to set men free. This brought him in conflict with the rabbis, priests and sectarian leaders, who sought his death. At passover time A.D. 33, with the aid of the traitorous apostle Judas Iscariot, they seized

---

13. How did Jesus on earth fulfill his anointing? and with what outcome to him as a man?

Jesus, gave him a mock trial, handed him over to the Gentiles for trial by Pontius Pilate and Herod Antipas, and then blocked his release by stirring up the misguided Jewish people to cry for Jesus to be hanged on a torture stake like a seditious lawbreaker and blasphemer. He died obedient to God, without renouncing God's kingdom.

[14] On the third day of his being dead in the grave his immortal Father Jehovah God raised him from the dead, not as a human Son, but as a mighty immortal spirit Son, with all power in heaven and earth under the Most High God. Says the Jewish witness Peter: "He being put to death in the flesh, but being made alive in the spirit." (1 Peter 3:18, NW; Dy) For forty days after that he materialized, as angels before him had done, to show himself alive to his disciples as witnesses. He then ascended to heaven and appeared in God's presence with the value of his human sacrifice as God's High Priest, and this he applied in behalf of all those who should believe in him.—Hebrews 9:11, 23, 24; 10:12, 13.

[15] God exalted his Son Jesus to be higher than he was before he lived and died as a man. If Jesus had been "equal in power and glory" with the Supreme One, then Jehovah God could not have elevated his Son any higher than he was in his prehuman state. But now Jesus is made the Head under Jehovah of God's capital organization over the entire universe. Says the apostle Peter: "Through the resurrection of Jesus Christ. He is at God's right hand, for he went his way to heaven, and angels and authorities and powers were made

14. What took place on the third day of his death and during the forty days after that?
15. In what way has the resurrected Jesus been exalted?

subject to him." (1 Peter 3:21, 22, *NW*) This proves Jesus did not take his human body to heaven to be forever a man in heaven. Had he done so, that would have left him ever lower than the angels. By his becoming a man, "we behold Jesus, who has been made a little lower than angels, crowned with glory and honor for having suffered death." (Hebrews 2:6-9, *NW*) God did not purpose for Jesus to be humiliated thus forever by being a fleshly man forever. No, but after he had sacrificed his perfect manhood, God raised him to deathless life as a glorious spirit creature. He exalted him above all angels and other parts of God's universal organization, to be next-highest to himself, the Most High God. What Jesus does in this exalted capacity, we leave to succeeding chapters to tell.

CHAPTER IV

TRANSMITTING
THE TRUE RECORD

"JEHOVAH said unto Moses, Write this for a
memorial in a book." That was in 1513 B.C.
It is the first divine command to write, and
it indicates Jehovah's purpose to have important
matters recorded. Memorial of them was not to
be entrusted to oral transmission subject to corruption by fallible human memory. The finished
product of this divine purpose is God's Word, the
Bible. Its sixty-six books have a common origin,
being inspired by God; yet they were written by
more than thirty-five men over a period of more
than sixteen centuries. Moses started its writing
no later than 1513 B.C., and the apostle John
penned its last book around A.D. 98. These historical dates give rise to two questions. Since Moses
in the Bible's first book, Genesis, wrote of creative
works and historical events that happened thousands of years before his lifetime, how did he get
reliable information? And since nearly nineteen
centuries have passed since the last Bible book
was written, how do we know all of this has
reached us in accurate and reliable form?

2 Jehovah could have revealed the information in
Genesis to Moses. God's spirit or active force could

---

1. When did Bible writing begin and end? and what
questions are raised?
2. How might Jehovah have revealed the information
in Genesis to Moses?

have accomplished that. His spirit did work in the Bible's production, as the writers themselves are quick to acknowledge. David said: "The spirit of the LORD spake by me." Luke declared: "He, through the mouth of his holy prophets from of old, has spoken." Peter added to the testimony: "No prophecy of Scripture springs from any private release. For prophecy was at no time brought by man's will, but men spoke from God as they were borne along by holy spirit." Paul left no room for further doubt or exceptions when he sweepingly said: "All Scripture is inspired of God." (2 Samuel 23:2; Luke 1:70; Acts 1:16; 2 Timothy 3:16, 17; 1 Peter 1:10, 11; 2 Peter 1:20, 21, *NW*) So Moses, one of God's "holy prophets from of old", could have received the Genesis record word for word in direct revelation; but there is nothing to indicate that such was the case. Or he could have received the information by oral tradition, handed down by word of mouth. Only five human links were needed to connect Moses with Adam (Methuselah, Shem, Isaac, Levi and Amram). But the Bible does not indicate this either.

[3] Modern archaeological discoveries in Bible lands indicate that the art of writing existed before the Flood, and lead us to conclude that Moses compiled Genesis from earlier written records. At Ur of the Chaldees Sir Leonard Woolley found seals belonging to men that lived before the Flood, and often included the owner's name in the cuneiform writing of that time. Thousands of clay tablets with cuneiform writing have been found that existed in Noah's time. Statements made by

---

3. What evidence establishes that there was writing before the Flood?

Ashurbanipal (called Osnappar in the Bible) indicate writing before the Flood. He said: "I had my joy in the reading of inscriptions on stone from the time before the flood." And going right back to mankind's beginning and indicating that Adam wrote or possessed written records, we have the statement at Genesis 5:1: "This is the book of the generations of Adam."

Letter in cuneiform with front of clay envelope broken away. It is of Noah's time, found at Ur of Chaldees.

⁴ This expression "the generations of" and its use are highly significant. It occurs first at Genesis 2:4: "These are the generations of the heavens and of the earth." But it is evident that unintelligent heavens and earth do not generate or beget offspring, and it indicates that it is incorrect to translate as "generations" the original Hebrew word *toledóth*. It should be translated "history", or "historical origins". Darby's translation renders the word "histories" at Genesis 2:4, but not in later occurrences. At Genesis 2:4 Moffatt's translation uses "story" and *An American Translation* uses "origins"; but neither follows through consistently thereafter. After Genesis 2:4 and 5:1, this expression "the generations of" occurs nine times, and in each case is followed by a proper name or a designation of certain individuals, namely Noah, sons of Noah, Shem, Terah, Ishmael, Isaac, Esau (twice) and Jacob.—Genesis 6:9; 10:1; 11:10, 27; 25:12, 19; 36:1, 9; 37:2.

---

4. How should "generations" in Genesis be translated, and why?

[5] Another misconception most Bible scholars have of this expression is that it introduces what follows, whereas actually it concludes what precedes it. Hence *An American Translation* is wrong in inserting the word "following" in its translation of Genesis 2:4: "The *following* are the origins of the heavens and the earth." It is obviously wrong because the story of origins preceded this verse. Moffatt recognized this, so he lifted Genesis 2:4 right out of its place and put it ahead of Genesis 1:1. But this is an unnecessary violation of the writing style of that time. In Moses' day, and in the centuries preceding him, it was the literary style for a historical document to be concluded with the words, "These are the generations," or, better translated, "This is the history," of So-and-so, and thereby indicate who was the writer or owner of the document. In a modern book this information would come at the beginning, on the title page; in Moses' day and prior thereto it was put at the end. Modern archaeology has firmly established these facts.

[6] Moses himself used this type of conclusion to certain sections of his own writings. The last verse of Leviticus reads: "These are the commandments, which the LORD commanded Moses for the children of Israel in mount Sinai." He was obviously concluding the instructions given at Mount Sinai, and not introducing the account of travels in the book of Numbers that followed. He ended the book of Numbers with the words: "These are the commandments and the judgments, which the LORD commanded by the hand of Moses unto the children

5. What does this expression indicate, despite what misconception?
6. Wherein did Moses follow this literary style himself?

of Israel in the plains of Moab by Jordan near Jericho." These words did not introduce the book of Deuteronomy that followed. Hence in both the above verses *An American Translation* reads: "These WERE the commands."

[7] From all of the foregoing it is clear that Moses compiled the material for Genesis, down to chapter 37, verse 2, from eleven earlier written documents. Adam doubtless wrote the first one about creation, he is identified as the writer of the second, and the writer or owner of the remaining ones is in each case identified by the conclusion. By inserting these conclusions or colophons, as they are called, Moses stuck to the writing style of the time and showed his written sources, establishing as authentic his compilation of Genesis. From Genesis 37:3 forward the expression "These are the generations of" occurs no more, indicating that Moses himself composed the remainder of Genesis and the Pentateuch (first five books of the Bible). For this purpose he could gather information about events before his time through his father Amram from Joseph's brother Levi.

[8] After Moses' death other faithful Hebrews wrote under inspiration, until more than a thousand years later the last of the thirty-nine books of the Hebrew Scriptures was written by Malachi, around 442 B.C. Nearly five centuries elapsed, without further Bible writing. Christ came, preached, died, and ascended to heaven to later pour out holy spirit upon his followers. It brought vital truths to their remembrance, truths that must be preserved for future generations, along

7. So what is the conclusion as to Moses' compilation of Genesis?
8. How was the Bible completed after Moses' death?

with facts about Christ and his earthly sojourn as a man, about many fulfilled prophecies of the Hebrew Scriptures, and new prophecies. So the spirit once again operated upon faithful Hebrews to write. Matthew wrote his history concerning Jesus Christ, likely between 41 and 50 (A.D.). Other Hebrew writers added their books and letters, until the apostle John wrote the last of the twenty-seven books of the Christian Greek Scriptures around A.D. 98.—John 14:26; Romans 3:1, 2.

PRESERVING THE RECORD UNTIL NOW

⁹ None of the original Bible writings are known to exist today, but their message was preserved by the making of many copies. The Hebrews kept Scripture manuscripts with the ark of the covenant at their central place of worship. (Deuteronomy 31:26; 2 Kings 22:8) When the first temple was destroyed by the Babylonians in 607 B.C. Bible manuscripts were preserved; Daniel studied them while in captivity. (Daniel 9:2) After the return from captivity Ezra is found reading the Law to the people, showing the preservation of Bible manuscripts through that perilous period. (Nehemiah 8:1-3) It is believed that Ezra compiled and put into final form the Hebrew Scripture canon, with the exception of the books of Nehemiah and Malachi. Then followed a period of intense activity in making many manuscript copies of the Hebrew Scriptures, for not all the Jews returned to Jerusalem after release from captivity. Many remained where they were and set up synagogues for worship there, and these

9. How were the manuscripts preserved, and why multiplied?

synagogues scattered far and wide had to be supplied with copies of Scripture. About 1,700 ancient manuscripts of the Hebrew Scriptures are extant today.

[10] The professional Hebrew scribes used the most scrupulous care in the copying of these manuscripts. They counted not only the words but the letters also. To write a single word from memory was considered gross sin. Before and during the time of Christ these Hebrew copyists were called *scribes* or *sopherim,* and while shunning mistakes they did take liberties in making textual changes, such as many times substituting "God" or "Lord" for "Jehovah". But after them came trained Jewish scholars called "Mas'oretes", and they exercised great care and fidelity in copying manuscripts, making absolutely no changes, but compiling notations that called attention to the changes made by the *sopherim.* They produced what is now known as the Masoret'ic text, on which our present copies and translations of the Hebrew Scriptures are based. The oldest dated copy of the Masoretic text is the Codex Babylonicus Petropolitanus of A.D. 916.

[11] A recent Bible manuscript find has strikingly confirmed the accuracy of the Masoret'ic text. In 1947 the now famous Dead Sea Scroll of Isaiah was found, and it is believed to have been written in the second century before Christ, or more than a thousand years before the oldest dated copy of the Masoret'ic text. Nevertheless, scholars were astonished to find that aside from certain admittedly minor variations in spelling this Isaiah scroll

10. What is the Masoretic text?
11. What confirms its accuracy?

is identical with the accepted Masoret'ic text. A thousand years of copying with no appreciable change! Remarkable testimony to the Bible's preservation!

[12] Just as in the case of the Hebrew Scripture manuscripts, so it was found necessary to make numerous copies of the original Greek Scripture writings, first in order to circulate the message widely and quickly, and later to preserve it against use and the ravages of time. Some 4,000 manuscript copies of the Greek Scriptures are extant today in the original language (plus 8,000 in Latin and 1,000 in other languages). The accuracy of the professional Hebrew scribes was passed on to a good degree to the nonprofessional copyists of

12. Why and by whom were Greek Scripture manuscripts made?

Photograph of a portion of the Dead Sea Scroll of Isaiah, showing Isaiah 28:2-12. Scholars who dated this scroll as of the second century B.C. were confirmed by science's radiocarbon clock, which showed the linen cloth in which the scroll was wrapped to be 1,900 years old, with a margin of error 200 years either way. The margin of error would allow for the second century B.C. date.

the Greek Scriptures. Of course, despite painstaking care copyist errors crept in, but these were largely insignificant as far as meaning is concerned.

[13] Just as the find of the very old Isaiah scroll confirmed confidence in the Masoret'ic text of the Hebrew Scriptures, so the comparatively recent finds of Greek Scripture papyrus manuscripts written in the second and third centuries establish beyond question the accuracy of this part of the Bible. Note the conclusion of the outstanding English scholar, Sir Frederic Kenyon: "The interval then between the dates of original composition and the earliest extant evidence becomes so small as to be in fact negligible, and the last foundation for any doubt that the Scriptures have come down to us substantially as they were written has now been removed."—*The Bible and Archaeology,* pages 288, 289.

[14] There are some who would try to preserve as a part of the inspired Bible certain books known as "Apocryphal". The Roman Catholic Church got its start in the fourth century after Christ, and at its Council of Carthage in 397 it adopted an enlarged Bible canon that included apocryphal books; but this move was widely opposed even in Catholic circles, and opposition continued by Hierarchy members down to the Protestant Reformation. How do we know these books do not belong to the Bible? Because for the first four centuries of the Christian era none of them was in the catalogues of inspired books accepted by Christian congregations. Because none of them was ever quoted from or even alluded to by Christ or his

---

13. How is the accuracy of these manuscripts established?
14. Why is the Apocrypha no part of the Bible?

followers, as shown in the Christian Greek Scriptures. And because none of them was included by the Jews in their Greek *Septuagint* translation as it first appeared. Apocryphal books made their appearance in the *Septuagint* only in later copies. Inspired canonical books of the Hebrew Scriptures were openly displayed for reference on the library shelves of the Jewish scribes, but other books not inspired by God were hidden away from the public and came to be called "Apocrypha", which means "hidden".

[15] Mention of the *Septuagint* brings up the matter of Bible translation. Bible translation was necessary to preserve the Bible's message. After the return from Babylonian captivity, when the scribes read from the Hebrew Scriptures they had to paraphrase the meaning in Aramaic. (Nehemiah 8:8) Hebrew became a dead language. Soon *koiné* or *common* Greek became an international language. It was for Greek-speaking Jews in Egypt that the *Septuagint* translation was made. It was started around 280 B.C., and eventually contained the entire Hebrew Scriptures in Greek. When after Jesus' death more Scripture writing was to be done, Jehovah's spirit caused it to be recorded in the language most widely understood at that time, the *koiné* Greek. He did not venerate and count specially sacred the dead language of Hebrew, like the Roman Catholic Church today does the dead language Latin. Jehovah was preserving the Bible to be read and understood by all, and not by merely a religious hierarchy.

---

15. Why was the *Septuagint* made? and why did Bible writing change to the Greek language?

[16] Not only is Bible translation necessary to keep it in a living tongue, but also it is vital to make it available in as many tongues as possible, to facilitate the reading and preaching of it in all nations. (Matthew 28:19, 20; Acts 1:8) Very early in their existence the Greek Scriptures were translated into Latin and other languages. Outstanding was the Latin *Vulgate* produced by Jerome, from 382-404. This version contained the entire Bible translated into Latin from the original Hebrew and Greek languages. It became the basis of Biblical scholarship for a thousand years. Today Bible translation has proceeded rapidly, until there are versions of the Bible, all or part, in more than 1,125 languages.

[17] However, this work of translating the Bible to keep it in living languages and make it understandable to the common people of many nations did not progress unopposed. History is emphatic that the chief opponent was the Roman Catholic Hierarchy, despite her claims of being the Bible's preserver. She seemed intent on preserving it only in a dead language that the common people could not understand. It was after the production of the Latin *Vulgate* that the Roman Catholic Hierarchy grew to tremendous power. She did not like for the people to be able to read the Bible in their own speech, and she rejoiced when Latin ceased to be understood by the people generally. In the eleventh century Pope Gregory VII expressly thanked God for this circumstance. But she could not keep the Bible in the dark shrouds of a dead language. The

---

16. Why and how has Bible translation proceeded until our time?
17. How only did the Roman Catholic Hierarchy seek to preserve the Bible?

first to complete the Bible in English were John Wycliffe and his associates, toward the end of the fourteenth century. Other translations followed, as the Hierarchy fumed and persecuted. Her record of hunting down possessors of Bibles in the common tongue as if they were wild beasts, of burning them at the stake with their Bibles tied around their necks, makes some of the bloodiest pages in history.

[18] Through the fifteenth and most of the sixteenth century the Hierarchy vented its rage against the Bible in the vernacular, but it finally became apparent that she had lost her fight. Unable to stop it, she sought to counteract it. That she did by belatedly bringing out an English translation of her own, known as the *Douay Version*. She published the Greek Scripture part in 1582, and the Hebrew Scripture portion not until 1610. It was a stiff, awkward rendering, using many unintelligible words; and the *Catholic Encyclopedia* says that this was done so that "an ordinary reader, finding the word unintelligible, would pause and inquire its meaning". The good Catholic would of course make this inquiry of the priest, who could give the text the desired twist.

[19] Probably the most valuable Bible manuscript is the Vatican 1209. It was written in the fourth century. Neither this manuscript nor any other really old and valuable manuscripts have been found in territories under Hierarchy domination. She came into possession of Vatican MS. 1209 in the fifteenth century. Who preserved it until that late date? Not the Hierarchy. And when she did get her hands on it she would let no non-Catholic

18. What did she belatedly do?
19. How are her false claims further exposed?

scholars carefully examine it. Only after another
famous fourth-century manuscript, the Codex
Sinaiticus, was found in the nineteenth century
did the Hierarchy publish facsimile copies of her
manuscript, to prevent it from being eclipsed. She
may defend her burning of Bibles on the grounds
that they were non-Catholic translations. Then
why did she not make a Catholic translation in
English, and properly fill the need, instead of trying to suppress other versions and keep the Scriptures in the dark of a dead language? For the
same reason she kept her Vatican MS. 1209 under
wraps. The facts are overwhelming that she goes
only as far as she is forced to in letting light
shine on the Bible. And it is only in the more advanced and democratic countries today that she
poses as favoring Bible reading; she does not do so
in backward, solid-Catholic countries.

[20] But despite opposition, God's Word will endure
forever, and it will allow him to be found true. He
is its preserver. The Jewish *sopherim* tried to alter
it, but their changes are known. The Roman Catholic copyists and theologians maneuvered spurious
passages into it, but modern scholarship is exposing such. An outstanding example is the spurious
trinitarian text at 1 John 5:7. Modern translations,
benefited by advancing knowledge of the original
languages in which the Bible was written and by
recent discoveries of older manuscripts, are bringing us ever closer to the true meaning of the orig-
inals. The evidence is now overwhelming that the
record that has been transmitted to us from
Adam's day is the true Record.—Isaiah 40:8;
1 Peter 1:25.

---

20. Who is the Bible's preserver? and how is it being
purified today?

CHAPTER V

SATAN THE DEVIL

S O ALIKE has been the course of the nations which for four thousand years have successively dominated the affairs of this world that historians have advanced the theory that "history repeats itself". The way in which world powers had their beginnings, rose to prominence as world powers, and then declined to a state of obscurity is noted as common to all. Wars were featured by each. Oppression and intimidation were their stock in trade. Religion was an influential part of each.

[2] Observing this similarity of experience down into our modern world, thinking men have voiced the questions, "Is it possible that a common invisible power has dominated all nations? Has the same guiding force been responsible for their similar acts of violence? Why should history seem to repeat itself? Will it always be thus?"

[3] There is no point in guessing at the matter when the Bible, God's written Word, makes the evidence so plain. In the history of man, dating from his very creation, God proves that the idea of some intelligent superforce of wickedness in-

---

1. Why have historians advanced the theory that "history repeats itself"?
2. What questions have thinking men observing this voiced?
3. Why do we not have to guess at the matter?

fluencing both men and nations is no idle imagination. It is a fact.

⁴ Consider the occasion of Christ at the beginning of his ministry here on earth. We are told, at Matthew, chapter 4, that immediately after his baptism in Jordan river Christ was led by the spirit into the wilderness "to be tempted by the Devil". Part of that tempting took the form of three proposals by the Devil to Christ, the third of which was as follows:

⁵ "Again the Devil took him along to an unusually high mountain, and showed him all the kingdoms of the world and their glory, and he said to him: 'All these things I will give you if you fall down and do an act of worship to me.' "—Matthew 4:8, 9, *NW*.

⁶ From this it is unreasonable to think anything else than that all world governments were the Devil's property. How else could he have offered them to Christ? He was the invisible ruler of them. For that reason Christ was compelled to say: "My kingdom is no part of this world." "The ruler of the world is coming. And yet he has no hold on me." (John 18:36; 14:30, *NW*) The Devil's attributes of greed, cruelty and selfishness have characterized every government on earth. He is "the god of this system of things".—2 Corinthians 4:4, *NW*.

⁷ From where did Satan the Devil come? Why has a righteous God let him remain to influence men to wickedness? Will it always be that way?

4, 5. What event occurring at the beginning of Christ's ministry sheds much light on the matter?
6. What conclusion must we draw from the scripture at Matthew 4:8, 9? and, for the same reason, what was Christ compelled to say?
7. What questions are now appropriately asked?

Is there no way for honest men to keep from under that influence?

[8] The one now the Devil was not always such. Time was when he enjoyed a high position in God's family. He was a spirit son of God. Contrary to the opinion of some, he was not an ugly creature with horns and tail, but was beautiful. The Bible figuratively describes him at Ezekiel 28:12, 13: "Thou sealest up the sum, full of wisdom, and perfect in beauty. Thou hast been in Eden the garden of God; every precious stone was thy covering."

[9] In keeping with his being a son of God, he was given a position of great trust and responsibility: that of overseer of humankind. The designated term for this office was, as stated in the Bible, at Ezekiel 28:14, "the anointed cherub that covereth."

[10] God had placed the perfect human pair in the garden of Eden, and it was the spirit cherub's duty to help them keep God's requirements and to educate them in their proper relationship to their Creator. That is why it could be said of him, "Thou hast been in Eden."

[11] For a time all went well in the universe and there was perfect peace throughout that righteous world. But it did not last. Greed and avariciousness entered in. The covering cherub had great visions. He saw a race of human creatures on a perfect earth, all with one accord giving their every devotion to Jehovah and acknowledging him

---

8. From where did the Devil come? and how may he be described?
9. In keeping with his being a son of God, what position was given him?
10. What duties did the position of the "anointed cherub" entail?
11. How did the theocratic arrangement at Eden come to an end, and what has the Bible to say on this?

as the great King and Giver of everything good. He wanted that devotion and worship for himself, and so his heart became malicious. He rebelled against the theocratic arrangement. This is indicated by the new name given to him, namely, Satan, for that name means "opposer".—1 Chronicles 21:1; Job 1:6-12.

[12] So the covering cherub fell from his perfection and innocence. Why? God's sentence of destruction against him says: "Thou wast perfect in thy ways from the day that thou wast created, till unrighteousness was found in thee. Thy heart was lifted up because of thy beauty; thou hast corrupted thy wisdom by reason of thy brightness." —Ezekiel 28:15, 17, AS.

[13] His self-admiring, self-seeking heart condition was first manifested by his cunningly and stealthily introducing sin into the world. God had told the perfect human pair not to eat of the tree of knowledge of good and evil that they might not die. The covering cherub, however, induced Eve to disobey. Through his visible mouthpiece, the serpent, he said to her: "Ye shall not surely die." That was the first lie. It branded the cherub as the "father of the lie".—John 8:44, NW.

[14] Although God pronounced sentence of death upon the cherub rebel, the wording of that sentence indicated there would be a long period of deferment before its execution: "I will put enmity between you and the woman, between your seed

12. How was it that the cherub fell from his perfection and innocence?
13. How was the cherub's heart condition expressed, and what did the utterance he inspired make him?
14. Why was not the death sentence immediately executed upon the cherub, and what was he henceforth called?

and her seed; he shall crush your head, and you shall lie in wait for his heel." (Genesis 3:15, *CB*) The cherub rebel must have time to bring forth some seed. From this point on in the Bible he is referred to as Serpent, Satan, Devil and Dragon. —Revelation 12:9.

15 He turned the first pair away from God in disgrace, and he now reasoned that he was able to turn all human offspring into rebellion against Jehovah's universal sovereignty. He now appeared to have grounds for tauntingly addressing God and challenging him with the words: 'Jehovah, you are not able to put on earth men whom I cannot by some means turn away from you.'

16 Those words do not actually appear in the Bible, but the evidence that he said them in effect is clear and unmistakable. For such evidence, turn to Job 1:6-11 (*AS*) and read: "Now it came to pass on the day when the sons of God came to present themselves before Jehovah, that Satan also came among them. And Jehovah said unto Satan, Whence comest thou? Then Satan answered Jehovah, and said, From going to and fro in the earth, and from walking up and down in it. And Jehovah said unto Satan, Hast thou considered my servant Job? for there is none like him in the earth, a perfect and upright man, one that feareth God, and turneth away from evil. Then Satan answered Jehovah, and said, Doth Job fear God for nought? . . . thou hast blessed the work of his hands, . . . But put forth thy hand now, and touch all that he hath, and he will renounce thee to thy face."

15. What did he now reason and seem to have grounds for doing?
16. What is the evidence of Satan's taunting Jehovah?

[17] That conversation discloses an issue of long standing between God and Satan. God's question, 'From where do you come, Satan?' and Satan's reply, 'From walking up and down in the earth,' indicated a license or permission on Jehovah's part to Satan to have a free hand to produce his seed or children from among men. In addition to disproving Satan's claim of ability to overthrow Jehovah's universal sovereignty, the issue included the matter of man's keeping integrity toward his Creator.

[18] Job was an actual character of history. He was a great-grandnephew of Abraham and lived about 1,700 years before Christ, or some 2,300 years after the rebellion at Eden. All those 2,300 years men were given opportunity to prove their integrity to the Most High God. The issue was not new in Job's day.

PROVED A LIAR

[19] The pages of the Bible are full of accounts of those who failed their Creator under attack by Satan. On the other hand, there were those who, like Job, were able to take all that the adversary offered and by their course of action under such conditions prove him the "father of the lie" and entirely incapable of being a universal ruler like the Most High God.

[20] The Jews gave a national example of failure.

---

17. What does that conversation disclose as of long standing, and what does the issue include?
18. How do we know the issue was not new in Job's day?
19. What does the Bible disclose as to those who have been under attack by Satan?
20. What national example have we, and how did Jehovah treat the various conditions arising?

When they, as a nation, made conscientious effort to serve Jehovah and keep his commandments he was with them, fought their battles for them, and gave them economic prosperity. When they succumbed to the Devil's offers and fell for the popular practices of the heathen nations round about them, Jehovah withdrew his protection and as a nation and as individuals they suffered at the hands of Satan.

²¹ At no time, however, has Satan the Devil succeeded in turning all creatures away from the Creator. At every period of history from Abel on there have lived faithful men and women whose integrity to God was above reproach and whom the Devil did not succeed in turning away from the true worship.

²² It was so with Christ Jesus. Although he died an ignominious death at the hands of Satan's agents, Satan was unable to prove by him that keeping integrity toward God was not possible for human creatures under any condition that the Devil might bring.

²³ It was Christ whom the Scriptures showed to be the promised Seed to bruise the Serpent's head; and at Revelation 12:7-9 (NW) appears the vision of his taking steps toward that act immediately upon coming into his kingship: "War broke out in heaven: Michael and his angels battled with the dragon, and the dragon and his angels battled but it did not prevail, neither was a place found for them any longer in heaven. So down the great

---

21. What outstanding fact does history show about those whom Satan has persecuted?
22. How did Jesus' death disprove Satan's argument?
23. How did Christ begin actively to take steps toward bruising the Serpent's head, and when?

dragon was hurled, the original serpent, the one
called Devil and Satan, who is misleading the entire inhabited earth; he was hurled down to the
earth, and his angels were hurled down with him."
The evidence is plentiful that this vision was realized during A.D. 1914-1918.

[24] Although history has appeared to repeat itself
at intervals, it must be agreed that present unsettled conditions of the world exceed anything
previous in scope and magnitude. The reason is
that Satan no longer has access to heaven but has
been cast down to this earth, and all his wicked
angels or demons with him. He is still the unseen
spirit ruler of disobedient humankind, and despite
his fall he is determined to rule or ruin.

[25] After his fall the cry rings out: "Woe for the
earth and for the sea, because the Devil has come
down to you, having great anger, knowing he has
a short period of time." (Revelation 12:12, *NW*)
We are in that short period of woe right now. Satan, knowing his time to prove his claims is limited, now turns his fury on all. In every field of
endeavor he influences leaders and common man
alike to acts of greed, selfishness and violence, and
all the world is in confusion. Many embittered people are doing just what Satan intended: turning
away from God, who they think is bringing the
sorrows, but who is in fact only permitting Satan
to prove, if he can, his boastful claims of supremacy and man's inability to keep integrity.

[26] The time limit for his attempts at proof is

---

24. Why do present unsettled conditions of the world
far exceed anything previous in scope and magnitude?
25. Why now are there more acts of greed and violence
than ever before, and how have many honest people
fallen into Satan's trap?
26. What is indicated by the scripture at James 2:19?

about up, and the Devil and his demons know it. They must shudder at the thought. "You believe there is one God, do you? You are doing quite well. And yet the demons believe and shudder." —James 2:19, *NW*.

[27] So subtle has been his attack over the thousands of years that today many people doubt the existence of either Satan or his wicked demons. To them sin, wickedness, and evil are merely abstract conditions inherent in humans. One way he blinds people to his existence is explained at 2 Corinthians 11:14 (*NW*): "Satan himself keeps transforming himself into an angel of light." His devices for fooling the people appear very innocent. A United Nations and other world security organizations, united church movements, and the like, are all his schemes to blind people to the real remedy.

[28] But it will not always be that way. Revelation 20:1-3 tells us of the time when the archdeceiver will be completely restrained from his activity. He will be bound and abyssed for a thousand years, to mislead the nations and peoples no more until it is God's time to loose him for a little while. In the meantime deceit, lying, and hypocrisy continue.

[29] Where do you stand in this matter of integrity? Are you by your course of action lending support to Satan's contention? Many meek persons are seeking Jehovah's approval and by faithful conduct are proving the Devil a liar. One way of gaining God's approval is stated at 2 Timothy

---

27. In what has the subtlety of Satan's attack resulted, and how does the Bible explain this?
28. Why will it not always be that way?
29. (a) What questions should we now ask ourselves? (b) What are the meek of the earth now doing, and why?

2:15 (NW): "Do your utmost to present yourself approved to God, a workman with nothing to be ashamed of, handling the word of the truth aright." It is God's Word which tells us of the subtle machinations of Satan, and by handling it aright we are able to withstand him. "Oppose the Devil, and he will flee from you."—James 4:7, NW.

[30] This does not mean we can now come to the point where we are immune from assault by the Devil. Until Satan is completely restrained that will never be. It does mean, however, that we will not be misled into supporting Satan's side of the controversy. Our principal fight now is against unseen forces. "We have a fight, not against blood and flesh, but against the governments, against the authorities, against the world-rulers of this darkness, against the wicked spirit forces in the heavenly places."—Ephesians 6:12, NW.

[31] The ultimate end of Satan is complete annihilation. This is made sure by Christ's words to those who have been deceived by the wicked one: "Be on your way from me, you who have been cursed, into the everlasting fire prepared for the Devil and his angels." (Matthew 25:41, NW) What is destroyed by everlasting fire is preserved nowhere, but is consumed for everlasting.

[32] The "lake of fire and sulphur" into which Satan is finally cast means everlasting death. "This means the second death, the lake of fire." (Revelation 20:14, NW) Christ Jesus will see to it that Satan the Devil does not live forever, for we read,

---

30. (a) What is the meaning of James 4:7? (b) With whom is our fight now?
31. What is the ultimate end of Satan, and how do we know?
32. What further Scriptural assurance do we have of this?

at Hebrews 2:14 (*NW*): "He also similarly partook of the same things, that through his death he might destroy the one having the means to cause death, that is, the Devil." Jehovah God also says to Satan, the unfaithful "covering cherub": "I will destroy thee, O covering cherub, from the midst of the stones of fire. . . . and never shalt thou be any more." (Ezekiel 28:16-19) Then the god of this system of things will no longer be able to control mankind and invisibly dominate them. Satan will be dead!

[33] So, be armed with knowledge. Inform yourself. "Keep your senses, be watchful. Your adversary, the Devil, walks about like a roaring lion, seeking to devour someone. But take your stand against him, solid in the faith, knowing that the same things in the way of sufferings are being accomplished in the entire association of your brothers in the world."—1 Peter 5:8, 9, *NW*.

---

33. What should we do to keep from under Satan's influence?

CHAPTER VI

WHAT IS MAN?

THROUGHOUT the centuries the questions, What is man? Has he an immortal soul? and, What is man's destiny? have been the subjects of great discussions among leaders of thought in this world. Men of religion, science and surgery have spent much time and effort in an attempt to answer these questions satisfactorily. The scientists and surgeons answer these questions from the facts they have learned in their study of the anatomy of man. Religious leaders of this world answer the questions from the knowledge they got in divinity schools or theological seminaries.

[2] The scientists and surgeons have come to the conclusion that man is simply a higher form of animal life, having a more complex organism and capable of exercising faculties beyond those of any of the other forms of animal life. They have not been able to find in man any definite proof of immortality. They cannot find any evidence that indicates man has an immortal soul. Yet the worldly religious leaders claim man has an immortal soul and that this is the major difference between man and the other forms of life. They say

1. (a) What questions are to be discussed hereinafter? (b) On what knowledge do men of religion, science and surgery base their answers?

2. (a) What is man according to the scientist and surgeon? (b) What is man according to the worldly religious leaders?

66

the soul is the immortal, spiritual part of man.

[3] To let God be found true our study of these questions will be to ascertain the answers of his Word, the Bible. Others may base their answers on the opinions and writings of men, but unless these opinions and writings are firmly based on the Holy Scriptures they will not correctly answer the questions. Since it is the correct answers that honest people desire, the Bible will be quoted as the authority for all that is stated. The psalmist expressed the proper attitude when he said: "Show me thy ways, O Jehovah; teach me thy paths. Guide me in thy truth, and teach me; for thou art the God of my salvation."—Psalm 25:4, 5, *AS*.

[4] Now to the question, What is man? The psalmist asked a like question, at Psalm 8:4-8, as follows: "What is man, that thou art mindful of him? and the son of man, that thou visitest him? For thou hast made him a little lower than the angels, and hast crowned him with glory and honour. Thou madest him to have dominion over the works of thy hands; thou hast put all things under his feet: all sheep and oxen, yea, and the beasts of the field; the fowl of the air, and the fish of the sea, and whatsoever passeth through the paths of the seas." Those words were in reality a prophecy, as the apostle Paul shows at Hebrews 2:5-10. There he applies the words to the Son of God, who became "the man Christ Jesus" and who was also called "the Son of man", and who was crowned with glory and honor in heaven.—Matthew 16:13, 27, 28; 1 Timothy 2:5, 6.

---

3. How can we get the true answers to our questions regarding man?
4. To whom does Psalm 8:4-8 really apply, and how do we know?

MAN THE SOUL

[5] In describing the creation of the original man Genesis 2:7 very simply states: "The LORD God formed man of the dust of the ground, and breathed into his nostrils the breath of life; and man became a living soul." Thus we learn that man is a combination of two things, namely, the "dust of the ground" and "the breath of life". The combining of these two things (or factors) produced a living soul or creature called *man*. If you have a Bible that shows marginal readings either alongside or below the columns of Scripture verses, you can look at Genesis 1:20, 30 and note that fish, birds and animals are in the "living soul" class—the marginal readings showing "soul" for "creature" and "life" in these verses. The Bible truth that beasts as well as men are *souls* is also indicated by Numbers 31:28, which says: "And levy a tribute unto the LORD of the men of war which went out to battle: one *soul* of five hundred [captured], both of the persons, and of the beeves, and of the asses, and of the sheep."

[6] So we see that the claim of religionists that man has an immortal soul and therefore differs from the beast is not Scriptural. The Bible shows that both man and beast are souls, and that man's pre-eminence is due to the fact that he is a higher form of creature and was originally given dominion over the lower forms of animal life. (Ecclesiastes 3:18-21) The first man, Adam, was created a living soul, and nowhere is it stated that he was given an immortal soul.—1 Corinthians 15:45.

---

5. (a) What is the Scriptural description of man as originally created? (b) What is a soul, and is man the only creature that is a soul?

6. Does man have an immortal soul?

[7] Under further examination we find that in the King James Version of the Bible the English word "soul" is used to translate the Hebrew word *nephesh* and the Greek word *psy·che'*. The word *nephesh* occurs 745 times in the Hebrew Scriptures, and the word *psy·che'* occurs 102 times in the Greek Scriptures (Westcott and Hort Greek text). By using an analytical concordance, such as Young's, a person can trace each occurrence of these two original words. The result of such a thorough search will be that you cannot find a single text in which either of those original words for "soul" is connected or associated with such words as "immortal, everlasting, eternal, or deathless". There is not one Bible text that states the human soul is immortal. Let us abide by the facts of God's Word, and not by the philosophies of men.

[8] The original words, *nephesh* and *psy·che'*, are translated into English by a number of other different English words in our common version of the Bible. Inasmuch as these original words include in their scope the various faculties, functions and properties of the human soul, the translators used various English words to convey the thought in correct language. Thus at times these original words are translated into English by such words as "life, mind, heart, appetite, body, self", etc.

THE HUMAN SOUL MORTAL

[9] The fact that the human soul is mortal can be

---

7. (a) What are the original Hebrew and Greek words translated "soul"? (b) How many times do these words occur in the Bible, and how could we trace these occurrences?
8. What are some of the other words used to translate *nephesh* and *psy·che'* into English?
9. What do the Scriptures prove regarding souls?

amply proved by a careful study of the Holy Scriptures. An immortal soul cannot die, but God's Word, at Ezekiel 18:4, says concerning humans: "Behold, all souls are mine; as the soul of the father, so also the soul of the son is mine: the soul that sinneth, it shall die."

[10] In the Hebrew Scriptures there are at least fifty-four texts where the word *nephesh* (soul) is used in such a way as to show that the soul can be slain or killed. An example of this is in Joshua 10:28-39. There you will find seven instances in which the soul is spoken of as being killed, slain, or destroyed.

[11] It is an acknowledged fact that every living fleshly creature has lifeblood surging through its body. The prophet Jeremiah, speaking to the Jewish organization in his day that had bloodguilt on her, states: "Also in thy skirts is found the blood of the souls of the poor innocents." (Jeremiah 2:34) This clearly proves that the term "souls" is used here as synonymous for flesh-and-blood creatures. There are many other examples similar to this in the Bible.

[12] In the Hebrew Scriptures there are 243 passages where the word *nephesh* is used for a person as being mortal, subject to various kinds of death, from which it is possible to be saved and delivered for life to be prolonged. One such example is at Psalm 22:20, 29: "Deliver my soul from the sword; my darling from the power of the dog. All they that be fat upon earth shall eat and worship: all they that go down to the dust shall bow before

10. (a) Can a soul be slain? (b) What is a Scriptural example?
11. What shows whether souls have blood or not?
12. How many times is *nephesh* used for man as proving him to be a mortal soul?

him: and none can keep alive his own soul." In the Greek Scriptures the word *psy·che'* is similarly used.

¹³ Isaiah, chapter fifty-three, containing the prophecy of the sufferings of the Messiah or Christ, gives very fine examples of the use of the word "soul" in the Bible. At verses 10-12 we read: "Yet it pleased Jehovah to bruise him; he hath put him to grief: when thou shalt make his soul an offering for sin, he shall see his seed, he shall prolong his days, and the pleasure of Jehovah shall prosper in his hand. He shall see of the travail of his soul, and shall be satisfied: by the knowledge of himself shall my righteous servant justify many; and he shall bear their iniquities. Therefore will I divide him a portion with the great, and he shall divide the spoil with the strong; because he poured out his soul unto death, and was numbered with the transgressors: yet he bare the sin of many, and made intercession for the transgressors." (*AS*) This doctrine of the ransom proves it was a soul (Adam) that sinned, and that in order to ransom man there had to be a corresponding soul (a man) sacrificed. Christ by 'pouring out his *soul unto death*' provided the ransom price for man. By this statement of Scripture it is clearly seen that even the man Christ Jesus was mortal. He did not have an immortal soul: Jesus, the human soul, died.

¹⁴ In the Greek Scriptures Matthew 10:28 (*NW*) presents an example where the word "soul" is used as meaning future life as a soul. It reads: "Do not become fearful of those who kill the body but can not kill the soul; but rather be in fear of him that

---

13. What does Isaiah 53:10-12 prove regarding the soul?
14. How is the word "soul" used at Matthew 10:28?

can destroy both soul and body in Gehenna." The gist of this text is that we should fear God, because he is able to destroy not only our present human body but the possibility of future life as well. The destruction in Gehenna here referred to means that death from which there is no resurrection to future life as a soul.

IMMORTALITY

[15] Now that we have examined the Scriptures on the matter of the soul, it is well to see what God's Word teaches regarding *immortal* and *immortality*. God's Word is true in saying that man (the soul) is mortal and subject to death. The question that now arises is, Who does possess immortality? Is it ever shared with others? In the King James Version Bible the words *immortal* and *immortality* occur six times. Let us now examine each such occurrence.

[16] The apostle Paul makes two statements regarding God and Jesus Christ as having immortality. One is found at 1 Timothy 1:17 and reads: "Now unto the King eternal, immortal [incorruptible, *Yg; NW*], invisible, the only wise God, be honour and glory for ever and ever. Amen." The other is found at 1 Timothy 6:16 and reads: "Who only hath immortality, dwelling in the light which no man can approach unto; whom no man hath seen, nor can see: to whom be honour and power everlasting. Amen." Jehovah God alone has always been immortal, and he bestowed immortality on Jesus Christ at his resurrection.

---

15. How many times do the words "immortal" and "immortality" occur in the King James Bible?
16. Who possessed immortality at the time Paul wrote Timothy?

[17] Immortality is held forth as something that the anointed Christian is to seek after: "To them who by patient continuance in well doing seek for glory and honour and immortality [incorruptible-ness, *NW; Yg*], eternal life."—Romans 2:7.

[18] Speaking of the congregation of faithful Christians who are counted worthy to have part in the first resurrection, Paul says: "For this which is corruptible must put on incorruption, and this which is mortal must put on immortality. But when this which is corruptible puts on incorruption and this which is mortal puts on immortality, then the saying will take place that is written: 'Death is swallowed up forever.'" (1 Corinthians 15:53, 54, *NW*) Like Jesus, the members of the Christian congregation do not get immortality till at their resurrection.

[19] The final mention of *immortality* in the *King James Version* is at 2 Timothy 1:10, where it says: "But is now made manifest by the appearing of our Saviour Jesus Christ, who hath abolished death, and hath brought life and immortality [incorruption, *NW*] to light through the gospel." In the Catholic Douay Version Bible the words *immortal* and *immortality* occur twelve times. This is because the *Douay Version* contains the apocryphal or spurious books, such as Wisdom or Ecclesiasticus. Ecclesiasticus 17:29 says: "The son of man is not immortal." But we prefer the testimony of the undisputed inspired apostolic books of Holy Scripture rather than lean on apocryphal

---

17. What shows whether Christians have immortality inherently?
18. What do those who have part in the first resurrection receive?
19. When did the opportunity to gain immortality come to light?

books written before the "manifestation of our
Savior, Christ Jesus".

[20] The Scriptures definitely show that immortality belonged originally to Jehovah God alone.
Christ Jesus was first to receive immortality as a
reward for his faithful course on earth, and it is
now also given in reward to those who are of the
true congregation or "body of Christ". Immortality is a reward for faithfulness. It does not come
automatically to a human at birth.

[21] Man being now a sinful mortal, his ultimate
destiny is death. God gave perfect Adam the command: "Of the tree of the knowledge of good and
evil, thou shalt not eat of it: for in the day that
thou eatest thereof thou shalt surely die." (Genesis 2:17) Adam disobeyed this command of God
and brought upon himself and his posterity the
condemnation of death. Had perfect Adam not
sinned, it would have been possible for him, though
mortal, to live on earth forever and to bequeath
life to his children. At Genesis 2:17 God spoke
very emphatically regarding the death sentence.
He said: "Thou shalt surely die." There is nothing
to indicate that God meant that sinner Adam
would only appear to die but that his soul would
live on forever. The only statement that the Bible
records that disobedient man would not surely
die is found at Genesis 3:4: "And the serpent said
unto the woman, Ye shall not surely die." Thus it
is seen that the serpent (the Devil) is the one that
originated the doctrine of the inherent immortal-

---

20. How may Bible teaching on immortality be summarized?
21. (a) What is man's ultimate destiny? (b) Who originated the doctrine of man's inherent immortality, and
how has this doctrine been used?

ity of human souls. This doctrine is the main one that the Devil has used down through the ages to deceive the people and hold them in bondage. In fact, it is the foundation doctrine of false religion.

[22] Do you know that men and beasts die alike? Ecclesiastes 3:19, 20 says so: "For that which befalleth the sons of men befalleth beasts; even one thing befalleth them: as the one dieth, so dieth the other; yea, they have all one breath; so that a man hath no preeminence above a beast: for all is vanity. All go unto one place; all are of the dust, and all turn to dust again."

[23] Speaking of man's death, Psalm 146:4 says: "His breath goeth forth, he returneth to his earth; in that very day his thoughts perish."

[24] The Scriptures thus show that the destiny of the sinner man is death. But the Bible offers also a ray of hope. Romans 6:23 says: "The wages sin pays is death, but the gift God gives is everlasting life by Christ Jesus our Lord." (*NW*) In that way the true hope is summarized for us. If a man turns to God through Jesus Christ and seeks righteousness through him, that man can gain eternal life in the righteous new world.—Zephaniah 2:3.

[25] The Bible's conclusion regarding the question What is man? is simple and logical. No vain philosophical teachings of pagans! And above all else, the Holy Scriptures alone offer real hope for those who do seek Jehovah God and strive to follow his ways.

---

22. Is man's death different from that of the beasts?
23. What does Psalm 146:4 say happens to man when he dies?
24. What hope do the Scriptures offer for man?
25. After considering the Bible answers to our questions, to what conclusion do we come?

CHAPTER VII

WHY EVOLUTION CANNOT BE TRUE

WHEN scientists are asked "What is man?" the majority will reply that he is merely the latest and highest development in the process of evolution of life, which began many millions of years ago with a microscopic living cell that somehow spontaneously popped into existence. And multitudes of their hearers will believe them. Why? Because of the proof offered? No; the hearers will accept the answer because scientists have accomplished much in certain fields and because they view scientists as shaping theories on only experimental fact and cold logic, unswayed by emotion or personal prejudice and certainly untainted by dishonesty in weighing the evidence. But this blind faith in them is not justified by their works relative to evolution. If, in keeping with the scientific method, we set aside their assertions and speculations and leave only facts on the scales, evolution's case is found to be weightless, and God is again found to be true and his account of man's creation stands vindicated.—Romans 3:4.

² Resemblance and relationship are not the same; yet one of the outstanding assumptions of evolutionary scientists is that they are. That is, when the assumption is convenient. When there is

1. Why do many believe evolution? but what will the facts show?
2. How do evolutionists inconsistently argue on resemblance?

76

a resemblance that does not help their theory they dismiss it on the grounds that there were parallel lines of evolution, producing organisms that resemble but which are unrelated. Thus they leave their hands untied, to pick and choose and reject at their whim. So they line up heads and skeletons, from fish to man, each resembling in varying degrees its neighbor in the line-up, and argue that the resemblance proves evolution. But they do admit that the animals in this line-up are only illustrative, that these particular animals are not the connected ancestry of man. First they argue that the resemblance proves evolution, then tell us the animals in their chosen resemblance chain are not related. In this line-up and next to man they put the ape, but they become indignant if anyone else says they teach we came from apes. It is like taking links of many shapes and sizes and lining them up according to resemblance and saying they originally formed one chain. It is like a flight of stairs,

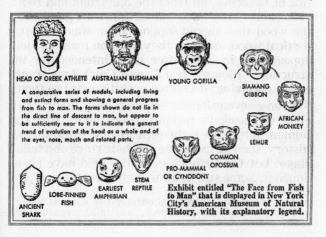

HEAD OF GREEK ATHLETE   AUSTRALIAN BUSHMAN   YOUNG GORILLA   SIAMANG GIBBON   AFRICAN MONKEY   LEMUR   COMMON OPOSSUM   PRO-MAMMAL OR CYNODONT   STEM REPTILE   EARLIEST AMPHIBIAN   LOBE-FINNED FISH   ANCIENT SHARK

A comparative series of models, including living and extinct forms and showing a general progress from fish to man. The forms shown do not lie in the direct line of descent to man, but appear to be sufficiently near to it to indicate the general trend of evolution of the head as a whole and of the eyes, nose, mouth and related parts.

Exhibit entitled "The Face from Fish to Man" that is displayed in New York City's American Museum of Natural History, with its explanatory legend.

with man as the top step, but all of the steps
ascending to it admittedly being imaginary. Such
is shallow philosophy, not sound science.

³ Frequently these scientific philosophers give
way to dishonesty in desperate endeavors to save
their sinking theory. Ernst Haeckel was a famous
evolutionist, and made wide use of diagrams to
prove resemblance between human embryos and
other animal embryos, and also skeletal resem-
blances between man and other animals. Once a
Dr. Brass supplied Haeckel with accurate diagrams,
but Haeckel doctored them before publication. He
later confessed: "I begin at once with the con-
trite confession that a small number of my diagrams are really forgeries in Dr. Brass' sense.
Hundreds of the best zoologists lie under the same
charge." (Müncher *Allgemeine Zeitung,* January
1909) But the diagrams keep appearing. It is like
what Anthony Standen said about Haeckel's evolutionary tree that shows present animals on the
tips of branches, all from the one trunk and root:
"Haeckel's trees have indeed fallen to pieces, for
the wood that should support them was all hypo-
thetical wood. And yet they keep on making their
appearance, in book after book intended for instruction." (*Science Is a Sacred Cow*) Appearanc-
es are deceiving; deceptive evolutionists use them.

⁴ Some evolutionists, though not many, still
cling to Haeckel's recapitulation theory that the
human fetus goes through man's evolutionary
history, such as fish stage and hair stage and tailed
stage; but the authorities in the field have abandoned it. Some still point to body structures appar-

---

3. How do evolutionists dishonestly use diagrams?
4. What about recapitulation, vestigial organs, and
blood tests?

ently no longer used, called vestigial, and say they prove evolution. The evidence is that they are not so much vestigial as it is that their use remains unknown. Anyway, evolution needs to show the gaining of new organs, not the loss of old ones. Blood tests were once pointed to as a means of showing relationship between man and certain animals near him in the evolutionary chain; but they proved this practice ridiculous and embarrassing when certain blood tests showed frogs and snakes and mice nearer to men than monkeys were.

[5] So-called "missing links" between men and apes have deceived many. A close study of them reveals to one's amazement the utter lack of evidence, and the tendency to twist the evidence to suit evolution's case. The Piltdown man is a fragment of human skull united with a chimpanzee jaw. Neanderthal man is admittedly no ancient ancestor of man. Modern-type men have been found in earth layers older than any of the famous "missing links"; so how can these be ancestral to modern man, if modern-type man existed before them? And when the evolutionists find a fossil man that does not help but hinders their theory, what do they do? They conceal the evidence, as evolutionist Hooton admits: "Heretical and nonconforming fossil men were banished to the limbo of dark museum cupboards, forgotten or even destroyed." (*Apes, Men, and Morons*) Of the famous "missing links" evolutionist Sir Arthur Keith said: "We cannot trace modern man back to any of these extinct types." Professor Branco of Berlin University said: "Paleontology tells us nothing on the subject—it knows no ancestors of man." Professor Virchow declared: "The man-ape has no

5. What eliminates "missing links" as proofs?

existence and the missing link remains a phan-
tom." Austin Clark of Smithsonian Institution
said: "Missing links are misinterpretations."

[6] The evolutionists allow the public to believe
that the geological record of the rocks proves evolution, that in the rock layers are fossils that trace
the ascending chain of life. Not so. There are innumerable fossils of forms living today, or of extinct forms but which are not transitional forms
from one animal family to another. But there is
no chain showing the change-over from one family to another, the deceptive claims of evolutionists
notwithstanding. Darwin himself admitted this,
in his *Origin of Species:* "Geology assuredly does
not reveal any such finely graded organic chain;
and this perhaps is the most obvious and serious
objection which can be urged against the theory."
The fact is that life appears suddenly in fossil form
in the rock layers, and in great diversity of forms
and families. The appearance is not gradual, with
increasing diversity, as evolution would require.
Deep down the rock layers have no fossils; life had
not started. Then all of a sudden an abundance
of fossils appear in the layers immediately above
these blank strata. It means creation, sudden and
with variety, and not evolution. The record of the
rocks proves God true and evolution false.

[7] Hear it from the mouths of evolutionists, and
be convinced. The Smithsonian Institution biolo-
gist Austin Clark said: "So far as concerns the
major groups of animals the creationists seem to
have the better of the argument. There is not the
slightest evidence that any one of the major
groups arose from any other. Each is a special

6. How do fossils prove God true and evolution false?
7. What testimony by evolutionists supports creation?

animal-complex, related more closely to all the rest and appearing, therefore, as a special and distinct creation." Of man he adds: "He appeared suddenly and in substantially the same form as he is today." (*Literary Digest,* February 16, 1929) Evolutionist Lecomte du Nouy admitted: "Each group, order, or family seems to be born suddenly and we hardly ever find the forms which link them to the preceding strain. When we discover them they are already completely differentiated. Not only do we find practically no transitional forms, but in general it is impossible to authentically connect a new group with an ancient one." About birds he lamented that they have "all the unsatisfactory characteristics of absolute creation". —*Human Destiny.*

NEW KNOWLEDGE FORCES EVOLUTION'S RETREAT

[8] Evolutionists once contended, and some still do, that life spontaneously generated itself millions of years ago, and that that beginning evolved into the myriads of complex forms of today. New knowledge forced a series of retreats from this position, until by the latter half of the nineteenth century "all biologists were convinced that spontaneous generation was definitely disproved for all forms of living organisms". (*Man and the Biological World*) "There is not a single fact or a single hypothesis, today, which gives an explanation of the birth of life or of natural evolution." (*Human Destiny,* 1947) With all their ingenious laboratory techniques modern scientists have tried and tried to create life, but have consistently failed. It has caused reasonable ones to acknowl-

---

8. Why do we say the first link of evolution's chain is a missing link?

edge that what they cannot do under various controlled conditions in the laboratory certainly could not happen by sheer chance. The first link of evolution's chain is a missing link.

⁹ But granting evolutionists the start they do not have, how would it evolve to manhood? More than a century ago evolutionist Lamarck said an organism acquired certain characteristics from its environment, which is true, and that these acquired characteristics were passed on to the offspring, which is not true. So he contended that environment changed the organism, and down through future generations the accumulations of acquired characteristics developed new animals. Now geneticists know better. "Until 1900 many biologists believed that characteristics plants and animals acquired from their environment were passed to their offspring. Modern genetics has proved they are not." (*Life,* March 17, 1947) In this connection note another of the many instances of dishonesty by evolutionists. In the 1920's a Dr. Paul Kammerer of Vienna claimed to have a specimen that acquired a characteristic from environment and passed it on to its offspring. The outcome: "The climax of Kammerer's case came recently when a certain American scientist journeyed to Vienna to investigate his claims first hand. Upon examination of one of the specimens which has, it was claimed, developed new structures, the visitor found that Kammerer had injected India ink under the skin to produce a swelling. Upon being confronted with the fake, Kam-

9. Why are acquired characteristics no help to evolution? and what instance in this connection again shows dishonesty?

merer picked up a revolver and shot himself."
—*Back to Creationism*, 1929.

[10] Next came Darwin with his theory of natural
selection and survival of the fittest. But new developments must arrive before they can be selected as fit to survive. As Professor Coulter of the
University of Chicago said: "The most fundamental objection to the theory of natural selection
is that it cannot originate characters; it only selects among characters already existing." Or as
evolutionist Hugo de Vries put it: "Natural selection may explain the survival of the fittest, but
it cannot explain the arrival of the fittest."

[11] Hugo de Vries tried to account for the arrival
by mutations, which refers to apparently spontaneous changes between parent and offspring,
and which changes are inheritable. This theory has
been seized upon today by many evolutionists as
the answer to their prayer. On the basis of mutations some try to avoid having evolution proceed
slowly, but say it happened fast, in big jumps. In
this way they are not embarrassed by the lack of
fossils to connect family groups; the change from
family to family came in jumps, not slow and gradual changes. Much experimenting has been done
with mutations, especially since the building of
atomic piles, for atomic radiation induces a flood
of mutations, which ordinarily are rare in nature.
The result? Innumerable mutations have been induced, but no new families produced.

[12] Moreover, if the mutations are small they
weaken, and if large they kill. Being harmful in-

10. What is the weakness of natural selection and survival of the fittest?
11. Do mutations explain or prove evolution? Why?
12. What facts about mutations eliminate them as proof
for evolution?

stead of helpful, they explain no upward evolving,
but downward devolving and degenerating. Consider: "I am afraid that many anthropologists
(including myself) have sinned against genetic
science and are leaning upon a broken reed when
they depend upon mutations. The evidence of modern experimental genetics seems to indicate that
most mutations are harmful, and that many of
them are even lethal, and that they are attribut-
able in the main to deterioration." (Hooton's *Apes,
Men, and Morons*) "No useful mutations have appeared, and none is anticipated." (*Life,* November 21, 1949) "It is conservatively estimated that
over 99 per cent of mutated genes are harmful."
(*Science News Letter,* November 4, 1950) "The
mutation theory of De Vries may now be relegated
to the limbo of discarded hypotheses," opines
Harvard University's Professor Jeffrey.

[13] These are the hard, cheerless facts facing the
evolutionists who had hoped that their failing
theory could gain salvation by mutations. From
the fog of wishful thinking the firm fact emerges
that neither acquired characteristics nor natural
selection nor mutations can form new families.
While allowing for many varieties within the family or Genesis kind, and which can interbreed and
produce offspring, the Creator's laws of heredity
ensure obedience to the divine decree to bring
forth "after its kind". (Genesis 1:11, 21, 24, *AS*)
So repeatedly the theories behind which evolutionists entrenched themselves have been smashed by
new facts, and these forced retreats should rout
evolution from the minds of sober thinkers.

[14] Actually, the findings of true science prove

13. So what facts now emerge?
14. What confirms the Bible, contradicts evolution?

the Bible account of Genesis. Science confirms the order of appearance of the different big divisions of life, as given in Genesis chapter 1, and the mathematical odds against the ancient writer's guessing this order are staggering. This first Bible book also shows the unchangeableness of families, that life would reproduce "after its kind", which fact the fossil record confirms. Geology shows complex life forms appearing suddenly and in great variety of families, as would be the case in creation. Bible truth dovetails with science's discovery that men of all races came from one pair originally, that archaeological findings prove civilization of a high order appears suddenly, that language studies show the oldest tongues are the most complex, giving no hint of evolving from animal grunts and growls. Degeneration instead of evolution upward is evident now, and the Bible's report of Adam's fall accounts for it. Man's creation in God's image harmonizes with man's ability to reason, determine right and wrong, manifest conscience, hold dominion over animals, worship the Creator; in short, it explains the tremendous gulf that separates man and any other animal. The Bible account fits so perfectly with the facts of true science; evolution is a misfit in every way.

[15] Then why do the majority of the men of science accept evolution? It is their faith; they stoop to many means to convert others, and they view the Bible as their competitor. Sir Arthur Keith said: "Evolution is unproved and unprovable. We believe it only because the only alternative is special creation, and that is unthinkable." Professor Watson of London University said: "Evolution

15. Then why do the majority of the men of science accept evolution?

itself is accepted by zoologists, not because it has been observed to occur or . . . can be proved by logically coherent evidence to be true, but because the only alternative, special creation, is clearly incredible." Dr. Calman of the British Museum said scientists *profess* to accept it "as a convenient weapon with which to meet the fundamentalists". Professor Bateson stated: "Though we must hold to our faith in the evolution of species there is little evidence as to how it came about, and no clear proof that the process is continuing in any considerable degree at the present time." Professor D. H. Scott contended: "Yet evolution remains— we cannot get away from it, even if we hold it only as an act of faith, for there is no alternative." Sir J. W. Dawson, professor of geology, said that to believe was "an act of faith, not that kind which is based on testimony or evidence, however slight, but of that unreasoning kind which we usually stigmatize as mere credulity and superstition". And finally, Professor T. L. More, University of Cincinnati: "The more one studies palaeontology, the more certain one becomes that evolution is based on faith alone; exactly the same sort of faith which it is necessary to have when one encounters the great mysteries of religion."

[16] The scientists have converted multitudes to their faith, a faith that is without works to prove it, and hence a dead faith. (James 2:26) Many Catholic, Protestant and Jewish clergymen have embraced it, and thus accept this dogma of ancient pagans along with some of their other pagan doctrines, such as trinity and immortal soul and eternal torment. Encyclopedias show Greeks and others before Christ believed evolution, and that sav-

16. Whom have the scientists converted to their faith?

age tribes in remote parts of earth believe it today. Space forbids extensive quoting to prove Christendom's acceptance of this, but since the pope of the Roman Catholic Church is foremost in Christendom's religious circles, we will cite him. In an encyclical of August, 1950, the pope said that it was permissible to study "the doctrine of evolution in as far as it inquires into the origin of the human body as coming from pre-existent and living matter". An Associated Press dispatch of September, 1951, elaborated: "Pope Pius XII says that the theory of evolution can be studied so far as it deals with origins of the human body but should not be allowed to raise questions as to divine creation of the human soul." Such religionists argue that God used evolution to do the creative work of Genesis chapter 1, but that position is contrary to his decree that his created works reproduce "after their kind".

[17] True Christians will not compromise. They will not be dazzled by the fake wisdom of this world that is foolishness with God, nor be preyed upon by the vain philosophies and empty deceptions of a world that has rejected Christ, nor endeavor to twist God's Word to fit the false stories of babblers. (1 Corinthians 3:19; Colossians 2:8; 1 Timothy 4:7; 2 Peter 3:16) They will not swallow the pagan pill of evolution, not even after modern science talks it up or Christendom's clergy sugarcoat it and offer it from their pulpits. Let worldlings allow their ears to be tickled and accept men as true though it make God false if they wish. As for Christians, they will "let God be found true, though every man be found a liar".

17. What will be the position of true Christians?

CHAPTER VIII

HELL, A PLACE OF
REST IN HOPE

"WHAT a horrible and disgusting subject! I do not want to discuss it. I have no desire to hear anything about that infernal place. We have plenty of hell here. Please do not start on such a subject!" In disgust so exclaimed a woman with whom one of Jehovah's witnesses was conversing.

[2] Do you blame this woman for expressing herself in such a way? We do not. It would be natural for her to speak so, and also for all those who have been taught by Christendom to believe the God-dishonoring doctrine of a fiery hell for tormenting conscious human souls eternally. But as you are an honest person, endowed by your Creator with an intelligent, inquiring mind, you will want to know what hell is. What does it look like? When, by whom and for what purpose was it created or discovered? Who go there, and for how long?

[3] In Old English versions the word *hell* is used to name the place, in German versions *Hoelle,* in Portuguese *inferno,* in Spanish *infierno,* and in French *Enfer,* and in Greek *ha'des.* In the old Hebrew Scriptures it is the word *sheol* that is translated by these words in the different languages.

1, 2. What is the general view about hell, and what questions arise in the inquiring mind?
3-6. How do various languages name the place, and how do English and foreign translators not agree in their translations?

[4] Throughout those sacred Hebrew Scriptures this word *sheol* occurs 65 times. In the *King James Version* the English translators rendered it 31 times "hell", 31 times "grave", and only 3 times "pit".

[5] In the Catholic *Douay Version* the English translators rendered *sheol* 63 times as "hell", and once as "pit" (Job 17:16), and once as "death" (Osee 13:14). This *Douay Version* says "hell" at Psalms 93:17 and 113:17, but the word *sheol* does not occur there, and in the corresponding places (Psalms 94:17 and 115:17) the *King James Version* says "silence". At Proverbs 2:18 and Ecclesiastes 9:3 the *Douay Version* says "hell", but the *King James Version* says "the dead". At Isaiah 7:11 the *Douay Version* says "depth of hell", but the *King James Version* simply says "depth". The *Douay Version* has the apocryphal books or writings, and in these the word *hell* occurs 19 times more and is translated from the Greek words *taphos* (burial place), *ha'des,* and *ábyssos* (abyss).

[6] Even in the foreign languages the various translators do not agree among themselves in translating the Hebrew word *sheol* and its Greek equivalent *ha'des.* But the very fact that the *King James Version* renders the one Hebrew word *sheol* three different ways shows that *hell, grave* and *pit* mean one and the same thing. Since *hell* means mankind's common grave or the pit of burial, it could not at the same time mean a place of fiery torture or a

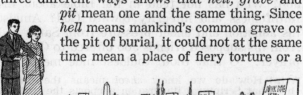

place of two compartments, one of bliss and one of fiery torment.

[7] How do we know *sheol* means mankind's common grave and not a place of torture? Holy Scripture, God's Word, interprets it so. At Genesis 37:35 and 42:38 Jacob, one of Jesus' forefathers, when mourning for his son Joseph, whom he thought to be dead, said to his sons and daughters who came to comfort him: "I will go down into the grave [*sheol*] unto my son mourning. . . . then shall ye bring down my gray hairs with sorrow to the grave [*sheol*]." In these verses the *American Standard Version* leaves *sheol* untranslated, the *King James Version* renders it "grave", but the Catholic *Douay Version* renders it "hell". Now, stop for a moment and think. Did Jacob believe that his son Joseph went to a place of torment to spend eternity there, and did he want himself to go there and meet him? Or rather was it that he merely thought his beloved son was dead and in the grave and he himself wanted to die? If he were to go to such hot and fiery place, his gray hairs would not last long. Whether Catholic, Protestant, Jew, or of other religion, stop! think! reason!

[8] Do good people go to hell? Yes, if by hell you mean the Bible hell. Who does not know about Job? Who has not read in the Bible about his faithfulness and integrity toward God? Amidst his affliction and under pressure from Satan and from his supposed friends Job offered to God this prayer: "O that thou wouldest hide me in the

7. (a) How do we know *sheol* means the grave? (b) What Scriptural illustration supports the truth of the matter?
8. Do good people go to the Bible hell, and how does faithful Job's prayer prove your answer?

grave [sheol, *AS;* hell, *Dy*], that thou wouldest keep me secret, until thy wrath be past, that thou wouldest appoint me a set time, and remember me!" (Job 14:13) If *sheol* means a place of torment and fire, would Job wish to go there and spend his time until God remembered him? This question calls for the use of your reasoning faculties rather than blind credulity. Evidently Job's desire was to die and go to the grave, that his sufferings might cease. Psalm 139:8 reads: "If I make my bed in hell [sheol, *AS*], behold, thou art there."

WHERE HELL IS

⁹ But where is hell located? The *Catholic Encyclopedia,* Volume VII, under the word "Hell", states: "Holy Writ seems to indicate that hell is within the earth, for it describes hell as an abyss to which wicked descend." But read what the Bible says about the location of hell. When the prophet Jonah was swallowed by a big fish to save him from drowning he prayed from its belly in these words: "I cried by reason of mine affliction unto the LORD, and he heard me; out of the belly of hell [the grave, *marginal reading*] cried I, and thou heardest my voice." (Jonah 2:2) Where was Jonah? In the belly of the fish which God prepared to swallow him. That cramped dark place would have been the prophet's grave had not God 'spoken to the fish and it vomited Jonah out upon the dry land'. But until that time he was in hell; he was as good as dead in sheol, the grave or tomb. Plainly, hell is not at the hot center of our earth, for it is no deeper than the grave.

---

9. According to false religion's teaching, where is hell located, but what does the Bible teach?

[10] And how about the soldiers who die in carnal warfare? Do they go to heaven or to hell? Your true answer is at Ezekiel 32:27: "The mighty that are fallen [in the battle] of the uncircumcised, which are gone down to hell with their weapons of war: and they have laid their swords under their heads, but their iniquities shall be upon their bones, though they were the terror of the mighty in the land of the living." So the soldiers who die in war are cast into hell, sheol or the grave, and their weapons too are laid with them in hell under their heads, in the land of the dead. Amos 9:2 reads: "Though they dig into hell, thence shall mine hand take them." How can men dig into hell if it is a place of literal fire and sulphur in the bowels of the earth? It is so plain that the Bible hell is mankind's common grave that even an honest little child can understand it, but not the religious theologians.

[11] At Numbers 16:32, 33, about those who rebelled against Moses, it is written that the earth "opened her mouth, and swallowed them up, and . . . they, and all that appertained to them, went down alive into the pit [into hell, *Dy*]". Here is one instance where *sheol* is translated "pit". It means the grave, down to which the earthquake brought those rebellious ones.

GETTING OUT OF HELL

[12] Is there any example in Scripture of where a

---

10. (a) Do soldiers who die in battle go to hell, or to heaven, or where? (b) Is it possible for men to dig into hell?
11. Can a man, descending into the Bible hell, take his belongings with him?
12. Is there a Scriptural example of where a man went to hell and was delivered from it? and in the Greek Scriptures what is the equivalent of the Hebrew word *sheol?*

man went to hell and was delivered from it? Yes;
Jonah was one. But the Bible gives another example, that of Jesus. He went to hell and stayed
there for three days, and then by the power of the
Almighty God he was resurrected. Hear what the
apostle Peter states about the martyred Jesus
Christ. Quoting from Psalm 16:10, Peter says:
"His soul was not left in hell, neither his flesh did
see corruption. This Jesus hath God raised up,
whereof we all are witnesses." (Acts 2:31, 32) The
Hebrew word at Psalm 16:10 translated "hell" is
sheol; but in Peter's Greek quotation it is *ha'des.*
So we see that *ha'des* is the Greek equivalent for
sheol. The original word in each language means
mankind's common grave, a condition where the
dead and buried ones are unseen. There is where
the Son of God went for three days, like Jonah.

[13] But are not Satan the Devil and his demons
down in hell keeping the fires and making it hard
for those who are in it? This is what is taught by
Christendom's clergy, but you will be surprised
to know the Devil never was in such a place. The
Devil's human servant, the king of Babylon, was
doomed to go to hell, the Bible hell. But Satan the
Devil who made himself Lucifer in his organization is really the one spoken to under the figure
of the "king of Babylon" in these words. "Hell
from beneath is moved for thee to meet thee at
thy coming: it stirreth up the dead for thee, even
all the chief ones of the earth; it hath raised up
from their thrones all the kings of the nations."
(Isaiah 14:9) If the Devil had been there constantly, how could hell be moved to meet him?

---

13. Is it true that Satan has always been in hell keeping up the fires? and what does Isaiah 14:9 state about
him?

Only because, as verse 15 prophetically says to him, "thou shalt be brought down to hell, to the sides of the pit." Clearly, then, Satan goes there for the first time at the battle of Armageddon to meet the dead. So hell here corresponds with the abyss where he is cast bound for a thousand years. —Revelation 20:1-3, 7.

[14] Many religious sects believe that for all those who have the misfortune to go to hell there is no hope whatever that they will ever come out from it. But Jesus got out of hell, and at Revelation 20:13 we read: "Death and hell delivered up the dead which were in them: and they were judged every man according to their works." Here the record states that hell let out *the dead* who were in it and that those released ones were judged according to their works.

[15] Now, it is a case of choosing who is true, God or the clergy? At verse 14 we read: "And death and hell [*ha'des*] were cast into the lake of fire. This is the second death." This is highly symbolic language. Death and hell are things that cannot reasonably be cast into a literal "lake of fire". Death itself, Paul says, will be destroyed: "Death is swallowed up forever." (1 Corinthians 15:54, 55, *NW*) None would be able to understand this symbolic language unless the Bible itself gave us the interpretation by saying: "This means the second death, the lake of fire." (Revelation 20:14, *NW*) From the second death there is no recovery or resurrection. At verse 10 the gladsome statement is made that the Devil himself is finally "hurled into the lake of fire and sulphur", which, accord-

---

14, 15. (a) Will hell last eternally? (b) What, then, is the "lake of fire" according to the Bible's own interpretation?

ing to the Bible, means "the second death". From this state the Devil will never return to molest the subjects of the King of the new world. The Devil's 'torments' in the lake of fire mean he will stay in the second death forever.

GEHENNA

[16] How, now, are we to explain Jesus' words at Mark 9:47, 48? Here the *King James Version* reads: "If thine eye offend thee, pluck it out: it is better for thee to enter into the kingdom of God with one eye, than having two eyes to be cast into hell fire: where their worm dieth not, and the fire is not quenched." This text is seized upon by hell-fire screechers to prove there is a place of fiery torture where the wicked are suffering conscious pains. But close examination of the words of Jesus reveals that what dies not is the worms, not the creature man. So according to the clergy theory the worms are immortal. This is wholly unscriptural and unreasonable. Jesus said nothing about creatures being conscious there and suffering torment in fire.

[17] What, then, did Jesus here mean? This: that it is better for a man to be deprived of anything that is as dear to him as an eye or a hand or a foot than to hold on to that and be destroyed in Gehenna. Here the Greek Bible text uses, not the word *ha'des*, but the word *Gehenna*. According to the Hebrew Scriptures this has reference, not to hell, but to the "Valley of Hinnom". This valley

---

16. What text is seized upon by hell-fire screechers to prove hell is a place of torture?

17, 18. (a) What, then, do Jesus' words at Mark 9:47, 48 mean? (b) What was Gehenna, and how was it used by the Jews?

lay outside of the south and west walls of Jerusalem. It was used as a crematory or incinerator where the Israelites dumped the city's offal and garbage as well as the dead bodies of animals and of vile criminals to be destroyed by burning. No live creatures, however, were cast there, as this was against the Jewish

VALLEY OF HINNOM (GEHENNA)

law. The fires were kept burning continually and, in order to increase their intensity, the Jews added brimstone or sulphur. Hence Gehenna, or the Valley of Hinnom, became a symbol, not of eternal torment, but of the condition of eternal condemnation. Its flames symbolized the complete, eternal destruction to which all the willful enemies of God and his kingdom will go and from which there is no recovery or resurrection.

[18] Gehenna is otherwise spoken of as a "lake that burns with fire and sulphur". (Revelation 21:8, NW) However, ha'des represents the death condition from which a resurrection is possible. If we were to take Jesus' words about Gehenna as meaning literal fire, then only the literally one-footed and one-eyed persons would ever get eternal life. See Matthew 23:33 where most translators mistranslate Gehenna as hell.

[19] In all places where hell is translated from the Greek word Gehenna it means everlasting destruction. The New World Translation correctly ren-

<hr />

19. (a) Is everlasting torment or everlasting destruction the punishment reserved for those who go to Gehenna? (b) How is this corroborated by the parable of the sheep and goats?

ders Gehenna. So note Jesus' words at Matthew 10:28: "Do not become fearful of those who kill the body but can not kill the soul; but rather be in fear of him that can destroy both soul and body in Gehenna." Since God destroys soul and body in Gehenna, this is conclusive proof that Gehenna, or the valley of the son of Hinnom, is a picture or symbol of complete annihilation, and not of eternal torment. This is the meaning of the "everlasting fire" mentioned in the parable of the sheep and goats. There, after Jesus pronounced judgment on the "goats", who do not support God's kingdom to which Christ's brothers are called, he declares respecting the "goats": "These will depart into everlasting cutting-off [Greek, *kolasis*], but the righteous ones into everlasting life." (Matthew 25:46, *NW; ED*) So the everlasting punishment of the "goats" is their everlastingly being cut off from all life.

[20] The question may now well be asked, What have you to say about the rich man whom Jesus described as having gone to hell and Lazarus who "was carried off by the angels to the bosom position of Abraham"? (Luke 16:19-31, *NW*) Does this not show there is a fiery hell with people conscious in it? Not at all; for this is a parable. A parable is a symbolic and figurative statement which pictures some reality. It is unreasonable to suppose that one goes to hell because he is rich, wears good clothing and has plenty to eat; for nothing is charged against the rich man. On the other hand, it would be ridiculous to believe that in order to go to heaven one must be a beggar, lie

---

20. Why is it unreasonable and ridiculous to believe that the "rich man" went to a hell of torment and the "beggar" to the literal bosom of Abraham?

at some rich man's gate, eat crumbs falling from his table, be full of sores and have dogs come and lick them. How many Jews like Lazarus are there in the world today? Another thing, if the rich man were in a literal burning lake, how could Abraham send Lazarus to cool his tongue with just a drop of water on the tip of his finger?

²¹ By this parable Jesus uttered a prophecy which has been undergoing its modern fulfillment since A.D. 1919. It has its application to two classes existing on earth today. The rich man represents the ultraselfish class of the clergy of Christendom, who are now afar off from God and dead to his favor and service and tormented by the Kingdom truth proclaimed. Lazarus depicts the faithful remnant of the "body of Christ". These, on being delivered from modern Babylon since 1919, receive God's favor, pictured by the "bosom position of Abraham", and are comforted through his Word. For a detailed discussion of this parable we refer the reader to the book *What Has Religion Done for Mankind?* pages 246-256, 302-312, and also *The Watchtower,* February 15 and March 1, 1951. These will give a satisfying answer and great consolation to all readers of them.

²² Who is responsible for this God-defaming doctrine of a hell of torment? The promulgator of it is Satan himself. His purpose in introducing it has been to frighten the people away from studying the Bible and to make them hate God. Imperfect man does not torture even a mad dog, but kills it. And yet the clergymen attribute to God, who is

---

21. Briefly what is the parable's meaning and application?
22. Who, then, is responsible for this God-defaming doctrine, and what is his purpose?

love, the wicked crime of torturing human creatures merely because they had the misfortune to be born sinners. (1 John 4:16) The hell-fire doctrine was taught by pagans hundreds of years before Christ. It, as well as the doctrine of "purgatory", is based on another pagan false doctrine, that of the immortality of the human soul. To suffer eternal torment in consciousness after death the human soul would have to be immortal and indestructible.

[23] The doctrine of a burning hell where the wicked are tortured eternally after death cannot be true, mainly for four reasons: (1) It is wholly unscriptural; (2) it is unreasonable; (3) it is contrary to God's love, and (4) it is repugnant to justice. From this it is appreciated more that Gehenna is the condition of destruction where the Devil, his demons and all human opposers of Jehovah's theocratic government will go and from which condition there is no resurrection or recovery. But hell, *sheol* or *ha'des* means mankind's common grave, the condition where humans, good and bad, go and rest in hope of a resurrection under God's kingdom.

---

23. For what four reasons cannot this hell-fire doctrine be true? and what is clearly seen from this short chapter?

CHAPTER IX

IS THERE A TRINITY?

A FUNDAMENTAL doctrine of so-called "Christendom" is that known as the "Holy Trinity". It is accepted as Scriptural truth and held sacred by millions of persons. The doctrine, in brief, is that there are three gods in one: "God the Father, God the Son, and God the Holy Ghost," all three equal in power, substance and eternity. As defined by the *Catholic Encyclopedia* under the heading "Trinity, The Blessed", "The Trinity is the term employed to signify the central doctrine of the Christian religion— . . . in the unity of the Godhead there are Three Persons, the Father, the Son, and the Holy Spirit, these Three Persons being truly distinct one from another. Thus, in the words of the Athanasian Creed: 'The Father is God, the Son is God, and the Holy Spirit is God, and yet there are not three Gods, but one God.' "

[2] Such a doctrine, with its attempted explanation, is very confusing. To excuse it with the word "Mystery!" is not satisfying. If one has in mind the apostle's words, "God is not the author of confusion" (1 Corinthians 14:33), it is at once seen that such doctrine is not of God. Well, one might ask, if God is not the author of this confusing doctrine, who is?

1. How is the "trinity" doctrine defined?
2. What points are raised that are cause for doubt as to God's being the author of the doctrine?

[3] The origin of the trinity doctrine is traced back to the ancient Babylonians and Egyptians and other ancient mythologists. It will not be disputed by Jews and Christians that these ancient peoples worshiped demon gods and that God's typical nation of Israel was warned not to mingle with them because of this. It follows, then, that God was not the author of this doctrine. Two more interesting facts are: (1) A religionist living in the second century, by the name of Tertullian, located in Carthage, Africa, introduced the term *trinitas* into Latin ecclesiastical writings, the term "trinity" not once being used in the inspired Scriptures. (2) The doctrine of the triad was first introduced into Greek ecclesiastical writings by a clergyman named Theophilus, also living in the second century. In the fourth century, or the year 325 (A.D.), a council of clergymen met under the jurisdiction of unbaptized Emperor Constantine at Nice in Asia Minor and confirmed the doctrine. It thus came to be declared the doctrine of the religious organization of Christendom, and the clergy have ever held to this complicated doctrine. The obvious conclusion is, therefore, that Satan is the originator of the trinity doctrine.

[4] One might ask, But what about the scriptures cited to support the "trinity"? Would they not prove the doctrine as taught by the clergy to be different from the trinity of ancient Babylon? Every honest and God-fearing person wants to know the facts. He realizes that knowledge is a defense against error and that to gain such knowl-

3. Where did the "trinity" originate, and how did it find its way into Christendom's religion?
4. What question arises as to proof? and why should the subject be frankly considered?

edge both sides of an argument must be frankly considered. To this end let us turn our attention to the main scriptures used to support the trinity doctrine.

[5] First, the text appearing at 1 John 5:7, *King James Version* and *Douay Version*. This reads: "For there are three that bear record in heaven, the Father, the Word, and the Holy Ghost: and these three are one." Second, John 10:30, which simply states: "I and my Father are one." Third, Paul's words regarding Christ Jesus, at 1 Timothy 3:16: "God was manifest in the flesh." And, fourth, the well-known text at John 1:1: "In the beginning was the Word, and the Word was with God, and the Word was God."

[6] When the clergy are asked by their followers as to how such a combination of three in one can possibly exist, they are obliged to answer, "That is a mystery." Some will try to illustrate it by using triangles, trefoils, or images with three heads on one neck. Nevertheless, sincere persons who want to know the true God and serve him find it a bit difficult to love and worship a complicated, freakish-looking, three-headed God. The clergy who inject such ideas will contradict themselves in the very next breath by stating that God made man in his own image; for certainly no one has ever seen a three-headed human creature.

[7] The position taken by true Christians is, "Let God be found true, though every man be found a liar." The standard they accept is: "Every word of

5. What four texts are commonly used to support the "trinity"?
6. How do the clergy try to uphold the doctrine, and how might a thoughtful person react to their attempt to explain?
7. What position do true Christians take, and why?

God is pure." (Romans 3:4, *NW;* Proverbs 30:5) Since the scriptures here quoted are from God's pure Word, the Bible, it is vital that they be given careful attention. With this in mind let us consider 1 John 5:7: "For there are three that bear record in heaven, the Father, the Word, and the Holy Ghost: and these three are one."

[8] That is a glaring example of adding to God's Word, though such adding is expressly condemned. In commenting on this text, a Greek Scripture translator, Benjamin Wilson, writes in his *The Emphatic Diaglott:* "This text concerning the heavenly witness is not contained in any Greek manuscript which was written earlier than the fifteenth century. It is not cited by any of the Greek ecclesiastical writers; nor by any of the early Latin fathers, even when the subjects upon which they treated would naturally have led them to appeal to its authority. It is therefore evidently spurious." The truthfulness of this statement is borne out by the fact that the modern translations (except Roman Catholic translations from the Latin versions) do not include the text.

[9] Our next scripture for consideration is John 10:30: "I and my Father are one." Reading this text by itself one might be justified in arguing that God and Jesus were one; but one in what way? Jehovah counsels, "Get wisdom: and with all thy getting get understanding." (Proverbs 4:7) This rule must always be applied, and no less in the present case.

---

8. What are the two facts regarding 1 John 5:7 that make it unnecessary for further comment?
9, 10. (a) What rule must always be applied when considering the Bible? (b) How does Jesus explain the meaning of John 10:30, and how does the apostle show he understood it so?

[10] What Jesus meant at John 10:30 he himself explains in his prayer to the Father on the night before his execution: "Neither pray I for these alone, but for them also which shall believe on me through their word; that they all may be one; as thou, Father, art in me, and I in thee, that they also may be one in us: that the world may believe that thou hast sent me. And the glory which thou gavest me I have given them; that they may be one, even as we are one." (John 17:20-22) Jesus was praying for those who would become members of his body, the congregation. Paul supports this thought, at 1 Corinthians 12:12: "As the body is one, and hath many members, and all the members of that one body, being many, are one body: so also is Christ." Illustrating this point he writes: "The husband is the head of the wife, even as Christ is the head of the church: and he is the saviour of the body." (Ephesians 5:23) And now tying Jehovah in as Head over all, the apostle writes further: "The head of every man is Christ; and the head of the woman is the man; and the head of Christ is God." (1 Corinthians 11:3) The plain truth reveals itself, that is, just as Christ and his body members are regarded as one, so are Jehovah and Christ regarded as one. They are all one in agreement, purpose and organization. If this were not the logical conclusion Jesus would never have said: "My Father is greater than I," and therefore, "Not my will, but thine, be done." (John 14:28; Luke 22:42) Hence all, including Jesus, are in complete subjection to the great Head, Almighty God.

[11] The claim which the clergy make that Al-

---

11. Why does 1 Timothy 3:16, *King James Version,* not prove Almighty God was made manifest in the flesh?

mighty God was manifested in the flesh to men on this earth brings up the text at 1 Timothy 3:16, which states: "God was manifest in the flesh." Says a footnote in *The Emphatic Diaglott* by Benjamin Wilson, on the said verse: "Nearly all the ancient manuscripts, and all the versions have *'He who,'* instead of *'God,'* in this passage. This has been adopted." The Catholic *Douay Version* of this verse reads: "And evidently great is the mystery of godliness, which was manifested in the flesh." The *American Standard Version* reads: "He who was manifested in the flesh"; and so does *Moffatt's.* Had this been God Almighty incarnated, which it would have to be if the trinity were true, then these words of John would be false: "No man hath seen God at any time; the only begotten Son, which is in the bosom of the Father, he hath declared him." (John 1:18) However, these words make clear the fact that Jesus, being at complete unity with the Father, was able to declare or explain him, both in word and in deed, before all men while in the flesh. Hence Jesus said: "He that hath seen me hath seen the Father."—John 14:9.

[12] David, speaking under inspiration, describes man as being made "a little lower than the angels". In Hebrews 2:9 we find the very same words quoted to describe Jesus: "But we see Jesus, who was made a little lower than the angels for the suffering of death." If the trinity doctrine is true, then God was lower than the angels while on earth; which is contrary to his supremacy. Yet we know that Jesus came to earth to provide a corresponding ransom by his perfect human life. The ransom, therefore, must be equal to the thing lost, namely,

12. Why could Jesus while on earth not have been God?

perfect human life as Adam had it in Eden. Hence
we read concerning Jesus: "Who, although he was
existing in God's form, gave no consideration to
a seizure, namely, that he should be equal to God.
No, but he emptied himself and took a slave's form
and came to be in the likeness of men. More than
that, when he found himself in fashion as a man,
he humbled himself." (Philippians 2:6-8, *NW*)
God's justice would not let Jesus, as a ransom,
be more than a perfect man. So he could not be
the supreme God Almighty in the flesh.

[13] The final text under consideration as to supporting the trinity is John 1:1: "In the beginning
was the Word, and the Word was with God, and
the Word was God." To dispose of any seeming
contradiction here let us refer to the word-for-
word translation of the Greek as it appears in the
sublinear reading of *The Emphatic Diaglott*. It
reads: "In a beginning was the Word, and the
Word was with the God, and a god was the Word."
Note the clause. "The Word was with the God."
In this instance "God" is written with the article
"the" before it, while in the following clause, "and
a god was the Word," you will note "god" is written with the indefinite article "a". This proves
that two persons are spoken of as being with each
other, and not two persons as being one and the
same God. So the *New World Translation* is correct in rendering John 1:1, 2: "Originally the
Word was, and the Word was with God, and the
Word was a god. This one was originally with God."

---

13. How do the wording and grammatical construction
of John 1:1 show that two separate persons are spoken
of?

¹⁴ Sober thinking upon this text will bring other enlightening facts to mind. Psalm 90:2 declares that God is "from everlasting to everlasting". Since this is true, then how could the Word, if being *the* God, have a beginning? The truth of the matter is that the Word is God's Son who became Jesus Christ and who did have a beginning. At Revelation 3:14, he distinctly says he was the beginning of the creation by God. That is why he is spoken of as the "only begotten" of the Father, at John 1:14: "And the Word was made flesh, and dwelt among us, (and we beheld his glory, the glory as of the only begotten of the Father,) full of grace and truth." The apostle Paul sustains this truth when he speaks of Jesus as "the firstborn of every creature". (Colossians 1:15) So again the trinity teachers must defend themselves by stating: "It's a mystery!"

THE HOLY SPIRIT

¹⁵ In the four scriptures which the clergy erroneously quote as supporting the trinity, only the first one (1 John 5:7, *Dy*) included the words "and the Holy Ghost", and these words were found to be spurious. The general thought about the "Holy Ghost" is that it is a spirit person, the third person of the "trinity" and equal with God and Christ in power, substance and eternity. In English the Greek word for *spirit* is translated by the Old English word *ghost* meaning "spirit" or "breath". A little searching of any Greek-English dictionary will reveal that the Greek word *pneuma* translated

---

14. How does Jesus' origin disprove the trinity instead of supporting it?
15. What are the facts regarding the "third person" of the trinity, and what is it actually?

"spirit" is the same word translated also in the Bible as "wind". Just as the wind is invisible to man, so is the spirit of God. When a man has God's spirit upon him it means he has been authorized by God to do a certain work, whatever that work may be. So the holy spirit is the invisible active force of Almighty God which moves his servants to do his will.

[16] For the sake of argument, let us assume that God and Jesus were one in equality, power and eternity during the time Jesus was on the earth, up until he was baptized. Where, then, was the third person of the "trinity", the "Holy Ghost"? The trinitarians will state they were all three in one throughout that period. But is it not true that the Bible states that at the time Jesus was baptized the spirit descended upon Jesus like a dove and immediately Jesus was led away by the spirit? Trinitarians will say that all three persons of the "trinity" were clearly in evidence on that occasion and will quote Matthew 3:16, 17: "Jesus, when he was baptized, went up straightway out of the water: and, lo, the heavens were opened unto him, and he saw the spirit of God descending like a dove, and lighting upon him: and lo a voice from heaven, saying, This is my beloved Son, in whom I am well pleased."

16, 17. What occurred at Jesus' baptism that raises questions in disproof of the trinity?

[17] However, the trinitarian teachers will have several embarrassing questions to answer on this text, such as, Whose voice came from heaven, saying, "This is my beloved Son"? Jesus' own voice? And where, till then, had the "Holy Ghost" or holy spirit been, seeing that first now it descended upon Jesus? And were not the heavens open to Jesus, if God, during the previous thirty years of his earthly sojourn? If he was God or a part of a trinity and equal in power, substance and eternity with God, he would always have access to the heavens. These and other equally embarrassing questions have convinced the clergy that it is far better to say it is all a great mystery.

[18] Yes, it would be a mystery if the trinity doctrine were true. One of the most mysterious things is the question, Who ran the universe during the three days that Jesus was dead and in the grave, or, for that matter, during his thirty-three and a half years on the earth while he was made a "little lower than the angels"? If Jesus was God, then during Jesus' death God was dead and in the grave. What a wonderful opportunity for Satan to take complete control! But the mere fact that he could not do so proves it was the only-begotten Son, and he alone, that was dead. The Scriptures state, at 1 Timothy 1:17, that God is "the King eternal, immortal". Therefore, if Jesus was the immortal God, he could not have died. During Jesus' earthly course the Devil had expended every effort to bring about his death; and now, surely, after he had finally succeeded, he would not permit Jesus' resurrection if it was Almighty God that was dead.

---

18. What complications as to rulership would have arisen if Jesus had been God Almighty while on earth?

How inconsistent it all is, according to the "trinity"!

[19] Here Jesus' words at John 14:28 are appropriate: "My Father is greater than I." That means "greater" not only as to office but also as to person. Faithful to his promise, the Father resurrected his Son on the third day. If Jehovah and the dead Christ were one in substance, the resurrection would have been impossible. The religionists will quote Jesus' words at John 10:17, 18: "I lay down my life, that I might take it again. No man taketh it from me, but I lay it down of myself. I have power to lay it down, and I have power to take it again. This commandment have I received of my Father." Thus they hope to prove that Jesus was God and able to resurrect himself.

[20] However, the logical conclusion, even from the *King James Version's* rendering of John 10:17, 18, is that Jesus, because of willingly laying down his life, was assured by his Father's commandment that he would be resurrected and given life again. He took back life when God gave it to him by resurrection. Here the *New World Translation* properly reads: "I surrender my soul, in order that I may receive it again. No man has taken it away from me, but I surrender it of my own initiative. I have authority to let go of it, and I have authority to receive it again. The commandment on this I received from my Father." This makes it clear that by obedience to God's will Jesus voluntarily laid down his life in ransom, and as a reward for faithfulness he had the authority

---

19, 20. What text is quoted to argue that Jesus had the power to resurrect himself, but what is the correct conclusion to be drawn?

to *receive* life again at the hands of the Father through his resurrecting him.

[21] The trinity doctrine was not conceived by Jesus or the early Christians. Nowhere in the Scriptures is even any mention made of a trinity. Therefore, if, as claimed, it is the "central doctrine of the Christian religion", it is passing strange that this complicated, confusing doctrine received no attention by Christ Jesus, by way of explanation or teaching. Stranger still that imperfect men living over a hundred years later should have the idea injected into their religion by pagans and should teach it as Scriptural truth. The plain truth is that this is another of Satan's attempts to keep God-fearing persons from learning the truth of Jehovah and his Son, Christ Jesus. No, there is no trinity!

---

21. What two strange facts stand out regarding this doctrine, and what is the plain truth of the whole matter?

CHAPTER X

"A RANSOM IN EXCHANGE FOR MANY"

ONE of the vital doctrines clearly taught throughout the Bible is that of the ransom which God provided through Jesus Christ for men who love God and have faith in him. For instance, Jesus' words at Matthew 20:28 (*NW*): "The Son of man came, not to be ministered to, but to minister and to give his soul a ransom in exchange for many." Jesus made other statements to the same effect, and so did his apostles. The prophets before Jesus' time wrote concerning this very important and loving provision of God which results in blessing for men, the *ransom*. It is one of the basic truths of God's Word.

2 This word *ransom* means that which loosens or releases, providing deliverance. In the Bible the word often has reference to deliverance from trouble, distress or calamity. An instance of this is found in Isaiah 43:3 (*AS*), which reads: "I am Jehovah thy God, . . . I have given Egypt as thy ransom." God gave Egypt, Ethiopia and Seba as a reward or ransom to the Persian conqueror of Babylon for the release of His people from Babylon. (Compare Ezekiel 29:17-20; Esther 1:1-3.) Used in this latter way, *ransom* is plainly not a

---

1. To what extent is the ransom truth taught in the Bible?
2. What is one of the ways in which the term "ransom" is used in connection with ancient Egypt?

ransom or deliverance from sin or from death due to sin.

3 The "ransom in exchange for many" mentioned by Jesus at Matthew 20:28 (*NW*) denotes a deliverance or saving too. Psalm 49:6, 7 states: "They that trust in their wealth, and boast themselves in the multitude of their riches; none of them can by any means redeem his brother, nor give to God a ransom for him." This scripture agrees with others in pointing out that the "ransom" is a redemption accomplished, not by wealth or ability of man, but by a provision of God. The Scriptural doctrine of the ransom is that in sending his Son Christ Jesus to earth Jehovah God provided through him and his death a redemptive price. Thereby those of men who have faith in God's provision may come into harmony with him and, serving him faithfully, they may receive the gift of life, being freed from inherited sin and from eternal death as a result of sin. To this effect it is written, at Romans 6:23 (*NW*): "The wages sin pays is death, but the gift God gives is everlasting life by Christ Jesus our Lord."

4 The ransoming is the action God performs in accomplishing this redemption of mankind through Christ. The ransom itself is that which serves as the redemptive price, the valuable thing with which the repurchase or r e d e m p t i o n is made, namely, "the man Christ Jesus."

5 Man's need of a ransom is shown in the fact that all men are born imperfect and sinful, as ad-

---

3. What kind of saving or deliverance is by the ransom referred to by Jesus, and so what is the Scriptural doctrine of the ransom?
4. What is the verb sense and the noun sense of "ransom"?
5. How was man's need for a ransom shown?

mitted by even godly David, who stated: "Behold, I was brought forth in iniquity; and in sin did my mother conceive me." (Psalm 51:5, *AS*) If sinful men are to receive everlasting life, then deliverance from this condemnation of sin and death must come, and this from the Creator, as man was and is helpless in this respect. Also, it is part of Jehovah's expressed purpose that men should receive everlasting life, as Jesus Christ stated it, at John 17:3 (*NW*): "This means everlasting life, their taking in knowledge of you, the only true God, and of the one whom you sent forth, Jesus Christ." To accomplish this purpose of giving life to men a purchase price or redemptive price, or ransom, is needed.

[6] That which is bought with the ransom price is identified in Jehovah God's statement to perfect Adam concerning what was to be lost by sin and disobedience: "Thou shalt surely die." (Genesis 2:17) That which was lost was perfect human life, with its rights and earthly prospects. That which is redeemed or bought back is what was lost, namely, perfect human life, with its rights and earthly prospects. God's just law, at Deuteronomy 19:21, was that like should go for like, hence a perfect human life sacrificed for a perfect human life lost. Who could provide the necessary ransom?

[7] The provider of the ransom is Jehovah God, the Source of life, the Creator. Jesus, his only-begotten Son, said: "God loved the world so much that he gave his only-begotten Son, . . . God sent

---

6. (a) What was lost when Adam sinned? (b) What is redeemed?

7. Who provides the ransom, and by what is he prompted?

forth his Son into the world." (John 3:16, 17, *NW*)
Justice was satisfied in mankind's suffering death,
the just penalty of sin. So the ransom is an expression of God's mercy, his undeserved kindness
toward mankind. What good and valuable thing
could there be which God was pleased to use to
ransom those appreciating his loving-kindness?

[8] It was his beloved Son. We read, at 1 Timothy
2:5, 6 (*NW*): "A man Christ Jesus, who gave
himself a corresponding ransom." Concerning his
birth as a man the account at Matthew 1:22, 23
tells us: "All this actually came about for that to
be fulfilled which was spoken by Jehovah through
his prophet, saying, 'Look! the virgin will become
pregnant and will give birth to a son, and they
will call his name "Immanuel".'" (*NW*) That this
one is the ransom or deliverer from sin and death,
Jehovah's angel said, in verse 21: "He will save his
people from their sins." Concerning him, too, the
apostle Peter explained, at Acts 4:12 (*NW*):
"There is no salvation in anyone else, for there
is not another name under heaven that has been
given among men by which we must get saved."
Of all God's faithful creatures in heaven, it pleased
him to use this One most dear to him, sending him
to earth to become a perfect man, so carrying forward among other things the ransoming work.
Hebrews 2:9 (*NW*) states: "We behold Jesus, who
has been made a little lower than angels, crowned
with glory and honor for having suffered death,
that he by God's undeserved kindness might taste
death for every man." How true, then, the glad
cry of John the Baptist upon seeing this One ap-

---

8. How is that which is the ransom Scripturally identified?

proaching: "See, the Lamb of God that takes away the sin of the world!"—John 1:29, *NW*.

⁹ The perfect human life which Jesus laid down in death is that valuable thing which accomplishes the purchase of what Adam's sin of disobedience lost for all his offspring. Jesus' blood spilled in death, his human life poured out in willing sacrifice, this is what the ransom is. It was provided here upon earth at Jesus' death. It was presented in heaven as a redemptive offering for sin by the resurrected and glorified Christ, for he was resurrected a spirit creature, immortal, no longer a human son of God. His perfect human life, with all its rights and prospects, was laid down in death, but not for sin and in punishment. It was not taken back by Jesus at his resurrection, for he was raised a divine spirit creature. After the heavenly Father gave to his faithful Son the reward of immortal spirit life, the sacrificed human life remained effective, a thing of value with purchasing power, hence with ransoming or redemptive power. The value of the perfect human life was now available for use on behalf of faithful men needing to be ransomed thereby. These wonderful truths are made clear at Hebrews 9:24-26 (*NW*), as follows:

¹⁰ "Christ entered, not into a holy place made with hands which is a copy of the reality, but into heaven itself, now to appear before the person of God for us. Neither is it in order that he should offer himself often, as indeed the high priest enters into the holy place from year to year with

---

9. (a) Where and how was the ransom provided?
(b) How and where was it presented to God?
10. How is this explained in Hebrews 9:24-26?

blood not his own. Otherwise, he would have to suffer often from the world's foundation. But now he has manifested himself once for all time at the consummation of the systems of things to put sin away through the sacrifice of himself."

[11] We see that by sin Adam lost perfect human life and was justly sentenced to death and eventually died, and all his descendants inherited sin and death from him. God made his beloved Son a perfect man, and Jesus was faithful, went into death, and was afterward resurrected by God's power and exalted to heaven, there presenting to God the merit or value of his perfect human life. But how does this operate on behalf of faithful men? How does this ransom "many"? Good questions these, and they deserve a Bible answer.

[12] Luke 3:38 names Adam "the son of God". As the human son of God, Adam was perfect, for Jehovah God created him, and "his work is perfect". (Deuteronomy 32:4) Adam was not made to be obedient to God automatically, as a robot. No, but he could choose to obey his Maker and enjoy the blessings of the life which he had been given, or he could willfully disobey and lose his life and all right to life. So, even though he was perfect, his faithfulness was subject to test. When he sinned, Adam ceased to be God's son, but was a deliberate sinner. "Adam was not deceived." (1 Timothy 2:14) And so the sentence of death for sin willfully chosen was passed upon Adam, and in due time he died. All his children, we and our ancestors, were born following his sin.

---

11. What questions now properly require a Bible answer?
12. What was Adam's relationship to God before and after he sinned, and when were his children born?

¹³ Adam's imperfect descendants could choose to serve God to the best of their abilities, or could choose to harden their hearts against his goodness during their few years of life. To imperfect Israelites Joshua said: "Choose you this day whom ye will serve; . . . as for me and my house, we will serve Jehovah." (Joshua 24:15, *AS*) But even those who set their minds and hearts to the worship of the true God were powerless to gain eternal life for themselves without God's action in their behalf. Romans 5:12 shows why: "Through one man sin entered into the world and death through sin, and thus death spread to all men because they had all sinned."—*NW*.

¹⁴ As a perfect man, Jesus stood in a position like that once occupied by the perfect man Adam in the garden of Eden. At Hebrews 5:8, 9 it is said concerning Jesus: "Although he was a Son, he learned obedience from the things he suffered, and after he had been made perfect he became responsible for everlasting salvation to all those obeying him." (*NW*) By a faultless obedience the perfection, not merely of human organism, but of devotion to his Father, was proved by Jesus. For this he was exalted and made the great High Priest to enter into "heaven itself" and offer the value of his perfect human sacrifice on behalf of "all those obeying him". In contrast with Adam's bringing of death upon all mankind through transgression of God's law, Jesus as the glorified High Priest, by presenting in heaven this redemptive

13. (a) Are men free to choose whom they will serve? (b) Can those who worship God gain life aside from his provisions?
14. As to the operation of the ransom toward man, what is Jesus Christ's office, what does he possess for use, and how is this valuable thing used?

price, is in position to relieve the believing ones of Adam's descendants from the inherited disability under which all are born. By his purchase he buys them, redeems them from sin and from death, applying the merit of his sacrifice on their behalf, that they may have a righteous standing before the Father through the Son.—1 Corinthians 6:20; 7:23.

WHO IS RANSOMED?

[15] The man Adam is not included in those ransomed. Why not? Because he was a willful sinner, was justly sentenced to death, and died deservedly, and God would not reverse his just judgment and give Adam life. He had perfect life, and this he deliberately forfeited. There is no provision in God's ransom for Adam. But in contrast with what Adam did to his big family born after him, Jesus Christ ransoms believing men with a corresponding ransom. He offsets the inherited condemnation on those "many" believers of Adam's family by applying in their behalf the merit of this redemptive price, and such are the ransomed ones.—Matthew 20:28.

[16] Would this take in non-Jews as well as Jews? Yes, because Romans 5:18 states: "Likewise also through one act of justification the result to men of all kinds is a declaring of them righteous for life." (NW) Galatians 3:13 shows the Jews that "Christ by purchase released us from the curse of the Law"; and Romans 4:11 speaks of the Gen-

---

15. Was Adam ransomed, and how do the effects of his course on mankind differ from those of Jesus' course?
16, 17. Are Jews and non-Jews subject to the ransom benefits? Individually or collectively? In the same way? Impartially?

tiles who exercise faith as "those having faith
while in uncircumcision, in order for righteousness
to be counted to them". (*NW*) So the course of an
individual determines whether he will ultimately
receive benefit from the ransom sacrifice of Christ
or not. Those willfully wicked and hardhearted
toward Jehovah's provision do not have ransom
merit and life forced upon them, but, as stated at
John 3:36 (*NW*), "He that exercises faith in the
Son has everlasting life; he that disobeys the Son
will not see life, but the wrath of God remains upon him."

[17] Thus is shown the impartiality of Jehovah,
the great Ransomer. The basis for the resurrection
of the dead who are in God's memory and their
eventual gaining of life is this same ransom provision. Jesus gave the "corresponding ransom for
all", all who enter into the covenant with God
through Jesus as Mediator. "For there is one God,
and one mediator between God and men, a man
Christ Jesus, who gave himself a corresponding
ransom for all."—1 Timothy 2:5, 6, *NW*.

[18] The ransom places upon those who want to
benefit from it an obligation and a marvelous
privilege. "The sting producing death is sin."
(1 Corinthians 15:56, *NW*) So in order for men to
be saved from death due to being stung by sin
they must inform themselves of God's mercy
through Christ Jesus and then have faith in the
provision He has made. This faith means to rely
on such provision confidently, to give God all cred-
it for it, and then to demonstrate this conviction
by devoting oneself to God and by informing others about the ransom. Such course of action by

18. What must men do to be saved from death by the
sting of sin, and how does Revelation 7:14 show this?

those of good will identifies them as being of those "many" for whom Christ died, including the "great crowd" described in Revelation 7:14, which says of them: "These are the ones that come out of the great tribulation, and they have washed their robes and made them white in the blood of the Lamb."—*NW*.

[19] Faith is based on reliable evidence. The Word of the Most High God is the dependable basis for faith. His Word makes plain the ransom provision and so makes possible faith in the redemptive price provided by Jesus. Those people of good will today who avail themselves of the provision and who steadfastly abide in this confidence will find Christ Jesus to be their "everlasting Father". (Isaiah 9:6) Their eternal life on earth under God's kingdom will be to the praise of the only true God, Jehovah, whose purpose in Christ Jesus is stated by this beloved Son, at Mark 10:45 (*NW*): "For even the Son of man came, not to be ministered to, but to minister and to give his soul a ransom in exchange for many."

---

19. How is a basis for faith provided for the 'many who are ransomed'?

CHAPTER XI

"THE CONGREGATION OF GOD"

MANY are the conflicting claims of numerous religious systems concerning "the church", about which so many good and heartening things are written in the Holy Scriptures. Some contend that their religious organization alone has exclusive right to represent God. They say that the individual seeking God's favor and blessing must attend prescribed religious meetings, must support the organization financially and otherwise, and must be submissive to the dictates of cardinals, bishops, fathers, vicars, pastors and other men charged with the oversight of such organization. Then, again, others maintain that one's belonging to any one of the religious systems will assure him membership in "the church", because all such organizations are "traveling the same path". Such confusing claims as these make the way of the honest and sincere inquirer difficult, and he is at first in a quandary as to the meaning of the religious expression "the church", in some Bible translations. What is "the church"? And how does it serve God's purpose?

[2] There are numerous so-called "Protestant" religious systems claiming to be "the church". The Jews also make claim of holding first place in

1. What confusing situation confronts the honest inquirer who is seeking to discover the true congregation?
2. Who lay claim to being "the church", and which religious system is outstanding among such claimants?

God's heart and honestly believe they as a people will yet be God's exclusive instrument. However, among the religious bodies professing to be God's channel the Roman Catholic religious system is outstanding. Therefore its claim is here specially considered. That Vatican-directed organization has spread its influence to the far-flung reaches of Christendom. On six continents and on islands of the seas are to be found its priestly representatives, conducting religious meetings and supervising the education of the young wherever possible.

[3] Catholic doctrine claims that the church of Rome is the *only* true church, built upon Peter as its foundation. The Hierarchy contends he was the first pope; also that the pope is the visible head of the church, is successor of Peter, is infallible, and is the only man authorized to interpret the Bible. In support of this claim they seize upon Jesus' words to Peter, as recorded at Matthew 16:18: "And I say to thee: That thou art Peter, and upon this rock I will build my church. And the gates of hell shall not prevail against it." (*Dy*) And so, claiming Peter as the first pope and the foundation of the church, Catholic doctrine has it that the Vatican religious organization operated by a "Sacred College of Cardinals" with the successor of Peter in the person of the pope at the head is God's church, His instrument, for the outworking of His purposes and the blessing of men. Clergymen teach that the duty of the church is to "save souls" and prepare men for the "next life".

---

3. What does Catholic doctrine teach regarding "the church", and to what Bible text does it often refer for support?

[4] However, there is a total absence of Scriptural proof that the apostle Peter was ever given the primacy in the Christian congregation. In proof that Paul, for example, was in no wise inferior to Peter, Paul says: "But when Cephas [Peter] was come to Antioch, I withstood him to the face, because he was to be blamed. For before that some came from James, he did eat with the Gentiles: but when they were come, he withdrew and separated himself, fearing them who were of the circumcision. And to his dissimulation the rest of the Jews consented: so that Barnabas also was led by them into that dissimulation. But when I saw that they walked not uprightly unto the truth of the gospel, I said to Cephas [Peter] before them all: If thou, being a Jew, livest after the manner of the Gentiles and not as the Jews do, how dost thou compel the Gentiles to live as do the Jews?" (Galatians 2:11-14, *Dy*) Peter wrote the first of his two epistles from Babylon, but there is no evidence that Peter even so much as visited Rome, although the Holy Scriptures definitely say Paul did. (1 Peter 5:13) Nor did the twelve apostles have any successors, for Jesus revealed at Apocalypse (or Revelation) 21:14 that there are only "twelve apostles of the Lamb". (*Dy*) Hence the claim that the pope as successor to Peter is the head of the church is without any foundation in Scripture or in fact. For men to build an organization on earth and label it "The Church", claiming that it is God's true church, is to do violence to God's Word, as will be shown hereinafter. Such an earthly body is not "the church" or "the congregation of God", nor can it ever be, because it

---

4. What is the evidence that the Catholic claim is unfounded?

is not of God's building and would not serve his purpose.

⁵ Scripturally "church" means a congregation called out from the world for God's purpose; and so the *New World Translation* renders the Greek word *ekklesia* by the English word "congregation". The doctrine concerning the church or congregation was for a long time a sacred secret. It was first revealed to those selected from among men as members of the congregation. (Mark 4:11) There is but one real and true congregation and it is referred to in Scripture as "the congregation of the living God". (1 Timothy 3:15, *NW*) God by means of his Son Christ Jesus is the builder of that congregation, for Hebrews 3:3, 4 (*NW*) says: "He who constructs it has more honor than the house. Of course, every house is constructed by someone, but he that constructed all things is God." It is the sanctuary, "the true tent, which Jehovah set up, and not man." (Hebrews 8:2, *NW*) The true congregation is the agency through which the Almighty God has purposed to vindicate his sovereignty and his name and to bring blessings to obedient men.

⁶ Knowing full well the important use to which the congregation would be put, the all-wise God has established it upon a tried and proved Foundation Rock. When Jesus advised Peter, "Upon this rock I will build my church," Jesus was referring to himself as the Great Rock upon which his church would be built. According to the Syriac manuscript Jesus said: "Thou art Cephas: and upon this rock [cephas], I will build my church."

5. What does the term *church* mean, and what is the true one?
6. Upon whom is the "church" built?

(Murdock's translation from the Syriac) In the Syriac Manuscript the pronoun *thou* is masculine and shows that the first Cephas is masculine and means the apostle Peter. But in this expression "this rock" the Syriac adjective for *this* is feminine, showing that the second *cephas* is feminine and here refers, not to Peter, but to someone else. It refers to Christ Jesus himself, who is the Great Rock. "The rock [*petra,* Greek; *cephas,* Syriac] was Christ." (1 Corinthians 10:4, *Dy*) Peter believed in that "Rock" and boldly proclaimed Christ Jesus to be the heavenly Foundation, The Rock, upon which the congregation of God is built. To the Jewish rulers Peter said: "This is the stone which was rejected by you the builders, which is become the head of the corner. Neither is there salvation in any other. For there is no other name under heaven given to men, whereby we must be saved."—Acts 4:11, 12, *Dy;* also see 1 Peter 2:3-10, *Dy.*

7 The apostle Paul confirms Peter's statement that Christ Jesus is the Chief One of the true church body, saying: "The Christ also is head of the congregation." "And he is the head of the body, the congregation. He is the beginning, the firstborn from the dead, that he might become the one who is first in all things." (Ephesians 5:23 and Colossians 1:18, *NW*) This is true because he is the only one who could qualify for that important place in Jehovah's heavenly ruling organization. The headship of the congregation was too lofty a position to entrust it to an imperfect, though faithful, man like Peter, to say nothing of

---

7. What further evidence is there concerning the Foundation and Head of the "church", and why must this view of matters be correct?

conferring the responsibility upon a succession of popes of Rome who are in no way imitators of Peter so far as adhering to Christian doctrine is concerned. Jesus Christ is "living for ever and ever" and does not need a man on earth as a visible head of the congregation or as his personal representative. (Revelation 1:18, NW) Alive in heaven, he sent the holy spirit and uses it to direct the congregation on earth. (John 15:26; 16:7, 13) The congregation is no earthly organization, but is Jehovah's own theocratic organization into which he brings faithful ones from among men.

⁸ In a typical or pictorial sense the nation of the twelve tribes of Israel under Moses was a church or congregation. (Acts 7:37, 38, Dy; NW) The Greater Moses, Christ Jesus, first received from his Father the apostles as twelve associate "pillars" of the congregation, of whom Peter was one. (John 17:6) This is pictured in symbol at Revelation 21:14, where the congregation is compared to a great city: "And the wall of the city had twelve foundations: and in them, the twelve names of the twelve apostles of the Lamb." (Dy) The twelve were laid as foundation stones of the congregation, but with Christ Jesus as the basic foundation. (Ephesians 2:20) Hence the apostle Peter says to all members of the true congregation, including the twelve apostles and all those since chosen: "Be you also as living stones built up, a spiritual house, a holy priesthood, to offer up spiritual sacrifices, acceptable to God by Jesus Christ." —1 Peter 2:5, Dy.

---

8. Who were the first members of it taken from among men, and to what are they compared?

MEMBERS

⁹ Those brought into the congregation are selected or chosen by God through Jesus Christ, the one first chosen. They do not gain entrance to the congregation of their own accord or desire, nor do they choose their positions of service in it; for "now God has set the members in the body, each one of them, just as he pleased". (1 Peter 2:4; 2 Thessalonians 2:13; John 15:19; 1 Corinthians 12:18, NW; John 3:27) After the selection of the "twelve apostles of the Lamb" as foundation pillars, the call went forth to the nation of Israel exclusively for three and a half years and God selected from among the Jews faithful persons to be associated with Christ Jesus in the heavenly congregation. These preached the Word of God, and many were added to the congregation.—Acts 2:41, 46, 47.

¹⁰ Later, at the home of a Gentile named Cornelius, Peter was privileged to extend the divine invitation for the first time to the non-Jews or Gentiles. These likewise began to preach God's Word, and many more Gentiles were added to the congregation. (Acts 10:44-48; 15:14) It is noteworthy that all those brought into association with the congregation were, like Jesus, preachers of the Word.

¹¹ After the selection of the apostles as the first members of the true congregation, Jehovah has continued selecting other "living stones" for his congregation. This selecting work has been going

9, 10. (a) In what manner are members brought in, and how did God proceed to select the members? (b) What is seen to be true of all the members?

11. For how long has the selection of members been going on, and what hope is held out to them?

on during the nineteen centuries since Jesus' resurrection and ascension into heaven. The Bible holds out heavenly hopes to these called to be part of the congregation, as is so well shown by Paul's words: "Our citizenship exists in the heavens, from which place also we are eagerly waiting for a savior, the Lord Jesus Christ, who will refashion our humiliated body to be conformed to his glorious body according to the operation of the power which he has, even to subject all things to himself."—Philippians 3:20, 21, *NW*.

¹² In order to be united finally with Christ in the heavenly congregation, the apostles and others afterward selected were required to finish their earthly course faithful to the death, as Jesus did. (1 Peter 2:21; Revelation 2:10) Though they were all received into the covenant for the Kingdom or heavenly congregation, they were at death not immediately taken to heaven and united with the Head of the congregation. They slept in the grave until the first resurrection at the coming of Christ Jesus to Jehovah's temple in 1918, when they were raised to glory with him their Head. (Luke 22:29, 30, *NW;* Revelation 20:6) Today there yet remain on earth some who are in line for association with Christ Jesus in the heavenly congregation, but they too must finish their earthly course faithful to the death. According to God's Word, any of these dying now are "changed, in a moment, in the twinkling of an eye", to an eternal spirit existence with Christ Jesus in his heavenly "body" or congregation.—1 Corinthians 15:42-54; Revelation 14:13.

12. What is finally required of all members before they are united with the Head Christ Jesus in heaven?

[13] At Revelation 14:1, 3 the Bible is conclusive in predicting that the final number of the heavenly congregation will be 144,000, according to God's decree. Because his true congregation was pictured by the twelve tribes of Israel under Moses, the heavenly congregation is likened to twelve tribes of 12,000 members each, under the Greater Moses, Christ Jesus. The congregation, then, is restricted to this select, predestinated number; and in heaven it is made the capital part or ruling body of Jehovah's universal organization. It is referred to in Scripture also as the "body" of Christ and as the "bride" of the Lamb Jesus Christ. (Revelation 7:4-8; 19:7; 21:9; Ephesians 1:20-23) All other creatures receiving life at God's hand through the Kingdom will not be a part of "the congregation of God", but will live on this earth under the rulership of Christ Jesus and his congregation in the heavens.

ITS COMMISSION

[14] Christ Jesus, the Head of the congregation, is called in Scripture "the faithful and true witness". (Revelation 3:14) From the time he was anointed till his lips were stilled in death on the torture stake he devoted his every effort to preaching the gospel or good news about God's kingdom, declaring the majesty of Jehovah's name and singing forth his praises. As Head of the congregation he quoted his commission, from Isaiah 61:1, 2 (AS): "The spirit of the Lord Jehovah is upon me; be-

---

13. How many members will there be in the congregation, and what about all other humans receiving life?
14. By what title is the Head known, and in what earthly activity did he engage in fulfillment of his commission?

cause Jehovah hath anointed me to preach good tidings unto the meek; he hath sent me to bind up the broken-hearted, to proclaim liberty to the captives, and the opening of the prison to them that are bound; to proclaim the year of Jehovah's favor, and the day of vengeance of our God; to comfort all that mourn." His was a preaching work. —Luke 4:18-21.

¹⁵ Jesus plainly declared that the same commission rested upon the members of the congregation. He said to them: "You will be witnesses of me ... to the most distant part of the earth." Peter confirms this commission of the congregation to preach the same as Jesus did: "You are 'a chosen race, a royal priesthood, a holy nation, a people for special possession, that you should declare abroad the excellencies' of the one that called you out of darkness into his wonderful light." (1 Peter 2:9, NW) That is why, on the occasion of his visit with his faithful disciples shortly prior to his ascension, Jesus said: "Go therefore and make disciples of people of all the nations, baptizing them in the name of the Father and of the Son and of the holy spirit, teaching them." (Matthew 28:19, 20, NW) The commission to preach about God's kingdom devolves upon all members of the congregation, for they are all anointed with God's spirit. They must minister to the spiritual needs of all men seeking life and blessings at God's hands. —Matthew 10:1-14; Luke 10:1-12; 1 John 2:20, 27; Isaiah 61:6.

¹⁶ The remnant yet on earth of the members of Christ's body or congregation are thus ministering by 'preaching this good news of the Kingdom

15, 16. What is the responsibility resting upon the congregation?

in all the inhabited earth for a witness to all nations'. (Matthew 24:14, *NW*) Those members now resurrected and united with Christ Jesus at the temple all proved faithful by a consistent course of preaching and ministering while on earth, and they are forevermore in heaven with the Head of the congregation as his joint heirs and co-rulers in Jehovah's glorious Theocracy.

[17] From the foregoing one thing is clearly seen: It is not the duty of the remnant of the congregation yet on earth, who are Jehovah's witnesses, to enter into political alliances with the nations of this world. Nor is it their duty and responsibility to build a huge earthly organization, backed by fabulous wealth and ornamented with costly and imposing structures for religious worship, and supervised by a special clergy class of men. (John 18:36; Matthew 6:19-33) No; the responsibility of the remnant yet in the flesh is to praise Jehovah's name and bear witness to his supremacy and glory. How? By ministering the spiritual "food at the proper time" to those hungering and thirsting for the truth, inviting all to partake of the "water of life freely". Theirs is the responsibility to see that Jehovah's name and Word are declared in every part of the earth where He makes such proclamation possible. That work is done in the very same manner as Jesus did it, namely, from house to house, city to city, province to province, and publicly. (Mark 1:38; Matthew 11:1; Acts 20:20, 21) Their faithfulness must be shown by performing their commission to preach in spite of any and all opposition, and in this way they prove their trustworthiness as Jesus did.

---

17. In what activity are the members yet on earth not to engage, and what is their all-important work?

[18] How is the true congregation fulfilling God's purpose on earth today? By seeing to it that the good news is preached as He commands. Bibles, books, booklets, magazines, tracts, voice recordings, public preaching, and every other Scripturally proper means is being used to publish abroad the Kingdom message. That this would be the right course, the only course for the congregation down at this "time of the end" of this world, was clearly defined by Jesus' prophecy to his apostles, at Matthew 24:14: "This good news of the kingdom will be preached in all the inhabited earth for the purpose of a witness to all the nations, and then the accomplished end will come." (*NW*) The congregation is responsible to do such preaching and to do it in the same way that Jesus did it. Only the true congregation is doing that work today and in that way. Therefore which is the true church or congregation and who are associated with it on earth is clearly to be seen. (Matthew 7:15, 20; 21:43) The true congregation is doing God's work as he has commanded. It will continue to do so until that portion of the congregation's work on earth is finished.

---

18. How is the remnant of the congregation fulfilling its commission today, how long will this activity continue, and how are the true members as a company on earth identified?

CHAPTER XII

"THE KINGDOM OF GOD"

JEHOVAH God is the universal and absolute Sovereign. But men not recognizing this fact have set up various governments of their own making during the past six thousand years. Whether these have been tribal rulerships, monarchies, city governments, dictatorships, or democratic political systems, yet it must be admitted that they have all come far short of satisfying the people's needs. This is because the rulers as well as the ruled have overlooked the one thing needed, namely, the establishment of the kingdom of God.

² The issue of world domination was raised at the time man took himself out from under God's righteous rule and started down the rough road of human government under Satan's invisible rulership. Therefore Jehovah gave his word of promise in the garden of Eden that in the then distant future he would himself set up a universal kingdom. That declaration, the first prophecy given to man, is recorded at Genesis 3:15. Being a solemn promise concerning a kingdom "seed", such declared purpose of God is a kingdom covenant.

---

1. How have men defied the Universal Sovereign? With what result?
2. What great issue was raised in the garden of Eden, and how will it be settled?

³ As time went on, God enlarged upon that original promise by making a kingdom covenant with his friends Abraham, Isaac and Jacob concerning the Seed for blessing all the families of the earth. Later it was revealed through Jacob that the Seed promised would come through the tribe of his son Judah. (Genesis 17:7, 8; 22:16-18; 26:3-5; 28:13-15; 49:10) Still later God set up a theocracy, this meaning a "God-rule", over Jacob's descendants, the nation of Israel. This, however, was not the kingdom that was promised in Eden. It did not crush the Serpent's head, nor did it bless all the families of the earth. It was merely a picture or type of the greater kingdom that was to come later.

⁴ In that typical arrangement the capital was located at Jerusalem, including Mount Zion. The palace of the king and the sacred ark of Jehovah were situated there. It being a government ruled by God, the king was said to sit on the "throne of Jehovah" as his visible royal representative. Accordingly, the people did not elect the king by vote, for God was the real Sovereign and he chose and anointed his own king to represent him. Because David was a man agreeable to God's own heart, of the tribe of Judah, Jehovah made an everlasting covenant for the kingdom with him for the kingdom to continue in his line of descent. (Acts 13:22; 2 Samuel 7:12-16) When that typical theocratic kingdom had served its purpose and approached its end, Jehovah declared: "I will overturn, overturn, overturn, it: and it shall be no

---

3. (a) In the development of the seed promised, what events occurred? (b) Was Israel's theocratic rule the kingdom promised?
4. (a) How did Israel's government picture the kingdom of God? (b) When the nation of Israel was overthrown, what promise did Jehovah there give?

more, until he come whose right it is; and I will give it him." (Ezekiel 21:27) The overturning came in 607 B.C. at Jerusalem's destruction. The one "whose right it is" to be king, namely, Jesus Christ, appeared A.D. 29.

⁵ Two historians named Matthew and Luke traced down the line of David's descendants individually, and both reached the same conclusion, that Christ Jesus was the rightful heir. He indeed proved to be the "Lion that is of the tribe of Judah". (Matthew 1:2-16; Luke 3:23-34; Hebrews 7:14; Revelation 5:5, *NW*) The angels unitedly glorified God at the birth of him who was to bruise the Serpent's head. Then, when he was baptized at thirty years of age and anointed to be King of the heavenly government, God's voice from heaven was heard saying: "This is my Son, the beloved, whom I have approved." Such declaration showed that Jesus was there begotten by God's holy spirit to be a spiritual son. A mere man could not be the king of the heavenly government.—Matthew 3:17, *NW; Acts 13:33; 1 Corinthians 15:50.

⁶ On one occasion this anointed Kingdom Heir said that a lesser one in the kingdom of the heavens would be greater than John the Baptist. (Matthew 11:11, *NW*) If that is so, what are the requirements for entering the Kingdom? Who and how many are able to enter it? The Revelation limits to 144,000 the number that become a part of the Kingdom and stand on heavenly Mount Zion. Thus it is seen that God never purposed to convert this old world and take all the good to

---

5. Who is the rightful heir to the throne of the heavenly kingdom, and when was he anointed to be King?
6. How many besides him will be associated in the Kingdom?

heaven. There are only a few that find entrance into this kingdom—only a "little flock" when compared with earth's population.—Revelation 14:1, 3; 7:4-8; Matthew 7:13, 14; Luke 12:32.

⁷ This may all seem like a mystery to those who have no knowledge of the Bible and its teachings. Indeed, it is the "sacred secret of the Christ". (Ephesians 3:4, *NW*) Only those who are "called, and chosen, and faithful" from among men reign with the "Lord of lords, and King of kings". (Revelation 17:14) Since "flesh and blood cannot inherit God's kingdom", these must become the spiritual sons of God. Even as Christ Jesus told Nicodemus: 'Except a man is born again, being born of the water of truth and of the spirit, he cannot see or enter the kingdom of God.'—1 Corinthians 15:50, *NW;* John 3:3-13; 1:12, 13; James 1:18.

⁸ These spiritual sons of God, receiving the "spirit of adoption", are able to say: "The spirit itself bears witness with our spirit that we are God's children. If, then, we are children, we are also heirs: heirs indeed of God, but joint heirs with Christ." (Romans 8:15-17, *NW*) Such heirs are brought into a covenant for the Kingdom, as Jesus stated: "I make a covenant with you, just as my Father has made a covenant with me, for a kingdom, that you may eat and drink at my table in my kingdom, and sit on thrones." (Luke 22:28-30, *NW*) In the capacity of priests and kings of God they reign a thousand years with Christ Jesus. This "royal priesthood" is spoken of by the apostle

---

7, 8. (a) How only can humans enter into and become a part of the kingdom of God? (b) Into what covenant are these brought, and what are their glorious privileges after that?

Peter as "a holy nation, a people for special possession", who inherit the Kingdom because they bring forth its fruits. All together, they constitute the royal family of God the Father.—Revelation 20:4, 6; 5:10; 1 Peter 2:9, *NW;* Matthew 21:43-45.

⁹ From all the above it is manifest that the Kingdom is not earthly, but heavenly. It is the invisible or heavenly part of the "new world". "I am not from this world," said Jesus, and again, "My kingdom is no part of this world." (John 8:23; 18:36, *NW;* Isaiah 65:17; 2 Peter 3:13) So the King Christ Jesus was put to death in the flesh and was resurrected an invisible spirit creature. Therefore the world will see him no more. He went to prepare a heavenly place for his associate heirs, "Christ's body," for they too will be invisible spirit creatures. Their "citizenship exists in the heavens".—1 Peter 3:18, *Dy;* John 14:19; John 14:2; Philippians 3:20, *NW.*

¹⁰ Further showing that the Kingdom is heavenly, Jehovah says: "The heaven is my throne, and the earth is my footstool." Christ Jesus says he sits down with the Father in His throne. (Isaiah 66:1; Revelation 3:21) It is wholly inconsistent to think that the Kingdom rulership over the entire universe will be administered from his lowly footstool, the earth.

¹¹ If it is to be a heavenly kingdom, who will be the subjects of its rule? In the invisible realm angelic hosts, myriads of them, will serve as faithful messengers of the King. And on earth faithful

---

9. Is the kingdom of God earthly or heavenly?
10. What conclusively proves that the Kingdom is heavenly?
11. What creatures will be privileged to live under the Kingdom's rulership as its subjects?

children of the King Christ Jesus, including faithful forefathers of his then resurrected, will be "princes in all the earth". (Psalm 45:16) A few of such princely representatives are mentioned in Hebrews, chapter eleven. Then, too, the "great crowd" of his "other sheep", described at Revelation 7:9-17 (*NW*), will continue to "serve him day and night", and many of them will also be "princes". Surviving the universal war of Armageddon, they will "multiply and fill the earth" in righteousness, and their children will become obedient subjects of the King Christ Jesus. And finally the "unrighteous" ones that are to be resurrected then, to prove their integrity, must joyfully submit themselves to theocratic rule. (Acts 24:15, *NW*) Those who prove rebellious or who turn unfaithful during the loosing of Satan at the end of Christ's thousand-year reign will be annihilated with Satan the Devil.—Revelation 20:7-15.

[12] The kingdom of God is a paternalistic government, its subjects receiving life from the Father through Christ Jesus, the reigning King. All, therefore, including the King, submit themselves in faithful obedience to Jehovah God. As King David said: "Thine, O Jehovah, is the greatness, and the power, and the glory, and the victory, and the majesty: . . . thine is the kingdom, O Jehovah, and thou art exalted as head above all." (1 Chronicles 29:11, *AS*) Unlike man-made democratic government, all the judicial force, legislative power and executive authority reside solely in the Theocrat. Says the prophet: "Jehovah is our judge, Jehovah is our lawgiver, Jehovah is our king." (Isaiah

---

12. What kind of government is the kingdom of God, and how does such differ in form from that of a democracy?

33:22, *AS*) And yet such rule is not a harsh, dictatorial and cruel authoritarian regime. Perfect are Jehovah's works and his ways are just. —Deuteronomy 32:4, *AS*.

NOW AT HAND

[13] If the Kingdom is to be heavenly, why did both John the Baptist and Christ Jesus proclaim: "The kingdom of the heavens has drawn near"? It was because the anointed King was personally in their midst proclaiming the thrilling Kingdom message. So when the faithless Pharisees demanded to know when the Kingdom would come, the King answered: "Look! the kingdom of God is in your midst." (Matthew 3:2; 4:17 and Luke 17:20, 21, *NW*) As long as Christ Jesus was in the midst of them the disciples likewise proclaimed the presence of the Kingdom. (Matthew 10:7; Luke 10:8-11) But there is no record that they continued to do so after his ascension on high. Such an announcement would not be appropriate until his return and second presence.

[14] On this point the disciples asked what sign would indicate Jesus' return, the consummation of the old system of things, and the setting up of his kingdom. (Matthew 24:3; Acts 1:6-8) Jesus knew a long period of waiting was foretold at Psalm 110:1, 2. He also knew that men would be unable to see the invisible heavenly kingdom when it was set up. So he told them what visible sign to look for. It was really a long-range prophecy leaping nearly 1900 years.

---

13. Why was the announcement made 1900 years ago, "The kingdom of the heavens has drawn near"?
14. Why was it necessary that a certain sign be given by Christ to indicate the establishment of the Kingdom?

[15] Since 1914 world-shattering events have followed one another in quick succession. These mark that year as the time when Christ Jesus began to rule in the midst of his enemies. It was a time when the nations became wrathful. The birth that year of the heavenly government pictured by a male child that would rule all nations with an iron rod precipitated a war in heaven, resulting in the ousting of Satan, who has since then brought great woe to the earth and the sea, just as foretold. —Revelation 11:17, 18; 12:1-12, *NW*.

[16] Another feature described by Jesus that would indicate the Kingdom's establishment was, "This good news of the kingdom will be preached in all the inhabited earth for the purpose of a witness to all the nations." (Matthew 24:14, *NW*) This is not the good news of a kingdom coming, but the news of one now established. So from and after 1919 the most sustained publicity campaign ever given on earth has been to the effect that "the kingdom of the heavens has drawn near".

[17] With the heavenly kingdom's establishment and Satan's ousting, God's will has now come to pass in heaven. It can therefore be said that his kingdom is here. This being so, is it proper when uttering the Lord's prayer to include the words, "Let your kingdom come"? If anything, it is even more proper since 1914 to pray so, for Satan has been ousted from heaven and hurled down to earth and Jehovah's will now is done only in the

---

15. If 1914 marked the time when the Kingdom was set up, what world events prove it?
16. What other visible feature proves the Kingdom here?
17. Since the Kingdom is now set up, what about the propriety of Christians to continue uttering the Lord's prayer?

heavens. Christians will therefore continue to pray for that kingdom to come in all its destructive fury against Satan's remaining forces at the battle of Armageddon. They will continue to pray that God's will come to pass, "as in heaven, also upon earth."

NOT SEDITIOUS

[18] But is it not seditious to say the Lord's prayer and announce that the Kingdom has drawn near? Why do we ask? Because Jesus was so charged for making a similar proclamation. As then, so now, the sectarian clergy charge that the Kingdom message proclaimed by Jehovah's witnesses is seditious. (John 18:28-32; Luke 23:1, 2) But no honest court of justice would make such a ruling, even if the coming to pass of God's will on earth means destroying present human governments and replacing them with the majestic kingdom of the heavens. For there is no power except by God. The Kingdom is of God.—Romans 13:1, 2.

[19] The very purpose of the Kingdom is to crush out all rebellion and restore righteousness universally. Hence Satan and his wicked organization will be destroyed beneath the irresistible power of that theocratic government. (1 Corinthians 15:25) Then under a righteous Kingdom rule the original purpose of the Creator will be carried out, namely, the populating of the earth with humans who will serve, praise and honor their loving God. All this will vindicate the name, word, purpose and

---

18. Is the announcement of the Kingdom message seditious?

19. (a) What purposes and aims will the Kingdom accomplish? (b) How is the Kingdom's importance shown in the Bible?

sovereignty of Jehovah God. Since it is the kingdom of the heavens that will accomplish this, it follows that the Kingdom is of greater importance than anything else. Such importance is also indicated for it in that the greatest doctrine, yes, the whole theme, of the Bible is the Kingdom. The prophecies given under inspiration by God, and Jesus' parables and teachings, all carry as their main burden "the kingdom of the heavens".

[20] Humans who will live under its rule must likewise make the Kingdom the most important thing in their lives. Why, the Creator loved the new world so much that he gave his only-begotten Son to be its King. The Son of God emptied himself and humbly became the target of Satan's fiendish attacks in order to qualify as God's vindicator. (John 3:16; Philippians 2:5-8; Hebrews 5:8, 9) He sold everything he had in order to purchase that treasure. The apostles, following Jesus' example, sought "first the kingdom". The way one of them expressed it, 'There is one thing about it, I press on toward the goal for the prize of the calling above, cost what it may.' (Matthew 13:44-46; 6:33; Philippians 3:13, 14, *NW*) People of good will who hope to live on earth in the new world do not split their affection and allegiance with this old satanic world, but make the Kingdom the all-important thing in their lives.

[21] The undefeatable purpose of Jehovah God to establish a righteous kingdom in these last days was fulfilled A.D. 1914. At the coming battle of Armageddon it will smite full force against the

20. Besides the Creator, how do creatures show their love and appreciation for the Kingdom?
21. What assurance are we given by the prophets that the Kingdom now established will last forever?

entire organization of Satan the Devil and destroy all its parts, high and low, visible and invisible, as foretold by the prophet Daniel: "In the days of these kings shall the God of heaven set up a kingdom, which shall never be destroyed: and the kingdom shall not be left to other people, but it shall break in pieces and consume all these kingdoms, and it shall stand for ever." (Daniel 2:44) Not only will it last forever, but of the increase of Christ's government and peace there shall be no end. (Isaiah 9:7; Daniel 7:14; Luke 1:33) It is beyond the imagination of frail men to conceive the blessings that this glorious kingdom will bestow on all who are privileged to live under its righteous rule.

[22] The climax of the centuries has been reached, and the great issue of universal sovereignty is about to be settled once and for all time by the Kingdom. So, awake, everyone who wants to live under that righteous government! Put not your trust in the princes of this old world who have set up a worldly international organization in defiance of God's rightful Kingdom rule. Obey the King Christ Jesus and flee, while there is still time, to the Kingdom heights. (Romans 13:11; Matthew 24:15-20) Time left is short, for "the kingdom of the heavens has drawn near".

---

22. Why is it now high time for the people to awake?

CHAPTER XIII

USE OF IMAGES IN WORSHIP

ACCORDING to the express statement of the Creator himself, man was made in the image of God. Not that man had the same form and substance as his Creator, but that he had God's attributes. To man as a creature with God's attributes was granted the privilege of holding dominion over the earth and its forms of life: the birds, fish and animals. Toward these he had the responsibility of exercising the same attributes as his Creator: wisdom in directing the affairs charged to him, justice in dealing with other creatures of his God, love in unselfishly caring for the earth and its creatures, and power in properly discharging his authority to carry on the right worship of the Universal Sovereign in whose image he was created.—Genesis 1:26-28.

[2] Man's exercise of earth's domination did not last long. He chose to deny the universal sovereignty of his God, and he set up images in supposed representation of his Creator. Instead of holding dominion over the lower forms of animal life, man set them up as objects of worship. He made carved images in wood and stone and molten ones in metal. To these he bowed and prayed. Man lost his dominion.—Romans 1:23, 25.

---

1. In what way was man made in the image of God?
2. How did man lose his position of dominion over the earth and animals?

[3] Some of earth's population, however, chose to recognize the Almighty God. (Genesis 35:2) To safeguard the Israelites from any worship of images in denial of His supremacy he gave them his law forbidding just such imagery and worship: "Thou shalt have no other gods before me. Thou shalt not make unto thee any graven image, or any likeness of any thing that is in heaven above, or that is in the earth beneath, or that is in the water under the earth: thou shalt not bow down thyself to them, nor serve them." (Exodus 20:3-5) This law was given them out of clouds and thick darkness and fire, and no form of any kind was discernible, for the very purpose of preventing man's attempt at making an image of the Almighty God. Thus his law became a hedge, a safeguard to a people constantly surrounded by image-worshiping nations.—Deuteronomy 4:15-23.

[4] In all cases of those outside that law, the claim is made that what is worshiped is not the image itself, but what is represented by the image. That is the theory of this claim, but does it work out that way in actual practice? Among the "learned" class, the images of the gods are mere representations, mere picture aids to devotion; while among the less educated the image is real, and they offer it incense, food and drink, and kiss, worship, bow and pray to it. In India "the common people indubitably worship the image itself, but the better educated repudiate such worship". So reports Du Bois, one of the early Roman Catholic mis-

---

3. What safeguard was given to God's worshipers, under what circumstances was it given, and for what reason?

4. What claim is made by worshipers of images, but does actual practice agree with the theory of the claim?

sionaries in India. In China "only the higher intelligence regards the holy hill as holy because a spirit lives in it or gives oracles there. To the less developed mind the hill itself is divine". (*Origin and Evolution of Religion* by E. Washburn Hopkins, Ph.D., LL.D., pages 19 and 21) Such has been the theory and practice of nations not confessing any responsibility under Jehovah God's law. (2 Kings 17:35) But what attitude was taken by God's chosen nation to whom his law was directly given?

[5] God's covenant declared to them: "Ye shall make you no idols, neither shall ye rear you up a graven image, or a pillar, neither shall ye place any figured stone in your land, to bow down unto it: for I am Jehovah your God." Coupled with this command was the divine warning that if the Israelites would not listen to God but would conduct themselves contrary to him, "then I will walk contrary unto you in wrath; and I also will chastise you seven times for your sins. And I will destroy your high places, and cut down your sun-images, and cast your dead bodies upon the bodies of your idols; and my soul shall abhor you." (Leviticus 26:1, 28, 30, *AS*) Yet, with that clear statement before them, the Israelite practice swung like a giant pendulum back and forth between the flat rejection of all forms of image worship and the direct violation of God's law by the open worship of images of animals, stars and men and the gods of the heathen nations about them.—Judges 2:11-17; Ezekiel 16:17; Amos 5:26; Acts 7:43.

[6] Jehovah's approval or rejection of the rulers

5, 6. What did Jehovah's covenant oblige Israel to do, but what was the attitude of the nation and its rulers toward images, and with what result?

of Israel hinged directly on the action they took toward idols and image worship. Periodically faithful rulers and judges, such as Gideon, David, Hezekiah and Josiah, made a clean purge of such mockery of Jehovah's supremacy to swing the nation back into his favor. (Judges 6:25-27; 2 Samuel 5:20, 21; 2 Chronicles 34:1-7, 33) But the nation swung too many times away from the proper worship of the Universal Sovereign, until at last, for the very reason of image worship in denial of Jehovah's supremacy, the nation was rejected and broken up.—Deuteronomy 4:23-28; Jeremiah 22:8, 9.

[7] But God was not to be without witnesses to his supremacy. With the announcing of the kingdom of the heavens by Jesus Christ came the selecting of another people for Jehovah's name, as Christians. (Acts 15:14) Since the first disciples were from among the Jews, they were at first considered just an offshoot or sect of Judaism, for they stuck rigidly to God's law against images. Hatred of such idolatrous usage was a thing that set apart the Christians in an age and in lands that had innumerable gods and deities represented in images of stone and wood. Says McClintock and Strong's *Cyclopœdia*, Vol. IV, page 503: "Images were unknown in the worship of the primitive Christians; and this fact was, indeed, made the ground of a charge of atheism on the part of the heathen against the Christians." Their position in this regard was fully in accord with the apostle Paul's authoritative counsel: "Therefore, my beloved ones, flee from idolatry." (1 Corinthians 10:14, *NW*) They were witnesses of the living and

7. How was a new people for God's name selected, and what was their attitude toward image worship?

true God Jehovah and were aware of the nothingness of images: "We know that an idol is nothing
in the world and that there is no God but one. For
even though there are those who are called 'gods',
whether in heaven or on earth, just as there are
many 'gods' and many 'lords', there is actually to
us one God the Father, . . . and there is one Lord,
Jesus Christ." (1 Corinthians 8:4-6, *NW;* Isaiah
43:10-12; Acts 17:29) As announcers of his kingdom Jehovah's servants were admonished to keep
apart from such image worship.—1 John 5:21;
1 Corinthians 10:7.

MODERN IDOLATRY

[8] Religious organizations today, however, do not
take the same position as did those early Christians. The official Catholic position is stated as follows: "The Christian religion has allowed the use
of statues and paintings to represent the Incarnate
Son of God, the saints, and angels, and these
images are a legitimate aid to devotion, since the
honour that is given them is but relative, being
directed through them to the beings they represent." The growth of Catholic usage of images
they explain in this way: "As soon as the Church
came out of the catacombs, became richer, had
no fear of persecution . . . they began to make
statues . . . The principle was quite simple. The
first Christians were accustomed to see the statues
of emperors, of pagan gods and heroes, as well as
pagan wall-paintings. So they made paintings of
their religion, and, as soon as they could afford
them, statues of their Lord and their heroes, without the remotest fear or suspicion of idolatry."

8, 9. What is the official Catholic position toward images,
and where did the use of images originate?

—*Catholic Encyclopedia,* Vol. XII, page 742; and
Vol. VII, page 666.

[9] "In the fourth century the Christian Roman
citizens in the East offered gifts, incense, even
prayers (!) to the statues of the emperor. It would
be natural that the people who bowed to, kissed,
incensed the imperial eagles and the images of
Caesar (with no suspicion of anything like idolatry), who paid elaborate reverence to an empty
throne as his symbol, should give the same signs
to the cross, the images of Christ, and the altar."
(*Catholic Encyclopedia,* Vol. VII, page 667) With
this unmistakable pagan background for image
worship, it can readily be understood why Cardi-
nal Newman in his book *An Essay on the Development of Christian Doctrine,* page 373, admitted
that, among a long list of other things, " . . .
images at a later date . . . are all of pagan origin
and sanctified by their adoption into the [Roman
Catholic] Church."

[10] It does no good to argue that such honor given
to images is merely "relative", for in actual practice among less-educated Catholics the worship
of the image itself is real. This too is admitted by
the *Catholic Encyclopedia,* Vol. VII, page 668,
which, speaking of the eighth century, says: "At
the same time one must admit that things had
gone very far in the direction of image-worship.
Even then it is inconceivable that anyone, except
the most grossly stupid p e a s a n t, could have
thought that an image could hear prayers, or do
anything for us. And yet the way in which some
people treated their holy [images] argues more
than the merely relative honour that Catholics

10. What actual practice toward images is admitted as
carried on among the less-educated Catholic people?

are taught to observe toward them. . . . [Images] were crowned with garlands, incensed, kissed. Lamps burned before them, hymns were sung in their honor. They were applied to sick persons by contact, set in the path of a fire or flood to stop it by a sort of magic." This was in the eighth century; and after twelve centuries of unlimited opportunity to educate the people of Italy, yet, in 1944, when Mount Vesuvius erupted, the humble folk placed their images in the path of the flowing lava to prevent disaster. To this very day the unlearned Catholic people of Mexico, Central America and South America do exactly as the Catholic people of the eighth century, even to placing before them daily offerings of food and drink. —Psalm 115:4-8; Habakkuk 2:18, 19.

[11] Still, are not prayers addressed through images of angels and saints in *relative* worship allowable? No. Prayer is to be directed to God, who says: "I am Jehovah, that is my name; and my glory will I not give to another, neither my praise unto graven images." (Isaiah 42:8, *AS*) Prayer, instead of being addressed to images of Jesus, saints or angels, is to be addressed to the Father in heaven and through the living invisible Christ Jesus, not through a lifeless object of wood or stone. (Matthew 6:6-15; John 15:16; 14:13) *Relative* honor to God through an angel was reproved in these words: "Be careful! Do not do that! . . . Worship God." (Revelation 19:10; 22:8, 9, *NW*) At Caesarea and Lystra the apostles Peter and Paul likewise rebuked others' bow-

---

11. Is "relative" worship of God through images Scriptural, and how should prayer be addressed to God?

ing before them as *relative* worship of God. (Acts 10:24-26;
14:11-18) Any such *relative* worship through images as visual aids
to the worshiper runs directly counter to the Christian principle, stated at 2 Corin-
thians 5:7 (*NW*), "We
are walking by faith, not
by sight."

WORSHIP OF INSTITUTIONS

[12] Image worship is nothing else than demonism.
A continuing in such practice results in a trap.
Israel took up worship of pagan gods: "And served
their idols, which became a snare unto them. Yea,
they sacrificed their sons and their daughters unto
demons." (Psalm 106:36, 37, *AS;* Deuteronomy
7:16; 32:17) Those demons led men to set up other images besides those of wood and stone and
metal for worship and adoration. Political organizations claim divine right and authority, and it is
therefore argued that obedience to the cross-
patch of earth's political organizations is a *relative*
obedience and worship of God. The claim of many
religious sects is that worship of God must be
through one or the other of multitudinous religious systems, with their big and little clergy as
'representatives' of God. So all these are images,
works of men's hands, and due for destruction
with all other forms of image worship.—Micah
5:13; Exodus 22:20; Zephaniah 2:11.

---

12. What is the source of image worship, and what other
images are set up besides those of wood and stone?

[13] At all times men who have chosen the worship of the living God instead of images have been targets of assault by the wicked demons and men. From Daniel's three faithful Hebrew companions who under penalty of death refused to worship the golden image of the state, and on to the early Christians who chose death by the stake or being torn by wild beasts in the Roman arena rather than acknowledge any image as God, and down to our very day, Jehovah's witnesses likewise refuse to heil men, salute flags, or worship the totalitarian state. During our twentieth century this has resulted in their spending years in concentration camps and prisons, and in suffering the things the faithful worshipers of Jehovah did in ages past. But, like them, they now uphold Jehovah's supremacy and are assured of deliverance by him. —Daniel, chapter 3.

[14] In direct contrast, men who do not see the issue involved in image worship will find no difficulty in bowing down and worshiping the greatest image of all. Christ Jesus warned that, after beastly World War I, a two-horned world power would cause an image of imperial authority to be set up, claiming the right and authority to rule the earth. (Revelation 13:14, 15; 14:9-11; 17:11) Finding its beginning in 1919 in the League of Nations, that political image has been revived now in a new form, an international organization for peace and security. This stands as a great image, a substitute for God's established kingdom. Flying in the

---

13. What has always been the attitude of Jehovah's worshipers toward images, and with what result?
14, 15. What great image is now raised up, who worship it, and with what consequence to the image and its worshipers?

face of the Kingdom's announcement, Christendom rebelliously rejects God's kingdom and lauds man's feeble efforts for earth's domination.

[15] This is open rebellion against God. In the face of knowledge it becomes stubbornness and idolatry which leads to death. (1 Samuel 15:23) At the time of the destruction of that and all other political images the worshipers are taunted with the words: "Where are their gods, their rock in whom they trusted, . . . let them rise up and help you, and be your protection." (Deuteronomy 32:37, 38) All who support and give worship to images are due for bitter disappointment and death.

[16] Jehovah's universal sovereignty is what is at issue. He has declared that men shall know he is Almighty God, though it be in the destruction of all who refuse to recognize that fact. (Psalm 83:18) Whether an image be of wood or stone, or be an organization of men, or any other form; whether the worship or praise be direct or *relative,* such image worship runs counter to God's law and will merit final destruction from him at Armageddon. When all deniers of the living God's supremacy and all substitute mockery of his kingdom are wiped out, and when Jehovah's universal rule is established for all time by his reigning King Christ Jesus, no more will man set up and worship images of men, animals and organizations. The time will then be when obedient man, in the image of God, will again exercise proper dominion over the lower animals and direct his praises to God. —Psalm 150:6, *AS.*

---

16. How will Jehovah establish his sovereignty, and how and when will man again wield God-given dominion over the earth?

CHAPTER XIV

THE WAY TO GOD IN PRAYER

IN THIS upside-down, unhappy world it seems to be the general course to take the good things for granted, to drift along the line of least resistance and only when unfortunate circumstances arise, to seek relief by resorting to prayer. Then, if the prayers are not at once answered, the feeling arises that the Lord God has fallen down on the job. Prayers for health, peace and prosperity go unanswered, even when addressed in sincerity to a god believed to be the Almighty. This ought to cause thinking persons to pause and give serious thought to this important matter. Seeking the right way, they ought to ask: How should we pray? To whom should prayer be addressed? Are there any special requirements for imperfect men to reach the Almighty? Indeed, why pray at all?

[2] The answers to these questions, and to many more of equal importance, are found in the Bible, the great Textbook of those who would be heard in prayer. Since all life depends upon the Creator, it is mandatory for those who want eternal life to know how to reach him in prayer, how prayer should be used, and what it can accomplish.

[3] Prayer is not a new thing to the human race.

1, 2. What seems to be the general attitude toward prayer? and what important questions come to mind on this matter?

3. What was the origin of prayer, and what examples serve to bear this out?

It early became apparent to righteously disposed men that many problems that arose in their lives could not be solved by their own efforts. "O Jehovah," confessed Jeremiah, "I know that the way of man is not in himself; it is not in man that walketh to direct his steps." (Jeremiah 10:23, *AS*) Probably first to realize this was the righteous man Abel. He offered to God an acceptable sacrifice, accompanied undoubtedly by words of supplication and praise. Abel was followed by others who sought God through prayer. Among them was David. When hemmed in by enemies who sought him, he cried: "Hear my prayer, O Jehovah; give ear to my supplications: in thy faithfulness answer me, and in thy righteousness." When God delivered him, David uttered words which are a comfort to us now, saying: "Jehovah is nigh unto all them that call upon him . . . in truth." (Psalms 143:1; 145:18, *AS*) Certainly one who realized his own inability to escape from a seemingly hopeless situation was Jonah when in the darkness of the belly of a great fish. For rescue, "Jonah prayed unto Jehovah his God out of the fish's belly. And Jehovah spake unto the fish, and it vomited out Jonah upon the dry land." (Jonah 2:1, 10, *AS*) Men today must realize their dependence upon Jehovah.

[4] It is not necessary, when praying, to assume some special pose or position. Certainly it is fitting to kneel when seeking God in prayer, as Daniel insisted on doing before he was thrown to the lions, for such a posture shows due humiliation. Paul said: "I bend my knees to the Father"; but

4. What is the proper position to assume in addressing God in prayer?

he further stated: "With every form of prayer and supplication you carry on prayer." (Ephesians 3:14; 6:18, *NW*) Here he could hardly have meant that it was necessary to remain always in a kneeling position. Jesus told his disciples: "When you stand praying, forgive." (Mark 11:25, *NW*) On one occasion God's servants "bowed their heads, and worshipped Jehovah with their faces to the ground". (Nehemiah 8:6, *AS*) It is not the position that matters. One may pray while in his bed at night, while at a meal, or while going about his daily tasks.

⁵ Let it be noted that it is Jehovah, not some strange heathen god, who is able to answer the prayers of his servants. An outstanding example in proof of this is found in 1 Kings, chapter 18. Repeatedly, but in vain, the prophets of the heathen god Baal entreated their god to bring fire down out of the heavens. Though they prayed from morning until night, Baal was unable to answer. Then the prophet Elijah prayed to the true God, and Jehovah answered by sending down fire which completely consumed the sacrifice, even though it had been purposely wetted down to guard against any trickery. Jehovah can "do more than superabundantly beyond all the things we ask or conceive".—Ephesians 3:20, *NW*.

⁶ Jehovah is able to hear the prayers of men, his powers of perception being such that he is able to understand the very thoughts of one's heart. While in Persia, Nehemiah sadly thought of the broken-down state of Jerusalem's walls. He was interrupted by the king whom he served as cup-

---

5. What incident serves to show who is capable of answering prayer?
6. Why is that One able to hear prayer?

bearer and who demanded to know the reason for Nehemiah's sadness. Before making known his desire to repair the walls, Nehemiah "prayed to the God of heaven". (Nehemiah 2:4) Although the prayer was inaudible to the king, it was heard and acted upon by God. To him all men of flesh must come, as well stated by David: "O thou that hearest prayer, unto thee shall all flesh come." (Psalm 65:2) But let them not be among those who ask and receive not, because they ask amiss. —James 4:3.

⁷ Since all flesh is imperfect and sinful, how can anyone approach a perfect and righteous God? For we read: "There is not a righteous man, not even one." "Jehovah is far from the wicked; but he heareth the prayer of the righteous." (Romans 3:10, *NW;* Proverbs 15:29, *AS*) If it is only the prayers of the righteous that are heard and there are none who are righteous, then whose prayers are heard? As shown throughout the Hebrew as well as the Greek Scriptures, there were men whose entreaties to Jehovah were heard and answered. All had something in common which made their communication with God possible. Without exception they had an unshakable faith in the existence of Jehovah and in his power and willingness to aid those who sought his ways. They believed him capable of fulfilling his promises, regardless of how impossible such might have seemed from a human standpoint. Because of this belief, God counted them righteous. Thus it was that, when Abraham's faith strengthened him to believe that God would give him a son in his old age, God

---

7. How has it been possible for imperfect, sinful man to direct his entreaties to a perfect and righteous God?

"counted it to him for righteousness". (Genesis 15:6) Faith is based upon knowing God's Word.

[8] In God's due time he sent his only-begotten Son, Christ Jesus, who gave up his life that it might serve as a ransom to redeem mankind from sin. Hence, to those who availed themselves of this loving provision, a new approach to God in prayer was opened up, the only avenue of approach now available to man. This was indicated when Jesus said: "No one comes to the Father except through me." (John 14:6, *NW*) Religious arguments to the contrary, this automatically bars any prayers from reaching Jehovah by way of a "back door"; whether it be through the pope at Vatican City or a numberless list of "saints" or, yes, even through Jesus' mother Mary. Not one scripture indicates prayers should be addressed through any of these. Jesus said: "If you ask anything in my name, I will do it."—John 14:14, *NW*.

[9] Little wonder it is, then, that so many of the prayers of the people and the nations fail to achieve any results, when they refuse to use the only avenue of approach that Jehovah has provided. But there are other reasons for God to reject their prayers. While he is ever ready to hear the prayers of those who seek to do his will, he takes no pleasure in the prayers of the wicked or those who turn their faces from obeying his righteous laws. "He that turneth away his ear from hearing the law, even his prayer shall be abomina-

---

8. What further provision has been made for men to approach God, and what fallacy does this knowledge make apparent?

9. Why have so many prayers failed to achieve the desired results?

tion." (Proverbs 28:9) Into this class must fall those religious clergymen who ignored God's law, "Thou shalt not kill," and uttered long prayers that the nation of which they happened to be citizens might be most successful at taking life. Does Jehovah favor one of their contending sides? "When ye make many prayers, I will not hear: your hands are full of blood."—Isaiah 1:15.

[10] Jesus' disciples realized the importance of prayer and asked him to teach them how to pray. He gave instructions that are indispensable to Christians today. (Luke 11:1-4) As we consider these instructions it should be our desire to conform ourselves to them, even though we might have to change from our present way of prayer.

[11] At Matthew 6:5, 6 (*NW*) Jesus said: "When you pray, you must not be as the hypocrites; because they like to pray standing in the synagogues and on the corners of the broad ways to be visible to men. Truly I say to you, They are having their reward in full. You, however, when you pray, go into your private room and, after shutting your door, pray

10, 11. (a) What did Jesus give his disciples when they asked to be taught to pray? (b) What important point did he make at the outset, and so what is seen regarding most prayers for peace?

to your Father who is in secret; then your Father who looks on in secret will repay you." When Jesus here instructed his followers to pray in secret he was very forcibly pointing out the folly of making public prayers solely for the purpose of being seen by men and receiving their admiration and praise. Since most prayers for victory, peace and prosperity are spread abroad in high-sounding, formal language over the radio and in the newspapers, it is obvious they are for the purpose of calling the attention of men to the ones offering the prayers. They receive the reward they seek, the plaudits of men. God hears them not nor does he act on their behalf.

[12] It would not be correct to assume from Jesus' words that any prayers offered outside the privacy of one's room would be hypocritical. Jesus himself prayed otherwise on numerous occasions, and he who set the perfect example would not have done so had it been improper. He prayed within the hearing of others, not to call attention to himself, but rather to give a witness to the glory of God's name and kingdom. So, when he offered public acknowledgment to God before he fed the five thousand; when he prayed in the audience of his disciples on occasions; and when they in turn prayed publicly for the purpose of enlightening others, neither Jesus nor they were interpreting his words, "Go into your private room," to mean prayers must always be said out of the sight and hearing of all others. As a prayer audible to others Jesus said to God: "I knew that you always hear me; but on account of the crowd standing around

---

12. What may we not assume from the admonition to "go into your private room", and why not?

I spoke, in order that they might believe that you
sent me forth."—John 11:42; 6:11, *NW*.

[13] Jesus further instructed his disciples: "When
praying, do not say the same things over and over
again, just as the people of the nations do, for they
imagine they will get a hearing for their use of
many words. So, do not make yourselves like them,
for God your Father knows what things you are
needing before ever you ask him." (Matthew
6:7, 8, *NW*) The heathen Buddhists and Lamas
employ a prayer wheel, a hollow drum into which
prayers are put, and each time the wheel is turned
the prayers contained in it are supposed to be said.
Today, millions follow the same routine with
rosaries and oft-repeated prayers from prayer
books. Those perceiving that such a practice is exactly what Jesus spoke against and sincerely desiring to pray in harmony with God's will are
glad to obey his injunction, "Do not say the same
things over and over again, just as the people of
the nations do." They heed his further instructions.

MODEL PRAYER

[14] Jesus' next words set forth a model prayer;
not one to be glibly repeated without thought of
its meaning or contents, but one that demonstrates
to whom prayer should be addressed, and for what
a believer should properly pray. He told them to
pray this way: "Our Father in the heavens, let
your name be sanctified. Let your kingdom come.
Let your will come to pass, as in heaven, also upon

---

13. (a) How do the heathen say the same things over
and over again, and those today who are like the heathen in this respect? (b) What will those who are sincere and who perceive this do?
14. What was the purpose of the model prayer Jesus
gave, and what, briefly, did it contain?

earth. Give us today our bread for this day; and forgive us our debts, as we also have forgiven our debtors. And do not bring us into temptation, but deliver us from the wicked one."—Matthew 6:9-13, *NW*.

¹⁵ This model prayer is unselfish in every respect. In addressing God as "Our Father" the one praying recognizes there are others who are children of the Most High and his thoughts are taken away from his personal desires. Furthermore, it indicates that those who thus pray have availed themselves of Christ's ransom sacrifice and are either spiritual sons of God or prospective earthly sons. A remnant of spiritual sons are still on earth. Joined together with them since A.D. 1918 is an ever-increasing crowd of men of good will. These also may address Jehovah as "Our Father", for, during Christ's thousand-year reign, they become the earthly children of the Life-giver Christ Jesus and hence are technically in the position of being "grandchildren" of God. In Scripture the grandfather is often referred to as father.

¹⁶ Since vindication of Jehovah's name and sovereignty is the foremost doctrine of the Bible, his name and kingdom find first place in the model prayer. Even though the Kingdom has already been established in the heavens, it has yet to come against Satan's entire world of wickedness and completely destroy it. Until such time, the servants of God will continue to pray for its coming. While such things as food and shelter are necessary for life, requests for these things take a

---

15. How does this prayer tend toward unselfishness, and who may properly employ the term "Our Father"?
16. How does the prayer show the order of importance of things?

secondary place. It is permissible to ask for them in amounts sufficient to take care of the daily needs, and they should be received with thanks to Jehovah, who knows our every need even before we ask.

[17] "Let your will come to pass," Jesus taught. World leaders selfishly pray that God help them to put across their schemes for world domination, and in this the clergy assist with their prayers for victory. Never did Jesus pray for the success or continuance of any of the worldly nations. Exactly to the contrary, he said: "I make request, not concerning the world, but concerning those you have given me." (John 17:9, *NW*) What of it if a nation selects a Day of Prayer and unitedly requests that its will be recognized and followed by God? Or if a Family of Nations is brought about and God's blessing asked upon the arrangement? Mere numbers or volume of prayers can have no effect on the matter. Prayers not in accord with God's will are never heard by him. But if one of his faithful children properly prays to God, saying, "Not my will but yours be done," or says, as the beloved David did, "Teach me to do thy will; for thou art my God," the prayer will not only reach the lofty throne of Jehovah but also be acted upon favorably. "A righteous man's supplication when it is at work has much force."—James 5:16, *NW*.

[18] In harmony with Jesus' instructions, we pray that our debts (sins) be forgiven. This cannot mean we can willfully pursue a wicked course and, by simply repeating these words, be absolved of any further responsibility for the past and be free

---

17. In what way do the prayers of present world leaders and those of Christ and his followers differ?
18. What is meant by the request "Forgive us our debts"?

to repeat such wickedness as opportunity affords. This prayer is designed solely for those who sincerely endeavor to follow the Lord's instructions but who transgress against his righteous requirements because of being imperfect and hence unable to follow a perfect course of action. The transgressions are forgiven through Christ Jesus, and the sins are cleansed away by his blood. But to be forgiven our transgressions by God's mercy, we must be merciful to those transgressing against us and must forgive them in a godlike manner. "Happy are the merciful, since they will be shown mercy."—Matthew 5:7; 6:14, 15, NW.

¹⁹ Jehovah is never guilty of tempting his servants to sin, but all such temptation comes from the wicked one, Satan. The expression, "Do not bring us into temptation, but deliver us from the wicked one," asks that God will never test or try us beyond what we are able to bear. (Matthew 6:13, NW; 1 Corinthians 10:13) Without Jehovah's loving guidance and protection his servants would be at the mercy of the wicked one the Devil, who "walks about like a roaring lion, seeking to devour someone". (1 Peter 5:8, NW) Jehovah delivers us from the power of the tempter and his world, and invites us to pray to God for succor in time of need. The words added to Matthew 6:13, "For thine is the kingdom, and the power, and the glory, for ever. Amen," are spurious and are omitted from all modern Bible translations.

²⁰ When Noah came out of the ark after the flood

19. How does God not bring us into temptation, but delivers us?
20, 21. How may persons now living on earth be like Noah and his family, and how is this invitation now being extended to them?

waters had receded, his first act was to build an
altar and offer up sacrifices and prayer to Jehovah
in thankfulness for the deliverance of him and his
family. To God, Noah's prayer and acceptable
sacrifice were as a "sweet savour". (Genesis 8:21)
Now, just prior to Armageddon, faithful servants
of God are going from city to city and extending a
gracious invitation to all who will hear. What is
that invitation? Zechariah 8:21, 22 gives the answer to that question, saying: "The inhabitants of
one city shall go to another, saying, Let us go
speedily to entreat the favor of Jehovah, and to
seek Jehovah of hosts: I will go also. Yea, many
peoples and strong nations shall come to seek
Jehovah of hosts in Jerusalem [heavenly New
Jerusalem], and to entreat the favor of Jehovah."
—AS.

²¹ Do you want to be among these "many peoples" who "seek Jehovah of hosts" and who, as
pictured by Noah's family, will survive Armageddon's war to offer up sweet-savored prayers to
Jehovah throughout eternity? If so, abandon the
foolish and repetitious prayers of this dying old
world. Instead, pray for God's kingdom by his Son,
Christ Jesus, and always seek it first.

CHAPTER XV

THE SABBATH: IN SHADOW AND REALITY

"IN SIX days Jehovah made heaven and earth, and on the seventh day he rested, and was refreshed." (Exodus 31:17, *AS*) His resting or desisting from work was because he had accomplished his creative work as he had purposed. Hence he ceased from his creative work as respects the earth. At such a height of accomplishment he surveyed his finished earthly work; and "God saw every thing that he had made, and, behold, it was very good". (Genesis 1:31) For such a reason, then, Jehovah God could feel refreshed. That is, he could enjoy the exhilarating pleasure of having accomplished his will. Only as regards our earth did he desist from creative activity, having finished his work on it to the extent that he desired. It is neither reasonable nor Scriptural to think that he halted operations as respects all the rest of his universe.

2 "Thus the heavens and the earth were finished, and all the host of them. And on the seventh day God ended his work which he had made; . . . And God blessed the seventh day, and sanctified it: because that in it he had rested from all his work which God created and made." (Genesis 2:1-3)

---

1. (a) What was the Creator's personal experience on the seventh day of the creative period? (b) In what respect did he desist from all his work on the seventh day?
2. Just how long is the day, and is it over?

This seventh "day" on which God desisted from his work toward our planet is not to be understood as a 24-hour day. This seventh day follows upon the preceding six days of creation. The Scriptural evidence is to the effect that all those six preceding days were much longer than 24 hours each. In fact, they were great periods of time thousands of years long. Measured by the length of the "seventh day", on which God desists from work and is refreshed, each of those days was 7,000 years long. Man being created toward the close of the sixth day, he was put on the earth toward the end of 42,000 years of earth's preparation. So in course of time the grand cycle of seven "days" will add up to 49,000 years. The Bible time-schedule indicates that slightly more than a thousand years of this great cycle remains yet to be run.

[3] *Shä-vath'* is the particular Hebrew word used at Genesis 2:1-3 and it is translated "rested". The English word *sabbath* is drawn from it. Certain religionists argue that there, at man's very beginning, God fastened the sabbath-day law upon his human creatures; and to their aid they call Genesis 2:1-3 as proof. Let such persons and all others take note that the *day* which God blessed and sanctified back there was no 24-hour day. We are yet in that "seventh day", because its time-length is equal to that of each of the six preceding days of creative work. The way the seventh-day sabbath-keeping religionists calculate, they claim man was made after the animals on the sixth 24-hour day of creation. If so, then the first full day of man's existence had to be a sabbath rest day

---

3. From what is the word "rested" translated, and what difficulties arise from claiming the seventh day to be 24 hours long?

for man without his having completed or even begun a week's work. So he rested before he began working. However, the Bible makes it plain that God's seventh day is longer than from sunset to sunset, just as the word *day* must mean more than a 24-hour period when Genesis 2:4 says: "These are the generations of the heavens and of the earth when they were created, in the *day* that Jehovah God made earth and heaven." (*AS*) According to the Bible the "seventh day" is still continuing on the part of the Creator, Jehovah God.

⁴ At the beginning of the seventh day God blessed it, pronouncing it good and to his glory and for the benefit of faithful creatures. At its ending, about a thousand years from now, the *day* will likewise be blessed; for the present evil conditions will then be entirely removed. He sanctified this *day* to his holy purpose. How? In that from its very beginning he ordained that it should vindicate him as the Creator of what is good and vindicate him as the Maintainer and Preserver of such good. And the end of this "seventh day" will yet prove that his original purpose in making this earth and putting man upon it has not been blocked but has been gloriously realized in full proof of his Godship, supremacy and all-power. By the end of this "seventh day" the earth will be a beauteous paradise, everywhere like Eden's garden. It will be filled with righteous human creatures, all in harmony with the Creator and all acting as his representatives in having dominion over the birds, fishes, beasts, and other living things that creep upon the earth.

---

4. How has Jehovah blessed and sanctified the seventh day?

[5] When God blessed the perfect Adam and Eve and gave them his mandate to fill the earth with righteous offspring and to subdue the earth and have dominion over the lower living creatures, God included no command with reference to a sabbath-day observance. The temptation by Satan, and the sin by Adam and Eve, did not have to do with breaking any 24-hour-long sabbath law. If God did not give them such a law in Eden before they sinned, then certainly he did not give them such a law after driving them out of Eden as sinners. There is no record that he did so. —Genesis 2:15-17; 1:28.

[6] What, then, about the number seven which occurs 61 times in the book of Genesis alone? For instance, with regard to Noah: He and his family and the animals went into the ark during a seven-day period. "It came to pass after seven days, that the waters of the flood were upon the earth." (Genesis 7:1-10) Noah's ark grounded on the mountains of Ararat on the seventeenth day of the seventh month of the year. After waiting for the waters to subside Noah sent out a raven and a dove. The dove returned. "And he stayed yet other seven days; and again he sent forth the dove out of the ark." After its return with an olive leaf in its beak, Noah "stayed yet other seven days; and sent forth the dove; which returned not again unto him any more". Then, a full solar year after having been shut up in the ark, Noah and his family and the animals left the ark of preserva-

---

5. Why are there no grounds for claiming God subjected Adam and Eve to sabbath-day regulations?

6, 7. How did Noah show regard for the number "seven"? And yet why is there nothing to show he was placed under sabbath-day law regulations?

tion. (Genesis 8:14) All this reveals that Noah divided up the time into periods of seven days, but it does not show he and his family kept a strict sabbath-day rest on the seventh day, doing no work thereon.

[7] In the everlasting covenant which God made right afterward and symbolized by the rainbow he made no reference to any sabbath-day observance. And in repeating the mandate to Noah and his sons he did not include any command as to sabbath observance. This was not because they had already been keeping a sabbath law down till then so that the law needed no repeating. No, but it was certainly because no such sabbath regulation had been put on men till then.—Genesis 9:1-17.

[8] Genesis 26:4, 5 is no proof that Abraham was under a sabbath-keeping law. God's commandments to him included none concerning a seventh-day sabbath-keeping. God's commandments to his obedient creatures are not the same at all times, but some are commanded to do certain things and others are not. Only Abraham was commanded to offer up his beloved son as a burnt-offering, but none of God's servants since Abraham have been so commanded. Abraham was commanded to be circumcised first after he was 99 years old; but no follower of Christ need be circumcised.—Genesis, chapters 17 and 22.

[9] The later evidence is against any argument that Abraham was under a sabbath-day obligation by God's express commandment. While the seventh day of the week may have been looked upon as

---

8. Why is Genesis 26:4, 5 no valid argument that Abraham was under a sabbath commandment?
9. Why was it no lawbreaking for Abraham, Isaac and Jacob not to keep weekly sabbath?

specially marked by God with his favor, that does not prove he had enjoined a seventh-day commandment upon Abraham, Isaac and Jacob. When the sabbath-day law did not apply, it was no law-breaking not to keep sabbath. So Abraham's righteousness was no more dependent on sabbath-keeping than on his first being circumcised.—Romans 4:3-13.

INTRODUCTION OF REST DAY

[10] The Hebrew word *shab·bäth'* means "cessation; rest". It occurs first at Exodus 16:23 and marks the time of introducing the sabbath law, to the Jews. By miraculously keeping manna from falling on the seventh day, God enforced the seventh-day sabbath law that he had just announced to the Jews. (Exodus 16:23-30) Whereas it was given informally out in the wilderness, the sabbath-day law was embodied in the law code which Jehovah formally gave the Jews by Moses when inaugurating the law covenant at Mount Horeb. It was made the fourth of the Ten Commandments there given, and was stated in these words:

[11] "Remember the sabbath day, to keep it holy. Six days shalt thou labor, and do all thy work; but the seventh day is a sabbath unto Jehovah thy God: in it thou shalt not do any work, thou, nor thy son, nor thy daughter, thy man-servant, nor thy maid-servant, nor thy cattle, nor thy stranger that is within thy gates: for in six days Jehovah made heaven and earth, the sea, and all that in them is, and rested the seventh day: where-

---

10, 11. When, and to whom, was the weekly sabbath law first given? And in what was it incorporated?

fore Jehovah blessed the sabbath day, and hallowed it."—Exodus 20:8-11, AS.

[12] Now note what Deuteronomy 5:1-15 says: "And Moses called unto all Israel, and said unto them, Hear, O Israel, the statutes and the ordinances which I speak in your ears this day, that ye may learn them, and observe to do them. Jehovah our God made a covenant with us in Horeb. Jehovah made not this covenant with our fathers [Abraham, Isaac, and Jacob], but with us, even us, who are all of us here alive this day. Jehovah spake with you face to face in the mount out of the midst of the fire . . . , saying, I am Jehovah thy God, who brought thee out of the land of Egypt, out of the house of bondage. . . . Observe the sabbath day, . . . remember that thou wast a servant in the land of Egypt, and Jehovah thy God brought thee out thence by a mighty hand and by an outstretched arm: therefore Jehovah thy God commanded thee to keep the sabbath day."—AS.

[13] In those words it distinctly says that Israel's forefathers, including most prominently of all Abraham, Isaac and Jacob, and the twelve sons of Jacob, were not under this law covenant. Those forefathers were under no obligation to do what the Fourth Commandment says, namely, keep the weekly sabbath day holy by a complete rest on it. But, as Moses further said to their descendants: God "declared unto you his covenant, . . . and he wrote them upon two tables of stone. And Jehovah commanded me at that time to teach you statutes

12, 13. What proof did Moses give that Abraham, Isaac and Jacob were not under the Fourth Commandment? And why is it certain that the Gentiles were under no such commandment?

and ordinances, that ye might do them in the land
whither ye go over to possess it". (Deuteronomy
4:13, 14, *AS*) Thus the sabbath commandment
was a component part of God's covenant with
Israel, and it could not be separated from that
covenant. The Gentile nations were not and never
have been under God's Fourth Commandment of
the covenant. "He sheweth his word unto Jacob,
his statutes and his judgments unto Israel. He
hath not dealt so with any nation: and as for his
judgments, they have not known them."—Psalm
147:19, 20.

¹⁴ The sabbath was a distinguishing feature of
Jehovah's c o v e n a n t arrangement with Israel
alone: "Verily ye shall keep my sabbaths: for it
is a *sign* between me and you throughout your
generations; . . . It is a sign between me and the
children of Israel for ever: for in six days Jehovah made heaven and earth, and on the seventh
day he rested, and was refreshed."—Exodus 31:13-
17, *AS;* see also Ezekiel 20:12 and Nehemiah
9:13, 14.

ARE CHRISTIANS UNDER SABBATH LAW?

¹⁵ Why did Jesus observe the Jewish sabbath
law, especially by going to synagogue on that day
and preaching? Why did Paul go into the synagogue on the sabbath days, "according to Paul's
custom," and preach and reason with the Jews
there?* We reply: "God sent forth his Son, who

---

* Matthew 12:1, 9; Mark 1:21; Luke 4:16, 32; Acts 13:14, 44;
16:13; 17:2; 18:4, *NW*.

14. How is it pointed out by God's prophets that the
sabbath distinguished the Israelites alone of all peoples?
15. Why was it proper for Jesus to observe such law,
but why may his observance not be argued as binding
Christians thereto?

was produced out of a woman and who came to be under law." (Galatians 4:4, *NW*) Hence Jesus was obliged to keep that law, as long as he was in the flesh. He was circumcised in the flesh and kept passover and other feasts. Hence his keeping the Jewish sabbath does not mean his followers must do so, no more than his being circumcised and keeping Jewish feasts requires his disciples to do so. He said: "Do not think I came to destroy the Law or the Prophets. I came, not to destroy, but to fulfill." (Matthew 5:17, *NW*) His coming to fulfill such Law and the Prophets proves that the law covenant and the sabbath obligations are not binding upon his disciples.

[16] Destroying the Law by breaking God's law covenant is far different from fulfilling it and thus moving it out of the way and lifting its obligations from his disciples. Certainly the 'fulfilling of the Prophets' made their prophecies a thing of the past and no longer applying or requiring fulfillment. Likewise the fulfilling of the Law makes it a thing of the past and relieves his followers from its requirements. So, in order to fulfill the Law and the Prophets, Jesus by Jewish birth "came to be under law". To illustrate: The Law commanded the yearly celebration of the passover over a slain lamb. Jesus did not destroy the passover celebration, but moved it out of the way by fulfilling it, in that he became the real passover Lamb, "the Lamb of God that takes away the sin of the world."—1 Corinthians 5:7; John 1:29, *NW;* also Ephesians 2:13-15.

---

16. How does fulfilling the Law and Prophets differ from destroying such?

¹⁷ Jesus went to synagogue on sabbath days to preach to the crowds there, as he was anointed with God's spirit to do. (Isaiah 61:1-3; Luke 4:14-21) Just so, too, the apostle Paul went to synagogue to preach, on the sabbath day when the Jews met there.

SHADOW AND SUBSTANCE

¹⁸ At Colossians 2:12-17, Paul writes to Christ's followers: "By relationship with him you were also raised up together through your faith in the operation of God, who raised him up from the dead. Furthermore, though you were dead in your trespasses and in the uncircumcised state of your flesh, God made you alive together with him. He kindly forgave us all our trespasses and blotted out the handwritten document against us which consisted of decrees and which was in opposition to us, and He has taken it out of the way by nailing it to the torture stake. . . . Therefore let no man judge you in eating and drinking or in respect of a feast day or of an observance of the new moon or of a sabbath, for those things are a shadow of the things to come, but the reality belongs to the Christ." (NW) At Galatians 4:9-11 he asks certain deceived ones: "How is it that you are turning back again to the weak and inadequate elementary things and want to be slaves to them over again? You are scrupulously observing days and months and seasons and years. I fear for you, that somehow I have toiled to no purpose respecting you."—NW.

---

17. Why did Paul also go to synagogue on the sabbath days?
18, 19. (a) What did Paul say to the Colossians about the law covenant and being judged in regard to its features? (b) What, then, must Christians observe?

[19] Since God has taken the Jewish law covenant with its Ten Commandments out of the way by nailing it to the torture stake on which Jesus died, the Christians must observe, not the law-covenant shadows, but the reality.

[20] Showing that God's seventh day of rest continues 7,000 years, Paul writes, at Hebrews 4:9 (*NW*): "So there remains a sabbath resting for the people of God." In the surrounding verses Paul makes no reference to keeping a 24-hour seventh-day sabbath. Instead, he quotes Genesis 2:2: "And God rested on the seventh day from all his works"; which fact began applying over 4,000 years before Christ. Also, Paul refers to God's words at Numbers 14:28-35, that unbelieving Jews should die in the wilderness and not enter and find rest in the Promised Land. This sworn declaration of God was made over 1,500 years before Christ. Then Paul quotes David's words at Psalm 95:7-11: "Today if ye will hear his voice, harden not your heart, as in the provocation, and as in the day of temptation in the wilderness: when your fathers tempted me, . . . unto whom I sware in my wrath that they should not enter into my rest." This psalm of David was written about 1,077 years before Christ. So, from about 4,000 B.C. down to 1,077 B.C., Jehovah God is still speaking about his rest, and in David's day his rest was already almost 3,000 years long. Then what?

[21] Then Paul himself writes, still speaking about

---

20. What reference does the psalmist David make to God's rest? And how long had it continued by the time of David's writing?

21. How long was God's rest day by the time of Paul's writing? So how is it then figured out that it will be 7,000 years long?

entering into God's rest; and this makes God's
resting-time down to Paul's day more than 4,000
years long, for Paul wrote Hebrews more than 40
years after Christ's birth. Furthermore, Paul's
words about Christians' entering into God's rest
still apply, that is, apply now and today, in the
1950's, which is nearly 6,000 years from the time
of Genesis 2:2. And now the battle of Armageddon
is near and Christ's reign of 1,000 years will begin immediately after it, during which time redeemed mankind will be given the privilege of
entering into God's rest. All of this, therefore, extends God's rest to a length of 7,000 years. So
this makes up the length of the seventh day on
which he rests, sanctifying the *day* for vindicating
himself as Creator.

[22] From that standpoint Hebrews 3:13 to 4:11
can now be understood, and on it we comment:
"For we who have exercised faith do enter into
the rest, just as he has said [*about 1500 B.C.*]:
'So I swore in my wrath: "They shall not enter
into my rest,"' although his works were finished
from the foundation of the world [*about 4000
B.C.*]. . . . he again marks off a certain day by
saying after so long a time in David's psalm [*about
1000 B.C.*] 'Today'; just as it has been said above:
'Today if you would hear his voice, do not be hard-
ening your hearts.' For if Joshua [Moses' succes-
sor] had led them into a place of rest, God would
not afterward [*about 400 years afterward, in
David's time*] have spoken of another day. So
there remains a sabbath resting for the people of
God. For the man that has entered into God's rest

---

22. How, then, are we to understand Paul's words at
Hebrews 4:3-11?

has also himself rested from his own works just as God did from his own. Let us therefore do our utmost to enter into that rest, for fear anyone should fall in the same example of disobedience [given by the unbelieving Jews]."—Hebrews 4:3-11, *NW*.

[23] So, every day that Christians exercise faith and obedience through Christ, they are keeping sabbath, God's sabbath or rest. They judge no day of a week above another. (Romans 14:4-6, *NW*) They do their utmost to hold their faith and to keep faithful in God's active service as his witnesses, so as not to fall away and fail to enjoy complete rest with God during his *day,* which is not yet ended.

[24] Keep in mind that the Jewish law covenant set forth a "shadow of the good things to come, but not the very substance of the things". (Hebrews 10:1, *NW*) Of what good things to come was the Jewish weekly sabbath a shadow? It being the *seventh* day of a week, the weekly sabbath foreshadowed the last 1,000 years of God's rest day of 7,000 years. That thousand years God has assigned to the Lord Jesus, to reign then without disturbance from the Devil's organization in either heaven or earth. Such 1,000-year reign of Jesus Christ, as foretold at Revelation 20:1-6, begins after Satan is bound; in other words, after Armageddon, a war which all evidences indicate will begin inside our generation.—Revelation 16:14-16.

---

23. When and how do Christians keep sabbath?
24. Being the seventh day of the week, what did the weekly sabbath foreshadow?

²⁵ A glorious sabbath day that will be for mankind. It will be the sabbath of which Jesus spoke in a prophetic way when he said: "The sabbath came into existence for the sake of man, and not man for the sake of the sabbath; hence the Son of man is Lord even of the sabbath." (Mark 2:27, 28, *NW*) He was greater than the temple at Jerusalem, in which the Jewish priests under the old law covenant seemed to profane the sabbath day by carrying on their sacrificial duties and yet were guiltless. (Matthew 12:1-8, *NW*) Christ Jesus is the Head of the great spiritual temple of God made up of "living stones", his disciples. Therefore God has appointed him to be the Lord of the antitypical sabbath, namely, the 1,000-year period of the Kingdom.

²⁶ Because the Jewish sabbath foreshadowed this Kingdom sabbath, Jesus on the weekly sabbath day did many works of healing and of delivering believing persons from the bondage due to the Devil. He healed the blind, raised up the crippled, and, when criticized by the enemy for curing an infirm woman, he said: "Was it not due, then, for this woman who is a daughter of Abraham, and whom Satan held bound, look! eighteen years, to be loosed from this bond on the sabbath day?" (Luke 13:16, *NW*) Thus Jesus foreshadowed what wondrous works of deliverance and relief he will do on the 1,000-year sabbath day when he reigns as Lord, raising even the dead from their graves. God made or ordained that coming sabbath day

25. For whom will that be a glorious sabbath day, and who will be its Lord?

26, 27. How will sabbath-keepers and sabbath-breakers then be dealt with?

for man, for man's benefit, and not for man's oppression.

[27] Hence the believing and obedient ones then on earth will enter into a rest from slaving toil and from bondage of sin, Satan, totalitarian rule and false religion. And since God commanded sabbath breakers of the old law covenant to be killed, so those refusing to keep the Kingdom sabbath by faith and by ceasing from selfish works of sin and false religion will be executed by the Lord of the sabbath and be destroyed eternally.—Exodus 35:2.

[28] Consequently, at the close of Jehovah's 7,000-year sabbath or rest day, his earthly creation and mankind upon it will be perfect, pure, and fully enjoying his blessing, just as when he finished his work at the end of the sixth creative day. Foreknowing this, Jehovah God could keep on resting all during this long sabbath day. (Genesis 3:15) And thus, due to his kingdom under Christ, all of Jehovah's earthly works will show forth his handiwork and be for an eternal vindication of his name. His good purpose in making this earthly creation will not have failed. So in this triumph of success he reaches the end of his 7,000-year sabbath day greatly refreshed.

---

28. What, then, will be the net result at the end of Jehovah's great sabbath day, and why will he reach it greatly refreshed?

CHAPTER XVI

"NOT UNDER LAW BUT UNDER UNDESERVED KINDNESS"

ONE of the foremost students of theocratic law, the apostle Paul, wrote to the Christians at Rome: "You are not under law but under undeserved kindness." To the Hebrew Christians in general he wrote: "There occurs a setting aside of the preceding commandment on account of its weakness and ineffectiveness. For the Law made nothing perfect, but the bringing in besides of a better hope did, through which we are drawing near to God."—Hebrews 7:18, 19, *NW*.

² To make certain whose law was set aside or abolished, Paul wrote to the uncircumcised Gentile Christians at Ephesus, saying: "Keep bearing in mind that formerly you were people of the nations as to flesh; 'uncircumcision' you were called by that which is called 'circumcision' made in the flesh with hands—that you were at that particular time without Christ, alienated from the state of Israel and strangers to the covenants of the promise, and you had no hope and were without God in the world. But now in union with Christ Jesus you who were once far off have come to be near by the blood of the Christ. For he is our peace, he

---

1. Are Christians under the law of Moses, and is their hope by it?
2. What did Paul write to the Ephesians proving whose law it was that was set aside or abolished?

who made the two parties one and destroyed the wall in between that fenced them off. By means of his flesh he abolished the hatred, the Law of commandments consisting in decrees, that he might create the two peoples [Jews and Gentiles] in union with himself into one new man and make peace, and that he might fully reconcile both peoples in one body to God through the torture stake, because he had killed off the hatred by means of himself." (Ephesians 2:11-16, *NW*) This proves it was Jehovah's law that was annulled or abolished. Read also Colossians 2:13-17 and see further that no mere man blotted out the law of God here concerned.

³ The law which God nailed to the stake of Christ's death was the Mosaic law. It is called "the law of Moses", not because he originated it; for Moses did not do so. It was so called because he was the go-between in handing over the Law from God to the nation of Israel. (Exodus 34:27, 28; John 1:17) The Law being theocratic and being given under glorious, awe-inspiring conditions at Mount Horeb, it would seem to be perpetual, everlasting, beyond recall, as eternal as its Giver. So it amazes many when informed that such Law was abolished and brought to an end by Jehovah, and that no creatures on earth, not even the Jews, are any longer under it. Some who fear that such abolition of all the law covenant must produce bad moral effects put up a strange argument. They claim two laws were given to the Jews, (1) God's law, written by him, and (2) Moses' law, written by him. They claim the one was the moral law and the other was the ceremonial law; and that the

---

3. Why does such abolition amaze some religionists, and how do they argue in reply?

ceremonial law was abolished, but not the moral law contained in the Ten Commandments. They claim that in saying to Christians, "You are not under law but under undeserved kindness," Paul means the ceremonial law, not the Ten Commandments including the sabbath law.

[4] Such sectarians quote Jesus' words: "Do not think I came to destroy the Law or the Prophets. I came, not to destroy, but to fulfill; for truly I say to you that sooner would heaven and earth pass away than for the smallest letter or one particle of a letter to pass away from the Law by any means and not all things take place. Whoever, therefore, breaks one of these least commandments and teaches mankind to that effect, he will be called 'least' in relation to the kingdom of the heavens. As for anyone who does them and teaches them, this one will be called 'great' in relation to the kingdom of the heavens."—Matthew 5:17-19, *NW*.

[5] The heavens and earth here mentioned are God's earthly and heavenly creation. Jesus' words do not say that the Mosaic law could not be abolished before such heavens and earth are destroyed, for they will never be destroyed. So Jesus was saying that the literal heavens and earth would sooner pass out of existence than for God to let his law to Israel go unfulfilled and thus prove him a liar, even down to the smallest letter or particle of a letter.

[6] Someone, though, may say, Surely by the term *Law* Jesus meant the Ten Commandments, for in

---

4, 5. What words do some objectors quote from Jesus' sermon on the mount?
6. In Jesus' sermon, to what does "the Law" refer, and why?

his sermon on the mount he quoted the Sixth Commandment against killing and the Seventh Commandment against adultery, namely, two quotations. (Matthew 5:21, 27) This is true. But in the complete sermon on the mount Jesus quoted more from other parts of Moses' law than from the Decalogue or Ten Commandments. He called attention to the matter of bringing gifts for the altar, to granting an immoral wife a divorce certificate, to swearing falsely, to "eye for eye and tooth for tooth", and to loving one's neighbor as oneself. Prove this to yourself. Compare Matthew 5:23, 24, 31, 33, 38, 43 with Deuteronomy 16:16, 17; 24:1; Numbers 30:2; Exodus 21:23-25; Deuteronomy 19:21; and Leviticus 19:18. Hence by the term *law* Jesus meant not just the Ten Commandments but all the rest of Moses' law. So the Ten Commandments did not hold a place detached from the law covenant.

[7] Therefore, instead of saying that the law covenant, including the Decalogue, was as eternal as the literal heavens and earth, Jesus was saying this: That the law was typical and that its types and shadows of good things to come would all find

7. What, then, did Jesus' words at Matthew 5:17, 18 mean, and how do we see that fact today?

fulfillment in antitypical realities. They would be fulfilled down to the least letter or particle and thus prove God to be true and to be the One who holds to his law and its requirements and its meaning and purpose. The types and shadows of the Law must begin fulfilling in Christ Jesus. This would mean that the Law must be abolished with its types, in order to make way for bringing in the antitypes or realities by Christ Jesus. We are now in the "time of the end" of this world and can see that the Law's fulfillment began nineteen centuries ago. At that time the Law was abolished by being nailed to the torture stake on which Jesus died as the antitypical "Lamb of God that takes away the sin of the world".—John 1:29, 36, *NW*.

[8] Jesus gave the sermon on the mount in the second year of his ministry. The Law was then still binding on the Jews. Jesus came, not to destroy it, but to bring about its fulfillment, starting off the antitypical realities. The scribes, Pharisees and Sadducees, by means of traditions that transgressed God's commands and made them of no effect, were the men who were destroying the Law and teaching men to break the commandments. Yet these men pretended to be the greatest observers of the Law and to be righteous by it. They claimed to be the "sons of the kingdom", that is, to be in line for Messiah's kingdom. In view of their lawbreaking, hypocritical course, Jesus warned his hearers: "If your righteousness does not abound more than that of the scribes and Pharisees, you will by no means enter into the

---

8. As respects the Law, why did Jesus come? And why was the righteousness of the scribes and Pharisees not enough to enter the Kingdom?

kingdom of the heavens." (Matthew 5:20, *NW*) Such righteousness must be, not by keeping the Law, but by a faith in Christ.—Philippians 3:5-9.

[9] So, while the law covenant was still in force over Israel, Jesus kept it, taught it and sought its fulfillment. Hence, before making the above statement, he said: "Whoever, therefore, breaks one of these least commandments and teaches mankind to that effect, he will be called 'least' in relation to the kingdom of the heavens." (Matthew 5:19, *NW*) The Law foreshadowed the Christian realities that were to come. So, unless a person was in harmony with that Law, he could not enter the heavenly kingdom. If he broke the Law in the smallest regard and taught others to do the same he would be "least" in relation to the Kingdom, not be in it at all, because he would be practicing and teaching lawlessness toward God. Thus seen, Jesus' statement to those Jews under the Law in no way meant that the kingdom-of-heaven class are still under the Law since Jesus' death on the stake. They are not under that Law, and their greatness or their littleness is not to be measured by their degree of keeping that Mosaic law, Pharisee-fashion.—Acts 15:5.

HOW "PERPETUAL"

[10] Sabbatarians who claim that the Law was in two parts say that only the ceremonial law was abolished but that the moral law set out in the Ten Commandments was to be perpetual and for-

---

9. How is the lawbreaking teacher called *least* in relation to the Kingdom? And so are Christians still under that law?

10, 11. How do sabbatarians use Exodus 31:16, 17 in their argument? And had the Ten Commandments always existed before Moses?

ever. They refer us to Exodus 31:16, 17, regarding
the fourth of the Ten Commandments, namely:
"The children of Israel shall keep the sabbath, to
observe the sabbath throughout their generations,
for a *perpetual* covenant. It is a sign between me
and the children of Israel *for ever:* for in six days
the LORD made heaven and earth, and on the
seventh day he rested, and was refreshed."

[11] However, the use of the terms *perpetual* and
for ever as regards the weekly sabbath cannot be
interpreted to mean that the Fourth Commandment as well as the other nine was to continue to
apply forever and hence must apply to Christ's
disciples. Those Ten Commandments had not always been in existence toward men, not even toward the Jews. Moses, the mediator of the law
covenant with Israel, plainly says so, at Deuteronomy 5:1-21. The Ten Commandments had their
beginning, not with the forefathers, Abraham,
Isaac, Jacob and Jacob's twelve sons, but with the
Israelites who were alive and present at Mount
Horeb when Moses mediated the law covenant
with them. Hence if the Ten Commandments did
not exist before then and apply to those forefathers, then it should arouse no fear and dismay
in us if those Ten Commandments have been abolished since Christ's death.

[12] The law covenant cannot be taken apart, so
that a part of it, the ceremonial part, could be
abolished, and the other part of it, the so-called
"moral" part, remain. James 2:10, 11 makes this
point clear, saying: "Whoever observes all the
Law but makes a false step in one point, he has

---

12. Why cannot the law covenant be taken apart and
partly abolished? And how perpetual would the Fourth
Commandment therefore be?

become an offender against them all. For he who said, 'You must not commit adultery,' said also, 'You must not murder.' If, now, you do not commit adultery but you do murder, you have become a transgressor of law." (*NW*) In applying this point to the question of how perpetual are the Ten Commandments and all the rest of the Mosaic law, what do we see? This: that if the Fourth Commandment on the sabbath day was "for a perpetual covenant" with Israel and for a sign "for ever", then all Ten Commandments and all the Mosaic law were also for a perpetual covenant to last as long as the Fourth Commandment. Conversely, if the rest of the covenant was abolished, then the Fourth Commandment went out with it also.

[13] Just how long, then, do the words *perpetual* and *for ever,* as used in Exodus 31:16, 17 quoted above, mean? Not to eternity, so as to be beyond abolishment. In Hebrew the word for *perpetual* is *oh·láhm* and that for *for ever* is *l'oh·láhm*. These Hebrew words are used with regard to the Jewish priesthood, the priesthood that descended from Moses' brother Aaron. Exodus 40:15 says: "Their anointing shall surely be an *everlasting* [*oh·láhm*] priesthood throughout their generations." Leviticus 6:18, 22 says: "All the males among the children of Aaron shall eat of it. It shall be a statute *for ever* [*oh·láhm*] in your generations concerning the offerings of the LORD made by fire: . . . And the priest of his sons that is anointed in his stead shall offer it: it is a statute *for ever* [*oh·láhm*] unto the LORD." See also Leviticus 25:46 where *l'oh·láhm* is translated *for ever*.

13, 14. In connection with what else are the Hebrew words for "perpetual" and "for ever" used?

[14] The above laws regarding priesthood had a physical or fleshly basis. That is, they required the priests and their high priest to be descendants of Aaron according to the flesh.

[15] Now the English Bible uses the words *perpetual, everlasting,* and *for ever* as applying to the Aaronic priesthood and their official duties. From this a person might imagine that these would continue existing in force to all eternity. Yet today the Aaronic or Levitical priesthood has disappeared. It operates no more. Moreover, the apostle Paul explains that God, who first established the Aaronic or Levitical priesthood, abolished it. He no longer recognized it after Christ's death and resurrection. Christ Jesus was made God's High Priest, not according to a "carnal commandment", "the law of a commandment depending upon the flesh," the flesh of Aaron the Levite, but according to God's new law and by his sworn oath. So Jesus' priesthood is superior to Aaron's. It is after the likeness of Melchizedek, who was the priest-king of Salem long before the Aaronic priesthood. At Hebrews 7:11-24 Paul explains this. At verse twelve he says: "Since the priesthood is being changed, there comes to be of necessity a change also of the law." (*NW*) When Christ offered up and presented to God his human sacrifice as God's High Priest, that former Law and its Aaronic priesthood were abolished.

[16] This means, too, that the old law covenant, of

---

15. Because of using such words concerning priesthood, was the Aaronic priesthood to continue always? And why is Christ's priesthood superior?

16. (a) Why, then, does *perpetual* as regards the Fourth Commandment not argue against abolishing the Ten Commandments? (b) What makes the perpetualness of Christ's priesthood unending?

which the priesthood arrangement was a part, was abolished. So it means that the Ten Commandments were abolished too as a component part of that law covenant. The Hebrew word *oh·láhm* was used in connection with the Fourth Commandment respecting the weekly sabbath and was there translated *perpetual* and *for ever*. But that does not argue against the abolishing of the Ten Commandments any more than it argues against the abolition of the Levitical priesthood. *Oh·láhm* (from *ah·lám*, meaning to wrap up, hide, or conceal) simply means *indefinite* or *uncertain time*, whether it be eternity or a limited space of time, the limit of which is concealed from man and unknown beforehand to man. Christ's priesthood is unending. What makes it so is his having immortality, hence the "power of an indestructible life". —Hebrews 7:16, 24, 25, *NW*.

A RIGHTEOUS ACTIVE FORCE IMPARTED

[17] The law covenant with its Ten Commandments was not set aside without anything to take its place in the lives of God's people. No, for Jesus Christ acted as God's High Priest in offering up his human sacrifice for sins and he became the Mediator of a New Covenant, a "better covenant" as compared with the old Mosaic law covenant. That old covenant with its Ten Commandments written on stone tablets did not make the Jewish nation perfect or righteous. But under the new covenant the Christians are made righteous or justified through the Mediator Christ Jesus. His sacrifice upon which this new covenant is based

---

17. With Christians what takes the place of the old law covenant, and why is it better?

really cancels or takes away sins in God's sight. The glory with which the Ten Commandments engraved on stone tablets were given did not guarantee that the covenant would not pass away at some time then unknown to man. The very glory attending that covenant was a passing glory.

[18] The new covenant has a better Mediator, a better sacrifice, and a power for righteousness which is stronger than the Ten Commandments engraved in letters of stone. It has a glory that never fades. Its power for righteousness is God's spirit or active force. This active force makes alive, whereas the handwriting of the old law covenant showed up the Israelites as covenant breakers, sinners, and it assigned them to death. Consecrated Christians who are under the new covenant are made its ministers or servants. They receive their qualifications for serving it, not from some religious theological seminary, but from Jehovah God and by Christ. The apostle Paul shows that the law covenant with its Ten Commandments written by God's finger in stone was abolished and was replaced by the new covenant with its life-giving spirit. He says:

[19] "Our being adequately qualified issues from God, who has indeed adequately qualified us to be ministers of a new covenant, not of a written code, but of spirit; for the written code condemns to death, but the spirit makes alive. Moreover, if the code which administers death and which was engraved in letters in stones came about in a glory, so that the sons of Israel could not gaze intently

18. How is the glory of the new covenant greater than that of the old law covenant? And who are its ministers?
19. Why must the new covenant properly have a glory greater than that of the old covenant?

at the face of Moses because of the glory of his face, a glory which was to be done away with, why should not the administering of the spirit be much more with glory? For if the code administering condemnation was glorious, much more does the administering of righteousness abound with glory. In fact, even that which has once been made glorious has been stripped of glory in this respect, because of the glory that excels it. For if that which was to be done away with was brought in with glory, much more would that which remains be with glory."

20 Then Paul shows that the power for righteousness under the new covenant is not the abolished Ten Commandments, but is God's spirit, which transforms Christians to a Godly likeness: "Now Jehovah is the spirit; and where the spirit of Jehovah is, there is freedom. And all of us, while we with unveiled faces reflect like mirrors the glory of Jehovah, are transformed into the same image from glory to glory, exactly as done by Jehovah the spirit."—2 Corinthians 3:5-18, NW.

21 From this we can appreciate the force of Paul's further words: "If you are being led by spirit, you are not under law." (Galatians 5:18, NW) The Christians are the ones being led by God's active force or spirit in harmony with his Word. This fact proves that they are not under the old law covenant with its Ten Commandments, but are under the new covenant, by God's unde-

---

20. How does Paul then describe the Christians' power for righteousness under the new covenant?
21. (a) By what are Christians led, and why are they therefore not under Law? (b) Against which fruits is there no law?

served kindness. Under it they are being transformed by the spirit which God's undeserved kindness imparts in connection with the new covenant. They produce the fruitage of his spirit in their lives. There are no Ten Commandments against producing such fruitage. (Galatians 5:13-23) God's spirit in his people is powerful enough to produce this legal fruitage of righteousness without the Ten Commandments.

22 Although not under the Law, but under God's undeserved kindness, the faithful Christians still study the law covenant, and properly so. Why? Because its features "are a shadow of the things to come" and such coming things pertain to Christ and his ministry and kingdom. Christians recognize the Law as having a "shadow of the good things to come", and they see Christ Jesus "came as a high priest of the good things that have come to pass". (Colossians 2:17 and Hebrews 10:1; 9:11, *NW*) The types and shadows of the Law are an important part of God's Word, and they must be studied by Christians as correctly outlining in advance the purposes of God respecting his Christ. Paul's entire book of Hebrews is inspired proof of this fact. Therefore Christians have a right to quote portions from the old law covenant and its Ten Commandments, just as much as Paul had the right to quote from the Ten Commandments as proof supporting what he wrote. For examples of such quotations see Ephesians 6:1-3 and Romans 13:8-10.

---

22. Why do Christians still study the old law covenant, and why do they have a right to quote from it and its commandments?

23 God's commands to Christians are given in the writings of Paul and other disciples of Christ. For example, see the command against idolatry at 1 Corinthians 10:14; Galatians 5:20; Colossians 3:5; and 1 John 5:21. But since the second of the Ten Commandments was a shadow or preliminary pattern of this r e q u i r e m e n t upon Christians against idolatry, they have the right to quote the Second Commandment as corroborative proof for refusing to render idolatrous honors to men and emblems. By quoting from the Ten Commandments to back up what he wrote Paul was not arguing that Christians are under the Ten Commandments and the rest of the Mosaic law. He was simply using those Commandments as supporting proof, to corroborate the rightness of the admonitions he was giving the Christians to conduct themselves pleasingly to God. The law covenant from which he quoted was a shadow of coming good things. So it set the right pattern for Christians to follow in the relationship which they hold to God under his new covenant by Christ the Mediator.

24 Hence the apostle Paul's statement remains uncontradicted: "By this undeserved kindness, indeed, you have been saved through faith; and this not owing to you, it is God's gift."—Ephesians 2:8, NW.

23, 24. Does Paul's quoting from the Ten Commandments argue that Christians are still under the law covenant? And so why does his statement about undeserved kindness stay uncontradicted?

CHAPTER XVII

CHRIST'S RETURN

THE return of Jesus Christ is clearly taught by many scriptures. To his apostle John he said: "Yes; I am coming quickly." John prayerfully replied: "Amen! Come, Lord Jesus." His fellow apostle Peter also spoke of the "revelation of Jesus Christ".—Revelation 22:20 and 1 Peter 1:13, *NW*.

² Jesus Christ returns, not again as a human, but as a glorious spirit person. He is now the reflection of God's glory, the exact representation of God's very being, and he is seated on the right hand of the Majesty on high. He has been exalted above the angels, so that when the Father again brings him into the inhabited earth he says: "Let all God's angels worship him." He comes, therefore, this time, not in humiliation, not in the likeness of men, but in his heavenly glory, and all his angels with him.—Hebrews 1:2-6, *NW;* Matthew 25:31.

³ Some have wrong expectations regarding Christ's return. Reading the promise of the angel to Mary that Jesus, the "Son of the Most High", would be given the throne of his forefather David, they conclude that he will sit on a literal earthly throne. However, the throne of David was only

---

1. What are some scriptures proving that Christ would return?
2. What is his present station as compared with that at his first coming?
3. Why will he not then sit on an earthly throne?

pictorial of the throne of Jehovah's King. Thus "Solomon sat on the throne of Jehovah as king instead of David his father". (Luke 1:32, *NW;* 1 Chronicles 29:23, *AS*) If Jesus were to sit as a man on an earthly throne, he would be lower in station than the angels, even as man is lower than the angels. The task of judgeship and rulership assigned to Christ can be done only by a mighty spirit king, one higher than the kings of the earth and not like them.—Psalms 8:4, 5; 89:27; Revelation 3:21.

⁴ Some wrongfully expect a literal fulfillment of the symbolic statements of the Bible. Such hope to see the glorified Jesus come seated on a white cloud where every human eye will see him. They overlook Jesus' words before he left: "A little longer and the world will behold me no more." Since no earthly men have ever seen or can see the Father, they will be unable to see the glorified Son.—John 14:19, *NW;* Exodus 33:20; 1 Timothy 6:16.

⁵ Some may quote the words of the angels at Jesus' ascension: "This Jesus who was received up from you into heaven will come thus in the same manner as you have beheld him going into heaven." But note, this text does not say he will come in the same body, but says he will come in the same manner. The manner of his going away was quiet, thieflike, without sound of trumpet or public display, yet with the message, "You will be witnesses of me . . . to the most distant part of the earth," ringing in the disciples' ears. (Acts 1:8, 11, *NW*) His witnesses alone saw him leave.

---

4. What proves he will not be seen with human vision?
5. What is meant by his coming in the same manner as he went?

Logically, only his faithful witnesses would promptly recognize his return.

HOW SEEN

[6] His return is recognized by the eyes of one's understanding, such eyes being enlightened by God's unfolding Word. Christ's arrival and presence are not discerned because of a visible bodily nearness, but by the light of his acts of judgment and the fulfillment of Bible prophecy. This light spreads from east to west and everywhere. Those who are farsighted like the eagles perceive the judgment truths and gather to the "body" of spiritual food which God provides.—Luke 17:24, 34-37, *NW*.

[7] In Matthew, chapter twenty-four, the Greek word *par·ou·si'a* occurs at verses 3, 27, 37, 39 and is translated in the *King James Version* by the word "coming". It is rendered "presence" in the *New World Translation of the Christian Greek Scriptures,* Rotherham's *Emphasised Bible, The Emphatic Diaglott,* and Young's *Bible Translation,* and in footnotes of the *American Standard Version.* Moffatt's modern version translates it "arrival". The meaning of *par·ou·si'a* is more exact than the word "coming" contained in the general English versions. It does not mean he is on the way or has promised to come, but that he has already arrived and is here. In the *King James Version par·ou·si'a* is translated "presence" at Philippians 2:12, which reads: "Wherefore, my beloved, as ye have always obeyed, not as in my presence only, but now much more in my absence

---

6. How is Christ's return recognized?
7. What is the meaning of the Greek word *par·ou·si'a*, frequently translated "coming"?

[*ap·ou·si'a*], work out your own salvation with fear and trembling." Also in 2 Corinthians 10:10.

⁸ It is not necessary for Christ to be visible at his presence, even as his Father is not visible to human sight. Jehovah's presence was with his people as they journeyed out of Egypt to the Promised Land, yet he was not visible to the Israelites. On his deathbed in Egypt Joseph said: "I die: and God will surely visit you, and bring you out of this land unto the land which he sware to Abraham, to Isaac, and to Jacob." (Genesis 50:24) But God was not visible then or on any of the occasions where the Bible says he visited his people.—Ruth 1:6; Luke 19:44.

⁹ Today the evidence of Christ's presence is all about us, and yet so-called "Christendom" does not see it. How, then, is he manifest to his true followers and not to the world? To his followers he gave the promise: "Happy are those slaves whom the master on arriving finds watching! Truly I say to you, He will gird himself and make them recline at the table and will come alongside and minister to them." (Luke 12:37, *NW*) The Master Jesus is the provider of this spiritual food, "food at the proper time," and he provides it through a visible instrument or agency on earth used to publish it to his slaves.

¹⁰ The agency which the Master uses to distribute or dispense his truth is called his "faithful and discreet slave". Matthew 24:45-47 says: "Who really is the faithful and discreet slave whom his

---

8. What fact about Jehovah's presence helps to understand that of Christ?
9. How does the returned Christ serve his people?
10. What agency is used by the Master to serve spiritual food?

master appointed over his domestics to give them their food at the proper time? Happy is that slave if his master on arriving finds him doing so. Truly I say to you, He will appoint him over all his belongings." (*NW*) This clearly shows that the Master would use *one* organization, and not a multitude of diverse and conflicting sects, to distribute his message. The "faithful and discreet slave" is a company following the example of their Leader. That "slave" is the remnant of Christ's spiritual brothers. God's prophet identifies these spiritual Israelites, saying: "Ye are my witnesses, saith Jehovah, and my *servant* whom I have chosen." —Isaiah 43:10, *AS; Yg*.

[11] From and after A.D. 1918 this "slave" class has proclaimed God's message to Christendom which still feeds on the religious traditions of men. The truth so proclaimed does a dividing work, as foretold, the ones accepting the truth being taken to the place of security, and the others abandoned. Those who have been favored to comprehend what is taking place, and who have taken their stand for Jehovah's Theocracy, have unspeakable joy now. The light of his truth is not confined to a small place, or one corner of the globe. Its proclamation is world-wide. In the thirty-three years from 1919 to 1952 inclusive Jehovah's witnesses distributed more than half a billion bound books and booklets, hundreds of millions of magazines, tracts and leaflets, and delivered hundreds of millions of oral testimonies, in over 90 languages. Only by God's spirit and power could this witness have been given in the face

---

11. How extensive is the proclamation of the truth, and in what does it result?

of world-wide opposition and persecution; and the witness still continues and increases.

[12] Jesus said: "Just as the days of Noah were, so the presence of the Son of man will be." (Matthew 24:37, NW) The resemblance of the times is true not only as to men's self-indulgence in eating, drinking, marrying, building, and ignorance of the epoch in which they live, but also as to the divine message that is being given. Noah was a preacher of righteousness before the deluge then, and Jehovah's witnesses are such now, before the destruction of this world at the coming war of Armageddon. Peter said: "Jehovah's day will come as a thief, in which the heavens will pass away with a hissing noise, but the elements being intensely hot will be dissolved, and earth and the works in it will be discovered." (2 Peter 3:10, NW) Jehovah's witnesses give this warning now.

[13] For many years prior to 1914 earnest Bible students understood that the year 1914 marked the end of the Gentile times or the "appointed times of the nations". That date marked the beginning of the "time of the end" of Satan's rule, and therefore the time when Christ Jesus the righteous Ruler of the new world received control. (Luke 21:24, NW; Ezekiel 21:27) The fulfillment of prophecy there begun continues in unbroken course, showing that "the kingdom of the world has become the kingdom of our Lord and of his Christ". At this Jehovah's servants gave thanks, saying: "We thank you, Jehovah God, the Almighty, the one who is and who was, because you

---

12. How are the present days like those of Noah?
13. How is the year 1914 marked, and what is the angels' testimony as disclosed in the Revelation?

have taken your great power and begun ruling as king."—Revelation 11:15, 17, *NW*.

¹⁴ Jehovah's time to assert his universal sovereignty has arrived. He has become king toward our earth. His kingdom, pictured by a male child, at Revelation 12:5 (*NW*), was born in 1914. The invisible organization of the Devil in heaven sought to swallow up the newborn government. War in heaven broke out. The Devil and his demons were hurled down to the earth. Then the victorious angels announced: "Now have come to pass the salvation and the power and the kingdom of our God and the authority of his Christ." —Revelation 12:10, *NW*.

MESSENGER'S COMING TO THE TEMPLE

¹⁵ At that time no one on earth knew that shortly Jehovah by his Messenger would come to his temple. Through Malachi Jehovah had foretold his sudden appearance at the temple, adding: "Who can endure the day of his coming? and who can stand when he appears? For he shall be like a refiner's fire, and like fullers' soap." (Malachi 3:1, 2, *AT*) As Jesus cleansed the temple in Jerusalem three and a half years after he was anointed with God's spirit to be King, so three and a half years after he received kingly power in the autumn of 1914 he came to the spiritual temple as Jehovah's Messenger and began to cleanse it. So this occurred in the spring of 1918. That marked the beginning of the period of judgment and inspection of his spirit-begotten followers.

---

14. What followed the birth of God's kingdom in heaven?
15, 16. (a) How was Christ's coming to the temple marked? (b) What is the order of the resurrection of the spirit-begotten class?

[16] Paul wrote: "Christ Jesus . . . is destined to judge the living and the dead, and by his manifestation and his kingdom." (2 Timothy 4:1, *NW*) The dead Christians sleeping in the graves were raised with spirit bodies to join him at the spiritual temple. The living anointed Christians on earth could not precede those who had fallen asleep in death, but they have to keep on maintaining their integrity until their own death. When this remnant on earth die, they do not have to sleep awaiting their Master's return, but receive an immediate change to spirit life. They cease their earthly labors, but their service from then on continues without weariness.—1 Thessalonians 4:15, *NW;* 1 Corinthians 15:51, 52; Revelation 14:13.

[17] Many of Jesus' kingdom truths were spoken in parables. In the parable of the talents and that of the minas, Jesus pictured himself entrusting kingdom interests to his slaves on earth before he left for a distant land, heaven, to receive kingdom authority. Returning after a long time, he judges his slaves. To the faithful he gives greater privileges and the joy of their Master. The unfaithful are thrown into the darkness outside the theocratic organization. The citizens of this world hate the King of the new world who overthrows Satan the Devil. So they are due for slaughter.—Luke 19:12-27 and Matthew 25:14-30, *NW*.

[18] The testing of God's people c o n t i n u e s as prophesied: "Jehovah is in his holy temple; Jehovah, his throne is in heaven; his eyes behold, his

---

17. Briefly what do the parables of the talents and minas show?
18. How is the unworthiness of some for Kingdom truth shown?

eyelids try, the children of men." (Psalm 11:4, *AS*) Some Christians who selfishly expected to be at the marriage feast of the Christ have been left out, as pictured by the five foolish virgins, because they lacked understanding and the joy of the Bridegroom and so did not let the light shine. Others who gained entrance to the feast have later been put out because of not keeping on the identifying garment of a faithful Kingdom witness. (Matthew 25:1-13; 22:1-14) Christ has received his own faithful spiritual brothers into the temple condition as worshipers and servants of Jehovah and he approves their continued presence there.

[19] The testing by the great Judge continues and is taking in all nations. While present on the throne of his glory, Christ Jesus as Jehovah's representative at the temple separates the people of the nations into two classes, called *sheep* and *goats*. Though many are not aware of it, that separation is now going on. One's attitude toward the remnant of Jehovah's anointed witnesses and the message of his theocratic government reveals one's attitude toward Jehovah's installed King. The persecutors, opposers and indifferent, who identify themselves as goats, are doomed to destruction that will last forever. But the meek, righteously disposed persons of good will toward Jehovah God, his "other sheep", are in line for life eternal. The separation now of the people as his "other sheep" and as "goats" is part of the composite sign that Christ has returned and is present as King.—Matthew 25:31-46; John 10:16.

---

19. What further scripture shows that the King's presence is a testing time, and what two classes are manifest?

[20] Shortly the destiny of all people alive will be determined: "For the Son of man is destined to come in the glory of his Father with his angels, and then he will recompense each one according to his behavior." (Matthew 16:27, *NW*) The final revelation of the King draws nearer. The disaster of Armageddon, greater than that which befell Sodom and Gomorrah, is at the door. For, "on the day that Lot came out of Sodom it rained fire and sulphur from heaven and destroyed them all. The same way it will be on that day when the Son of man is to be revealed." (Luke 17:29, 30, *NW*) That revelation of his unseen presence by the execution of judgments is not for their blessing, but for their destruction: "At the revelation of the Lord Jesus from heaven with his powerful angels in a flaming fire, as he brings due punishment upon those who do not know God and those who do not obey the good news about our Lord Jesus. These very ones will pay the penalty of everlasting destruction from before the Lord and from the glory of his strength, at the time he comes to be glorified."—2 Thessalonians 1:7-10, *NW*.

[21] The nearness of that event is causing the selfish fearful ones to band together and hide themselves in human organizations for protection. It will avail them nothing. Anticipating an early end, they lament for fear of losing their ill-gotten gains and their worldly privileged position. Their eyes discern the King's invisible presence in the clouds of trouble that surround him. (Revelation 6:15-17; 1:7) Acceptance of the reigning King and his kingdom is the only security for anyone. Jesus warned: "Keep awake, then, all the time making supplica-

---

20. In what does the final revelation of the King result?
21. What source of protection will prove unavailing?

tion that you may succeed in escaping all these things that are destined to occur, and to hold your position before the Son of man."—Luke 21:36, NW.

²² Today persons of good will from all nations are taking their stand for Jehovah's Theocracy. This "great crowd" of other sheep are welcoming the new King by engaging in the Kingdom proclamation, even as the multitude welcomed Jesus on his triumphal ride into Jerusalem. (Revelation 7:9-17, NW; Luke 19:37-40) Back there the Pharisees wanted the multitude rebuked. So today religious leaders try to silence and suppress the message. Their efforts have failed and will fail.

²³ Christ returns before his thousand-year undisturbed reign to put all enemies under his feet at Armageddon. There he lays hold of the old Serpent, the Devil, and binds and abysses him and his demons a thousand years. By clearing out false religion, by restoring true worship, and by reestablishing the divine government toward our earth, he reveals his kingly power of which he proved himself worthy at his first coming. He becomes the new world's Judge and Leader, the Commander of the people. The vindication of his Father's name and sovereignty is his greatest joy, and also that of all those who are not "shamed away from him at his presence".—1 Corinthians 15:25, 26; Revelation 20:1-3; Isaiah 55:4; John 17:1; 1 John 2:28, NW; ED; Ro.

---

22. How do the people of good will welcome the King?
23. What is the purpose of Christ's coming, and how is that accomplished?

CHAPTER XVIII

RETURN OF NATURAL ISRAEL TO PALESTINE

WHILE World War II was raging and the Nazi hordes were overrunning nation after nation, horrifying reports came filtering through, testifying to the fact that the Jews were suffering renewed atrocities such as marked the Dark Ages of Christendom. This time it was not only persecution and oppression, but genocide, mass annihilation. After the conflict subsided in 1945, with a measure of peace restored, a census of the Jewish population of Central Europe was taken. It showed that, whereas the prewar population was 7,000,000, the Jewish population over the same area in 1946 was but 1,400,000. The Jewish question once more became a pressing international concern.

[2] Though Hitler's Nazi regime has been overturned, the religious and political power behind anti-Semitism is still strong. Impelled by the increased sufferings of the Jews Zionist organizations exerted all possible efforts to influence the leading powers to do something about it. They demanded that Palestine be converted into a Jewish state, a permanent homeland for the Jews as a nation.

---

1. How did World War II bring the Jewish question up again?
2. What did Zionist organizations endeavor and demand?

[3] The orthodox Jews and many religionists of Christendom believe that Bible prophecy foretold that the Jews would be once more regathered into their "Holy Land" in Palestine. They claim that that time is now here and that the regathering now taking place is in fulfillment of Bible prophecy.

[4] The Holy Bible proves beyond a question of doubt that the nation of Israel was for long God's chosen people. Many questions now arise in the minds of unprejudiced persons who consider the past and present experiences of the Jews. Since the natural Jews were at one time chosen as God's people, why were they cast off and scattered? Why have they been persecuted for centuries? Why such a wave of anti-Semitism sweeping the world today? Why are the Jews now regathered in Palestine under a modern republican government of their own, and did Bible prophecy foretell such a development? If not, what is the proper course for Jews to take to be saved from Armageddon?

[5] For centuries the Jews have been speaking the Yiddish and Spanish-Jewish tongue, but now the ancient Hebrew has been revived in the nation of Israel in Palestine and is the official language of the state. From Abraham on down through his grandson Jacob this race of people were known as Hebrews. Then God changed Jacob's name to Israel. Hence Jacob's descendants became known also as the children or sons of Israel, or Israelites. Jacob, or Israel, had twelve sons. These became the family heads of the twelve tribes of Israel.

---

3. What do orthodox Jews and many non-Jews believe that the Bible prophecies foretold?

4. In view of the past and present experiences of the Jews, what questions now arise in the minds of unprejudiced persons?

5. What was the origin of the Israelites?

—Genesis 14:13; 32:28; 35:23-26; 49:28; Acts 6:1; 2 Corinthians 11:22.

⁶ Just prior to Jacob's death he called his twelve sons before him and made a statement of prophecy over each. Judah was his fourth son by his wife Leah, and yet a royal blessing was bestowed upon him in these words: "Judah, thou art the one thy brothers shall praise, . . . Like a lion's whelp, O Judah, from the prey, my son, thou risest: . . . The sceptre shall not depart from Judah, nor a lawgiver from between his feet; until Shiloh come, and unto him shall the gathering of the people be." (Genesis 49:8-10, *Le*) This prophecy showed that the real deliverer of mankind would come through Judah's tribe. He would be the long-looked-for Messiah, the promised seed of Abraham. One of his names would be "Shiloh", meaning "peaceful one; rest".

⁷ "Judah" means "Let him (Jehovah) be praised". From this paternal name comes the name "Judean" or "Jew". Not only those who were the descendants of Judah were called Jews, but Jehovah recognized as Jews all Israelites who were faithful, regardless of the tribe from which they descended. They had faith in God's promise to Judah. A real Jew is one who has the faith of Abraham and who is devoted to the praise and service of Jehovah God.

⁸ In the outworking of Jehovah's purpose he organized the children of Israel into a special, holy,

---

6. What prophetic blessing did Jacob bestow upon Judah, and what does it mean?
7. Scripturally, who are the real Jews?
8. (a) How were the children of Israel organized, and by what rule were they governed? (b) Where was their law covenant inaugurated, and what conditions did they have to meet to win its benefits?

chosen nation. He did this for a specific reason,
namely, for his great name's sake. Moses told
them: "Thou art a holy people unto Jehovah thy
God: Jehovah thy God hath chosen thee to be a
people for his own possession, above all peoples
that are upon the face of the earth." (Deuteronomy 7:6, *AS*) This people organized into a nation
with Jehovah as their God and Sovereign Ruler
had a typical theocratic government. They were
therefore used to enact prophetic types and shadows of greater things to come. So says one Jewish
commentator at 1 Corinthians 10:11 and Hebrews
10:1. At Mount Sinai, where Moses was instructed
to assemble the children of Israel, Jehovah inaugurated the law covenant with them. The condition
under which they would receive the benefits of
the covenant was that of faithfulness. In the first
of his Ten Commandments to them Jehovah stated: "Thou shalt have no other gods before me."
—Exodus 20:3, *Le*.

⁹ All God's laws are perfect. So why did he give
a perfect law to an imperfect people and instruct
them to keep it? We may state four principal
reasons why the law covenant was given:

(1) It was meant to prove Israel by giving them
an opportunity to show their love and devotion to
Jehovah.—Exodus 20:20.

(2) The heathen nations round about the Israelites practiced demon religion. Hence the true
worship was given through God's law to protect
his people from being ensnared by demonism.
—Deuteronomy 7:16, 25.

(3) The Law served as a temporary addition
to Jehovah's promise to Abraham, that through

9. Why was the law covenant made with the Israelites?

him and his seed all the families of the earth should be blessed. (Genesis 12:1-3) Why was the Law added? A faithful Jew, Paul, answers: "It was added to make transgressions manifest, until the seed should arrive to whom the promise had been made, . . . Consequently, the Law has become our tutor leading to Christ, that we might be declared righteous due to faith."—Galatians 3:19, 24, *NW*.

(4) The Law was given to provide prophetic types and shadows of good things to come by and under the Messiah, the Christ: "The Law has a shadow of the good things to come."—Hebrews 10:1, *NW*.

[10] Time after time the Israelites failed to keep the Law and fell to demon religion and became slaves to the heathen nations. Then they would cry to their God Jehovah and he would hear them and deliver them. For centuries in Palestine they had judges whom God raised up to rule visibly over them. Then at their own request God gave them a visible king. By a special covenant with King David, God established the royal dynasty in his line.

THE NATURAL PEOPLE CAST OFF

[11] Finally, after more than 900 years of favor, the nation became grossly wicked and rebellious. Their last reigning king, Zedekiah, did evil in the eyes of God. He mocked and misused the prophets whom Jehovah sent and he despised God's words spoken by them. Thus God's wrath was kindled and his final decree to Zedekiah was issued:

---

10. How was a kingdom established over them in Palestine?
11. When and why was their kingdom overthrown?

"Thou, death-deserving wicked one, prince of Israel, whose day is come, at the time of the iniquity of the end,— ... Remove the mitre, and take off the crown: this shall not be always so; exalt him that is low, and make him low that is high. Overthrown, overthrown, overthrown will I render it: also this shall not belong (to any one), until he come whose right it is, and I will give it him." (Ezekiel 21:30-32, Le) This overthrowing of the kingdom of Judah took place in 607 B.C. The Jews were assaulted and taken captive by the Babylonians, and Jerusalem lay desolate in destruction for seventy years.—2 Kings, chapter 25; 2 Chronicles, chapter 36.

[12] But Jehovah foretold a release of the Jews from Babylon and a regathering of them to Palestine at the close of Jerusalem's seventy-year desolation. So a remnant of faithful Jews began returning to the homeland in 537 B.C. Their temple was rebuilt and also the city of Jerusalem. With the passing of centuries the restored Jews came under the power of the rabbis with their traditions of men and religious institutions, and they became victims of "rabbinism". This brought them into conflict with Messiah, and they rejected Jesus as king and called for him to be fastened to a torture stake A.D. 33. Thirty-seven years later, or A.D. 70, Jerusalem was destroyed by the Roman armies as foretold by Jesus, and A.D. 73 the last Jewish stronghold, at Masada, fell to the Romans and the Jews were scattered to the ends of the earth. From this it is evident that Jehovah cast them off as his people, letting them be without temple, priest or sacrifice, to this very day. This

12. When and why was the nation of natural Israel cast off by Jehovah, and what became of the law covenant?

is circumstantial proof that he abolished his temporary Law covenant with them, nailing it to the torture stake at the martyrdom of Jesus Christ. But as foretold at Jeremiah 31:31-34 God established a "new covenant" with Christ's followers, Jews inwardly with circumcised hearts, spiritual Israelites. The sacrificed Jesus was their Mediator, greater than Moses.

[13] With the Jews being cast off as a nation, does that mean that no Jews would ever have an opportunity to gain salvation and life? No, for nineteen centuries ago a small Jewish minority, a remnant of the nation, held true to Jehovah and kept in his favor. Jesus Christ rode into Jerusalem A.D. 33 and offered himself to the nation as their Messiah and King. Instead of joyfully receiving him, the majority followed their priests and rabbis and cried out, 'Let him be impaled! Let his blood be on us and our children!' (Matthew 21:5, 9, 42; 27:22, 25, *NW*) However, the small remnant received him and was chosen by Jehovah God. The apostle Paul states: "The very thing Israel is earnestly seeking he did not obtain, but the ones chosen obtained it. The rest had their sensibilities blunted."—Romans 11:7, *NW*.

[14] In the light of these facts, is it necessary for the Jews today to continue to have their holidays, ordinances and rituals as they did in olden times? Once again God's Word answers: "He kindly forgave us all our trespasses and blotted out the handwritten document against us which consisted of

---

13. (a) Was all opportunity for the Jews to gain salvation and life individually gone forever after they were cast off? (b) When did their true Messiah come, but how was he received?
14. What does the apostle Paul show regarding the Jewish religious practices today?

decrees and which was in opposition to us, and He
has taken it out of the way by nailing it to the torture stake. Therefore let no man judge you in eating and drinking or in respect of a feast day or
of an observance of the new moon or of a sabbath,
for those things are a shadow of the things to
come, but the reality belongs to the Christ." (Colossians 2:13, 14, 16, 17, *NW*) Those who are Jews
inwardly live in the realities and not in the "shadows" of the past. They do so by faith in Messiah
or Christ.

MODERN ISRAEL

[15] Because of the anti-Semitic spirit and the activities against Jews world-wide by so-called
"Christians", many movements have been organized to aid them. In 1897 the first Zionist Congress,
called together by Theodor Herzl, was held at
Basel, Switzerland, where 206 delegates assembled. That meeting marked the birth of what is
known as the "Zionist" movement, to "create for
the Jewish people a home in Palestine secured by
public law".

[16] The purpose of Zionism was to open up and
organize the land of Palestine into a Jewish state
so as to provide a permanent homeland for the
Jews. To such end the governments that had interests there were appealed to for their support and
co-operation. Many Jewish leaders believed the
Bible supports their being regathered a second
time to their "Holy Land of Palestine". As proof
these quote scriptures such as Jeremiah 32:37:
"Behold, I will gather them out of all the coun-

---

15. When, where and why was Zionism organized?
16, 17. What Scriptural proof do they offer to back up
the purpose of Zionism? But what do they fail to see?

tries, whither I have driven them in my anger, and in my fury, and in great wrath; and I will bring them back again unto this place, and I will cause them to dwell in safety."—*Le.*

[17] Failing to see that spiritual Israel has become the heir to God's promises, they do not appreciate that the first or miniature fulfillment of Jeremiah 32:37 applied to the Jewish remnant that returned from Babylon in 537 B.C. and that the second or major fulfillment applies to the "Israel of God" made up of those Jews inwardly, spiritual Israelites, who come out from captivity to this Babylonish world. (Galatians 6:16) From A.D. 1919 on, these have been regathered into the theocratic organization of Jehovah God as his witnesses and as ambassadors of his kingdom now set up in the hands of his Messiah.

[18] When on December 9, 1917, the British army delivered Jerusalem from the Turks and the British foreign secretary, Balfour, issued the "Balfour Declaration", the Jews felt that their long-looked-for hopes would be fulfilled. The League of Nations in 1922 mandated Palestine to the British. A "White Paper" was issued setting out the British government's policy respecting Palestine at that time. But in 1939 a White Paper stated: "His Majesty's government therefore now declares unequivocally that it is not part of their policy that Palestine should become a Jewish state . . . but rather that a Jewish home or community should be established within Palestine." The postwar appeal for the Jews by the president of the United

---

18. (a) When and why did the Jews feel their hopes were at last to be realized? (b) How did the British interpret the Balfour Declaration, and whom did they leave to cope with the matter?

States and others in 1945 was rejected by the British. They suggested that the League of Nations' successor, the United Nations organization, cope with the problem.

[19] The United Nations continued the League's recognition of the British mandate over Palestine. This mandate was due to expire at 12:01 a.m. Saturday, May 15, 1948. So the nationally minded Jews decided to set up their own political state and declare their independence. They did so, and on Friday, May 14, 1948, at 4 p.m. Palestine time, David Ben-Gurion, chairman of the National Council and the first premier of the new state, declared the State of Israel at Tel Aviv, the temporary capital. Britain's mandate expiring, Israel's foes in that area began attacking violently at once. After the national election in January of 1949, the first Jewish Parliament (Knesset) was formed on February 14, 1949, to draw up a constitution. On February 17 this Constituent Assembly at the new city of Jerusalem elected as Israel's first president Dr. Chaim Weizmann, who had till then been serving as provisional president. After that the heavy Jewish immigration into the new republic put a heavy strain upon the economies of the government.

[20] Did Israel heed Jehovah's warning at Isaiah 30:1-7 not to "go down into Egypt" for help? No! In proclaiming the new state the Israeli government appealed to the United Nations "to assist the Jewish people in the building of its state and to admit Israel into the family of nations". Early that

---

19. When and how was the new republic of Israel set up?
20. How has modern Israel 'gone down to Egypt for help'?

same Friday night the American president announced the recognition by the United States of the new Jewish state. Guatemala and other nations followed suit, Britain first granting de facto recognition January 29, 1949, as thirty-third in line to recognize the new state. The new Israel welcomed such worldly advances of friendship. When just two days old it applied to the United Nations for membership, on May 16, 1948, and also addressed itself to the United States for financial help. But it was first on May 11, 1949, after repeated applications by the new republic, that the General Assembly of the United Nations by a vote of 37 to 12, with nine members including Britain abstaining, admitted Israel to membership. By this Israel became the 59th member of the United Nations.

THE PROPER COURSE FOR INDIVIDUAL JEWS

[21] Nothing in the modern return of the Jews to Palestine and the setting up of the Israeli republic corresponds with Bible prophecies concerning the restoration of Jehovah's name-people to his favor and organization. In no way does it correspond with the restoration of the faithful, repentant Jewish remnant who forsook Babylon and returned to the land of Judah in 537 B.C. Their return set a historic pattern of how the major or final fulfillment of the prophecies of restoration would take place down here in this "time of the end" of this world. That ancient Jewish remnant returned to a land left desolate for seventy years and they returned primarily to rebuild Jehovah's temple at Jerusalem and to restore his pure theocratic worship there under his anointed high priest. But not

---

21. Why can modern Israel's return to Palestine not be construed as the fulfillment of the prophecies?

so the modern Israelis. They immigrated into a Palestine not lying desolate, but they bought up lands from the inhabitants and also induced the flight of other inhabitants from their lands under pressure of Israel's wars with neighbors. Neither was it their prime object to rebuild the temple on the temple site now occupied by the Mohammedan mosque of Omar. Neither have they restored Jehovah's worship with his accepted priesthood, that of the Greater Melchizedek. Hence the regathering of unbelieving natural Israelites to Palestine cannot be construed as fulfillment of prophecies.

[22] Israel's applying for admission into the United Nations and her accepting membership in that worldly body which assumes to take the place of Messiah's rule is a flat rejection of God's kingdom of the heavens. The remnant of spiritual Israelites, as Jehovah's witnesses, have proclaimed world-wide the establishment of God's kingdom in 1914. But again, as natural Israel did nineteen centuries ago, it has rejected its true Messiah, Jesus Christ, and has declared it has no king but Caesar. So again Jesus the King will refuse to give them a special sign for their mass conversion in Palestine to him. Therefore let individual Jews open their eyes of understanding to behold the great composite sign which Jesus foretold betokening this world's end, and let them join the great flock of "other sheep" which now seeks refuge under his kingdom. That way they will be gathered into "one flock" under "one shepherd" and be restored to divine favor and gain eternal life in the new world.—John 10:16; Revelation 7:9-17.

---

22. How has modern Israel rejected Jehovah's King, and what course remains for individual Jews to gain divine favor?

CHAPTER XIX

WHO ARE JEHOVAH'S WITNESSES?

EVERYWHERE Jehovah's witnesses are spoken against. (Acts 28:22) Why? Misinformed and prejudiced persons are the cause. There are two sides to every question. Honest persons who are fair desire to hear the truth. Accordingly they ask: "Who are these witnesses of Jehovah?" On this question everyone is entitled to hear the side of Jehovah's witnesses themselves. Any fair person can agree that Jehovah's witnesses are better qualified to state the facts from the record than is one who opposes them. In order that unbiased judgment can be exercised the evidence is given here from the record available to all.

² These Christians constitute a body or group of persons dedicated to do God's will under the leadership of his Chief Witness, Jesus Christ. They have drawn together for the purpose of declaring that he whose name alone is Jehovah is the universal sovereign and that he is the author and creator of the heavenly government of righteousness for the coming of which Jesus taught his disciples to pray. To everyone they point out the only way to that Kingdom which will permanently

---

1. (a) What does every honest person want to know about Jehovah's witnesses? (b) Who are best qualified to give the facts about them?
2. Who are they? For what purposes have they drawn together?

take the place of all present earthly governments doomed to be destroyed soon in the universal war of Armageddon.

³ For about sixty centuries Jehovah God has had his witnesses on earth. Here is how in modern times they drew together for organized work world-wide. In 1872 at Allegheny near Pittsburgh, Pennsylvania, United States, Charles Taze Russell began a Bible class that met regularly to study the Scriptures about Jehovah's kingdom and the second coming of Christ Jesus. Not many years after that similar groups of students of the Bible, having these same interests, were organized throughout the United States. In due time such Bible-study classes were established in other countries. By following the course of study outlined by the headquarters in America those classes were unified and the students became of one mind on what Almighty God teaches through his Word throughout the earth.

⁴ In time the printed courses of studies in the Scriptures used by such students were offered from door to door by special representatives in many lands for the purpose of spreading the understanding of the Bible among the people. As a result other schools or congregations of students were organized throughout the earth. Jehovah's witnesses have ever since been an international organization. They are to be found in every nation under the sun.

───────────

3. (a) For how long has Jehovah had active witnesses among men? (b) In modern times how and when did organizing of Jehovah's witnesses begin?

4. (a) How were others drawn to understand Bible truths and to have part in aiding still others to understand? (b) How widely has the work and the organization of it increased?

⁵ In 1884 the legal servant body of this international association was incorporated under Pennsylvania law. That nonprofit corporation (Watch Tower Bible & Tract Society) and the governing body of Jehovah's witnesses have been inseparably associated ever since. In 1909 the corporate headquarters were transferred from Pittsburgh to Brooklyn, New York, and then an associate charitable corporation was formed. It is a New York corporation now known as Watchtower Bible and Tract Society, Inc. In other lands other associate corporations are used, such as International Bible Students Association in Great Britain and in Canada.

THEIR NAME

⁶ Since the beginning of their modern-day organization these Christians have been called various names. Uninformed persons and enemies have falsely called them a "sect" and dubbed them Russellites, Millennial Dawnites, Rutherfordites, etc. Although for about half a century these servants of God used no distinctive names, referring to themselves as Christians, their friends and other interested persons called them "Bible students" or "international Bible students". In 1931 their representatives from many countries assembled in convention at Columbus, Ohio, and resolved that they 'desire to be known and called by the name which the mouth of the Lord God has named, to wit, *Jehovah's witnesses:* "Ye are my witnesses, saith

---

5. What is the legal servant body of Jehovah's witnesses, and what is some of its history?

6, 7. (a) In modern times what false names have Jehovah's witnesses been called, and by whom? (b) What true name was given to them, by whom, and why?

Jehovah." (Isaiah 43:10; 44:8, *AS*)' After that all local congregations or companies of these Christians throughout the earth declared themselves as recognizing this God-given name.—See 1941 *Yearbook of Jehovah's Witnesses*, pages 30-35.

[7] True, since the nineteenth century men such as C. T. Russell and J. F. Rutherford took a prominent part in this world-wide work as Jehovah's witnesses, even as in ancient days Christ Jesus, Paul, Peter, John the Baptist, Moses, Abraham, Noah, Abel and many others participated prominently in the work as Jehovah's witnesses. Yet it is Scripturally and factually clear that only Almighty God Jehovah himself founded or ordained and continues to ordain his witnesses, and in proof of this he gives them his name.—Jeremiah 15:16.

MANNER OF PREACHING

[8] The method of teaching and preaching employed by them is primitive. That is to say, they use the original method of preaching initiated by Jehovah's great witness, Christ Jesus. He and his apostles preached publicly and from house to house. (Acts 20:20) Every true Christian minister of the gospel is commanded to follow in their footsteps and must do as they did. (1 Peter 2:21; Luke 24:48; Acts 1:8; 10:39-42) Since Jehovah's witnesses take the message to the people, their preaching is distinguishable from that of the religious clergy, who require people to come to them and sit at their feet to be preached to.

---

8. (a) How and according to whose example do Jehovah's witnesses preach? (b) Why do Jehovah's witnesses preach in the primitive manner, and in doing so how do they differ from the clergy?

[9] Jehovah's witnesses do not waste time and money by building large church edifices to invite people to such to hear them preach. Experience and statistics prove that not all people can be reached in that way, because they will not all come to such buildings. In many countries more than half the people do not belong to any religious organization. Millions belonging to churches of the clergy do not attend. Many of those who do not choose to go to the clergy are, however, interested enough in the truth of God's Word to receive the message willingly at their homes when brought to them by a minister of the Lord Jesus Christ. Therefore Jehovah's witnesses establish free Bible studies in the people's homes. They go even farther than that by providing the people with opportunities to receive the message in public places and streets. There, throughout the world, they stand daily offering the Word of life in printed form to the people as they pass along the streets. —Acts 17:17-22.

[10] In their preaching work books and booklets are used by Jehovah's witnesses for the convenience of the people. Such publications contain the truths of the Bible in a permanent form for study by the interested person at his convenience. Today such persons cannot afford to have the minister stay with them hours and days at a time, as was customary centuries ago or in less recent years.

---

9. (a) Why do they not build and use costly cathedrals and temples for their preaching? (b) Where else are those served who have no opportunity to receive the message from Jehovah's witnesses at their homes?

10. (a) In their preaching, why, and in place of what, do Jehovah's witnesses use literature? (b) Do Jehovah's witnesses sell printed publications which they distribute, and, if not, how is their work carried on?

Literature used by Jehovah's witnesses is a substitute for the oral sermon or Bible discourse that is available to only the few. The literature is not printed and distributed selfishly for commercial gain or to achieve a large volume of profits. Indeed, the literature is offered on a contribution basis. Persons unable to donate toward the work but who are interested may have the literature free or upon such terms as they desire to receive it. (1 Corinthians 9:11-14) Contributions received when the literature is distributed are used to help defray cost of publishing and distributing more such literature. Any money deficit is taken care of by Jehovah's witnesses.

[11] Each of Jehovah's witnesses is a minister of the gospel. One who does not preach the good news as Jesus did is not one of Jehovah's witnesses. Because a man claims to be a minister does not, alone, make him a minister. It is his preaching in harmony with God's revealed Word that proves him to be a minister. Jehovah's witnesses are a society of ministers. As a body they are a missionary group. It is a group of evangelists, all being ministers, just as those in the first congregation of apostles and disciples of Christ Jesus were ministers, each and all. (Acts 2:44-47; 5:42) Each ac-

---

11. (a) Why is each one of them a minister? (b) Of what sort of group is each of them a part, and whom and where does he serve?

tive minister has as his congregation a group of people of good will to whom he ministers at their homes in territory assigned to him. Such minister goes to the people. They do not have to seek him out to learn about God's kingdom.

[12] While Jehovah's witnesses of today do not attend any theological seminary or religious universities in preparing for their ministry, neither did Christ Jesus or his apostles. Nor did any others of Jehovah's witnesses who performed their God-given ministry even in all the centuries before Christ Jesus. Today, however, they do receive an adequate and regular course of instruction and training before being ordained as ministers of Jehovah God and Christ Jesus. Each congregation or company of them maintains regular classes for the instruction of ministers and for students preparing for the ministry. The main textbook is the Bible. Other books and courses of instruction, free of all false religious traditions and dogmas, are provided to equip the student thoroughly for the good works of the ministry which he expects to enter. Moreover, actual practice in the ministry is provided the student under the direction of a mature minister in order for the training provided to be complete.

[13] Although school classes for ministers and students preparing for the ministry are continuous, considerable time must be spent by the student preparing for the ministry before he becomes equipped properly. Some establish their qualifica-

----

12. (a) How and why are they prepared to work as ministers? (b) Where and out of what textbooks do they receive instruction?
13. (a) Within what time does one qualify to minister as one of Jehovah's witnesses? (b) Before ministering as one of them, what requirements must he meet?

tions quicker than others. To acquire the needed knowledge might, for some, take many months, or even years; while others may become informed adequately in a few months. The Ethiopian eunuch received instruction from Philip during a chariot ride, then stopped his chariot and was baptized and thus became an ordained minister of the gospel of the Christ. (Acts 8:26-39) The time required depends entirely upon the diligence and ability of the student. In every case the student must show he has dedicated himself to Jehovah to do His will under Christ's leadership, and he must show he is apt to teach and preach. Such prime requirement is essential before the student is recognized and sent forth as a regularly ordained minister representing the Watch Tower Bible & Tract Society.—2 Timothy 2:24, 25.

ORDINATION

[14] Each such minister sent out is ordained or authorized primarily by Jehovah God. Christ Jesus was ordained in like manner simultaneously with his baptism in the Jordan river. (Isaiah 61:1, 2; Luke 4:17-19) The corporate legal servant body of Jehovah's witnesses authorizes each minister to represent it. It recognizes he is duly authorized to preach and that he has been regularly ordained in accordance with the regulations of the organization based on the Bible.

[15] The ministry is not confined to adult persons or to the aged. Women as well as men are priv-

---

14. (a) By whom and how are they ordained to preach? (b) What earthly evidence of authority to preach do they have?

15. To whom is the call for ministers and the privilege to preach as Jehovah's witnesses extended?

ileged to engage in the field service on the streets
and from house to house. Youths not only are permitted to preach but are invited to do so. (Joel
2:28, 29; Acts 2:16-18; Psalm 148:12, 13) All
children of Jehovah's witnesses should be brought
up "in the discipline and authoritative advice of
Jehovah", being trained for the ministry at a very
early age. After being thoroughly schooled, they
may enter the ministry, if they desire to, although
yet children or youths. Ancient outstanding examples are Samuel, Jeremiah and Timothy, whose
faithfulness as witnesses of Jehovah in very early
youth is proof of the propriety of children's acting
as ministers. (Ephesians 6:4, *NW;* 1 Samuel 1:24;
2:11; 3:1; Jeremiah 1:4-7) The apostle Paul declares he sent Timothy out as a minister. Timothy
was instructed by Paul to let none look down on
his youthfulness.—1 Corinthians 4:17; 1 Timothy
4:12.

[16] The literature distributed by Jehovah's witnesses costs more to print and distribute than the
sum of contributions received. Still, the organization is maintained by voluntary donations on their
part and that of people of good will. The part-time
minister contributes to the Society the cost of the
literature he puts out, and he receives contributions to help toward defraying the expense of distribution. The full-time minister is provided literature at less than its cost in order for some of
the contributions he receives to cover his expense
of distribution and also help him to provide necessities to sustain himself. This Scriptural and apos-

---

16. (a) Where do they get money they use in carrying
on their work? (b) While preaching, some full time,
others part time, how do Jehovah's witnesses sustain
themselves?

tolical p r a c t i c e Paul describes at 1 Corinthians 9:7-14. Additionally, f u l l-time ministers doing special missionary work may call upon the S o c i e t y each month for a nominal expense allowance to sustain them in their special work.

¹⁷ Jehovah's witnesses are not trying to convert the whole world. It is neither their purpose nor obligation to convert every person on earth to Christianity. Indeed they recognize that it is impossible to convert the wicked and ungodly. They seek to help toward God only those persons who are of good will and upright in heart, as he counsels. (Psalm 97:11) To set up God's glorious kingdom would be impossible if such were dependent upon conversion of the whole world, for many never would take their stand for Jehovah and his kingdom, regardless of how long and how persistently the good news might be preached among them. Announcements which witnesses of Jehovah make as to his kingdom and the way to it are a mere testimony or witness to all the people, the wicked as well as the righteous. Everyone who has a good heart will embrace the message. Scoffers and ungodly ones will reject the testimony as not worthy of credence.

¹⁸ Jehovah's witnesses preach from house to

---

17. (a) Are they trying to convert the whole world to Christianity, and, if not, why not? (b) What is the purpose of their carrying the message to the people?
18. (a) Why do they preach from house to house on Sunday? (b) How is it proved that such Sunday activity is no violation of laws against peddling and selling on Sunday?

house on Sunday, the cus-
tomary day of rest in Christendom. While some object,
nevertheless they continue
to preach on that day, for
Jesus and his apostles and
disciples did so on the Jew-

ish sabbath day. It is a most desirable day to do
missionary work from house to house, because
more people are to be found at home, and, as Jesus
said, it is lawful to do good on the sabbath or rest
day. (Luke 6:6-9) Since the clergy make use of the
day to preach from their pulpits, Jehovah's witnesses properly employ the same day to preach
from door to door. That they receive contributions
from some to whom they give literature does not
make their work commercial selling or peddling
any more than does the clergyman's taking up a
collection at Sunday church service. Therefore
laws prohibiting selling on the Sabbath or Sunday
do not apply to Sunday preaching activity of Jehovah's witnesses.

[19] It is often stated that Jehovah's witnesses are
against Catholics, Protestants, Jews, etc. That is
false. They are not against anybody because he
happens to be a Catholic, a Protestant, or a Jew.
They are not against any other person because of
his religion. All people of good will toward God
are loved by Jehovah's witnesses, regardless of
race, creed, color or nationality. Their love they
show impartially by offering from door to door

19, 20. (a) Do they attack Catholics and other religious
persons because of conflicting beliefs, and what is their
attitude toward such persons? (b) How do they deal
with false theories and practices of all religions, and
with what result?

the truthful message about the way to everlasting life under God's kingdom. The apostle declares that this is the way to incite others to love.—Hebrews 10:24, 25.

[20] On the other hand, unscriptural principles of all false religions are attacked by Jehovah's witnesses, who expose such harmful theories and traditions of men by the truth of God's Word, the Bible. But they do not attack the innocent people of good will who have been blinded or imprisoned by reason of relying on false doctrines of any religion. Persons of good will show their appreciation of the love extended from Jehovah's witnesses by studying the Bible with such witnesses. Exposing of religious errors and revealing of Bible truths do not disturb the honest person desiring to serve God.

[21] While they do not keep a membership roll as sectarian systems do, yet a record is kept of the preaching activity of all of Jehovah's witnesses. Everyone makes a regular report of his preaching activity, and the organization keeps a record of the work done by each of its ministers. Moreover, there is no man-made organization that one can join when he becomes one of the witnesses. Jehovah God is the One who draws his servants together to himself. (John 6:44) When any person drawn becomes associated with God's servants in the earth, then the Society recognizes such new servant. It authorizes him to preach in territory duly assigned to him. One's presence with Jeho-

---

21. (a) Do they enroll members as do sectarian organizations, and what record do they keep? (b) Is it possible to join an earthly organization under their control, and how does one identify himself as one of them and also with them?

vah's witnesses is shown by his work as a minister. He who does not actively preach as one of the witnesses is not *with* the organization. As long as one actively preaches with the organization he is recognized as being with it.

HOPES AND PROSPECTS

[22] Not all of Jehovah's witnesses expect to go to heaven. Indeed, only a small proportion, a "little flock", do. (Luke 12:32) Almighty God, who sets all members in his organization as it pleases him, has limited to 144,000 the number of the "body of the Christ", whose members will reign with Christ Jesus in God's heavenly kingdom. Only a small remnant, sufficient to complete the fullness of that body, now remain on earth.

[23] An unnumbered crowd of faithful persons now working as Jehovah's witnesses are sometimes called his "other sheep" or "Jonadabs", because they were foreshadowed by Jonadab, companion of King Jehu. (John 10:16; 2 Kings 10:15-28; Jeremiah 35:8, 18, 19) They do not expect to go to heaven. They have been promised everlasting life on earth, including the privilege of subduing, beautifying and populating the earth, if they, as Jehovah's witnesses, prove their faithfulness to him before his war of Armageddon. Jonadabs are witnesses, even though they are not of the remnant of the "body of the Christ". The same way faithful men and women were His witnesses before the Christ's body began to be made up by Almighty God with Christ Jesus as its Head. (He-

---

22, 23. (a) Do all of Jehovah's witnesses expect to go to heaven, and what future service assignment do those not going there expect to receive from God? (b) Who are Jonadabs, and why are they Jehovah's witnesses?

brews 11:1 to 12:1) Every person dedicated to do
God's will as a follower of Christ Jesus and who
acts as a witness of Jehovah can properly be called
one of Jehovah's witnesses. It follows that his
"other sheep" or "Jonadabs", too, are Jehovah's
witnesses.

²⁴ He who associates with them or who becomes
one of them can not and does not expect to receive
any selfish benefit. He does not privately profit
according to worldly standards of finance or social prestige upon becoming one of them. Indeed,
he must divorce himself from all such standards
and worldly ambitions in order to become one of
Jehovah's witnesses and to grow in favor with
Almighty God. (John 15:18-21) But because a witness of Jehovah gains no worldly or temporal ad-
vantage does not mean he personally receives no
benefits upon becoming one of Jehovah's witnesses.

²⁵ While from a material standpoint God promises to his faithful servant only his daily bread or
bare necessities of life, many spiritual blessings
are his portion even before God's kingdom wholly
displaces this world's commercial organization.
Among such blessings the foremost is the high
privilege of being an ambassador for the Most
High God and his theocratic government and ad-
vertising its blessings among all people. Other
benefits are the joys of hunting for his lost sheep
and fishing for people of good will and then bringing up such persons in the discipline and authori-

---

24. What material advantages does one not expect upon
becoming one of Jehovah's witnesses?
25, 26. (a) To what extent, before Armageddon, is material provision promised and given by Almighty God
to one dedicated to serve him? (b) What are some
satisfactions and benefits shared by one who faithfully
serves Jehovah?

tative advice of Jehovah till they reach the full
stature of a witness of His. There is also the mental satisfaction of being free from the fears, burdens and griefs of the present wicked system of
things which God Almighty will destroy at Armageddon; also the knowledge that a person is following the path of righteousness and truth which
leads to everlasting life. Moreover, he looks forward to seeing the dead arise under the kingdom
of God. By God's almighty power exercised
through Christ Jesus the dead who are in the
memorial tombs will be resurrected, upon earth,
and be given the opportunity to prove their integrity toward Jehovah the universal sovereign after
the war of Armageddon.

[26] Finally, and above all other benefits, comes
the satisfaction of seeing his heavenly Father's
name and sovereignty vindicated by the eternal destruction of Satan's wicked world with all its supporters. This will be followed by the unchallenged
exercise of full authority and sovereignty by Jehovah through his Son and King Jesus Christ over
all the earth. This will forever guarantee the free
and full worship of Jehovah everywhere on earth
for all his faithful witnesses and servants.

CHAPTER XX

"CAESAR'S THINGS TO CAESAR"

"CAESAR" is generally used to symbolize the civil or temporal rulership of the nations. In these days before the war of Armageddon various civil governments are urging the support of all peoples to the international organization, the United Nations. Efforts to regiment people under national, regional and international governments cause the issue of politics, political obligations and political ceremonies to rise to a higher level of interest and importance. As usual, all people are requested by the rulers to take part in such things. Often no consideration is given to the exemption from such obligations usually granted to ambassadors and ministers domiciled in foreign nations. (Revelation 13:15-17) Refusal by conscientious persons to participate in the political, commercial and religious activities requires them to answer a number of vital questions. Some of these we here review and put them up to the Bible to answer, to get an expression of God's will on these critical matters.

2 A minister is one who performs service in any office. An ambassador is such a minister of high rank. Almost always in modern times he is a resi-

---

1. Whose co-operation do worldly governments expect and require now, and why, and with what result?
2. (a) Who are ministers and ambassadors? (b) Why and for whom are Jehovah's witnesses ambassadors and ministers?

dent agent of a foreign government. Both a minister and an ambassador serve their sovereign state in an alien land. Holy Scripture clearly shows that a true follower of Jesus Christ is a witness of the universal sovereign Jehovah God and as such he is a minister or ambassador of God's kingdom. Since A.D. 1914 Jehovah's witnesses are ministers and ambassadors of the established kingdom of God Almighty with Christ Jesus at his right hand on the throne. (2 Corinthians 5:20; Ephesians 6:20; Jeremiah 49:14; Obadiah 1; Matthew 24:14) Since that government will stand forever it is the greatest of all governments. It follows that its ministers or ambassadors deserve the same rights and exemptions as such officials of this world enjoy.

[3] An ambassador of a foreign power is by the laws of this world exempted as an alien from giving allegiance to the government of the land in which he is resident. He is relieved of rendering political obligations of any sort. The nation where he resides is without authority to impose any regulation that burdens or abridges his performing his duty as such. Moreover, for like reasons, ministers of religion are exempt from burdens of government that are ordinarily imposed on all the people. The reason for these exemptions is that benefits and advantages flow to the people and to the government from the activities of such ministers, which relieve the government of certain work and responsibility. The influence on the people from preaching is said to contribute to welfare

3. (a) Ambassadors and ministers are generally exempted from what, and why? (b) Are Jehovah's witnesses entitled to claim such exemption, and what proves whether?

and morals, and so is good and great enough to justify exempting of religious ministers. Jehovah's witnesses, preaching the only message of real hope, are entitled to claim these exemptions granted to all ministers of religion.

⁴ The time, energy and life of a witness are dedicated exclusively to the service of Jehovah God. He has entered into an irrevocable obligation to the Supreme One to perform his God-given preaching duties faithfully as long as he lives, and never to turn away from them. Any turning aside from assigned duty so as to engage in serving another master, to perform other work assigned by the civil state, and any refraining from preaching because of complying with men's arbitrary commands to stop are in Jehovah's eyes unfaithfulness. God has declared that those false to agreements are worthy of death. (Romans 1:31, 32, *NW*) No man can excuse a minister for unfaithfulness to Jehovah. So no man can rightly oblige such minister to break his agreement with Jehovah. The exemption granted to ministers by liberal governments avoids such predicament.

⁵ Since Jehovah has chosen his witnesses out of the world to be ambassadors in behalf of his kingdom to the peoples of earth, they are no part of this world. As their allegiance is to the Most High God and his kingdom, they do not take part in local, national or international elections or politics. From such they are disengaged by the law of God,

4. (a) To whom and what are the time, energy and life of Jehovah's witnesses devoted, and why? (b) Abandoning their agreement with Jehovah results in what, and why can no man force them to abandon it?
5. (a) Can Jehovah's witnesses take part in worldly politics, and why your answer? (b) How and by whom was the example set for them to follow in this respect?

who commands them to remain unspotted from the world. Like Christ Jesus and his apostles, who set the example to follow, they are in the world but are no part of it. (James 1:27; John 17:16, 17; 15:17-19) Another reason why they abstain from the world is that the Devil is its invisible ruler, and they know that to be a friend of the world is to incur the enmity of God.—2 Corinthians 4:4; 1 John 5:19; James 4:4.

EXEMPTION

⁶ The preaching activity of Jehovah's ministers entitles them to claim exemption from performing military training and service in the armed forces of the nations in which they dwell. The exempt status of Jehovah's witnesses also relieves them of performing governmental work required of men who conscientiously object to both combatant and noncombatant military service, because Jehovah's witnesses are ministers of the gospel and are no political, academic or religious pacifists. They claim neutrality and the rights of neutrals because of their status as ambassadors of God's kingdom. This is exactly the same position Christ Jesus and his apostles took. Additionally, the early Christians who were thrown to the lions by the authoritarian rulers assumed that position in the Roman empire.—John 18:36; 2 Timothy 4:17.

⁷ The perfect and supreme law of God has always provided for his ministers to be exempt from

6. (a) What activity entitles Jehovah's witnesses to claim the legal exemption from military service? (b) What reasons do they give for claiming the exempt status?
7. (a) By whom was the exemption from training and service for civil duty first provided for God's ministers, and what was it? (b) Following that precedent, what have enlightened nations of modern times done?

performing extraordinary services to the civil state. Why, in the first conscription act of the nation of Israel, by which its manpower was conscripted for theocratic warfare, a provision was included to exempt priests and Levites who actively performed their ministerial duties. Obedience of the Israelites to all features of that conscription law was proper because theirs was a theocratic government and the conscription and the exemptions were at God's command. (Numbers 1:47-54; 2:33; 26:62) Following this precedent, nations claiming to be Christian have shown enlightenment by exempting ministers from military duty. Today one of the leading members of the United Nations, namely, the United States of America, has declared Jehovah's witnesses to be a recognized religious organization and that its ministers are exempt from training and service in the armed forces.

[8] For another reason each minister of the Most High God claims exemption as a follower of Christ Jesus from military training and service. He is already in an army, to serve as a "soldier of Christ Jesus". (2 Timothy 2:3, 4, *NW*) Since the war weapons of the soldier of Christ Jesus are not fleshly, he is not authorized by his Commander in Chief, Jehovah God, to engage in carnal warfare of this world. Furthermore, being enlisted in the army of Christ Jesus, he cannot desert the forces of Jehovah to assume the obligations of a soldier in any army of this world without being guilty of desertion and suffering the punishment meted out by Almighty God to deserters.

---

8. What other reasons support the stand of an active witness of Jehovah in his claim for exemption from military service?

⁹ Some politically named administrative boards arbitrarily and capriciously refuse the exemption claimed by Jehovah's witnesses. But this fact in no way proves that the minister actually preaching is no minister in truth and in fact. His actual ministerial status is not dissolved or nullified by such arbitrary administrative denial of e x e m p t i o n claimed. In such case the misinformed or prejudiced board members violate the law by imposing their ill-conceived private opinion as justifying such refusal. They are the ones that do the wrong rather than the minister who persists in claiming his exemption allowed by the law of the land and the law of God. Even the judicial courts before which the action of arbitrary boards has been brought for review have declared that, in order to preserve equal justice under the law, Jehovah's witnesses are entitled to the same treatment and consideration that the popular orthodox clergy receive.

¹⁰ Both the orthodox clergy and some of Jehovah's witnesses were classified as ministers of religion and exempted from doing military service. So they did not help to win World War II by carrying arms. However, people of all nations were served and greatly comforted by the preaching Jehovah's witnesses did during the war. No truthful person can prove they did not do as much for the people's benefit as the orthodox clergy did. From the Bible standpoint, Jehovah's witnesses did more and continue to do more to comfort the

<hr>

9. How have the true claims of some of Jehovah's witnesses been treated, and with what result?
10. (a) How did Jehovah's witnesses help the people during wartime, and with what result? (b) How does their activity in this respect compare with that of the clergy?

spiritually sick, to aid those bereaved by death of their loved ones, and to relieve mental suffering of the wounded. This they did and still do by carrying the consoling message of God's kingdom to every house possible. By this type of beneficent activity the faith, the hope and the good courage of millions, whether attending a church to hear a clergyman or not, were and are sustained. In this way people were helped more from the work of Jehovah's witnesses during World War II than from the work of the orthodox clergy.

NO WORSHIP DUE CAESAR

[11] Following the rise of the Nazis to power the political ceremony of heiling Hitler and saluting the swastika flag was imposed on all inhabitants of the German Reich. For reasons both Scriptural and legal, Jehovah's witnesses refused to heil Hitler and salute his swastika. So they were persecuted. Children were torn from parents. Faithful men, and women as well, were imprisoned in concentration camps. Some were killed because of their faithfulness to Jehovah God in refusing to engage in such patriotic ceremonies. These facts are too well known to be denied.

[12] Where the Nazi and Fascist scourge prevailed, the like fiendish practices and results followed in a great part of the earth. While the Nazis and Fascists prospered in their plans for world domination a similar patriotic move was launched in democratic lands as a supposed countermeasure to the Nazi-Fascist conspiracy. In those lands, not except-

11, 12. (a) What patriotic ceremony originated in totalitarian countries, and how were Jehovah's witnesses in those lands affected by it? (b) What happened along the same line in democratic lands, and with what result to Jehovah's witnesses?

ing the United States of America, the persecution of faithful Christians, Jehovah's witnesses, reached a height almost equal to that in Axis-dominated areas. In the United States those who refused to salute the flag were beaten by mobs that were unrestrained in their violence. Children were taken away from parents. Thousands of children were denied the right to an education in the public schools because of their conscientious refusal to do religious service to the national emblem. All this reached a climax of persecution when the U. S. Supreme Court declared on June 3, 1940, that the compulsory flag salute was legal, not unconstitutional. Three years later, on June 14, 1943, the Supreme Court reversed its decision, in favor of freedom of worship.

[13] The Fascist flag, the Nazi flag, and the Communist flag Jehovah's witnesses have refused to salute. It is not that they just refuse to salute the flag of the United States and other democratic nations. So they do not discriminate against any nation. Their position world-wide is based on the infallible Scriptures. Refusal to salute is based on the prohibitory laws of Almighty God expressed at 1 Corinthians 10:14 and elsewhere throughout the Christian Greek Scriptures as well as the Hebrew Scriptures. In the Ten Commandments we read: "I am Jehovah thy God, who brought thee out of the land of Egypt, out of the house of bondage. Thou shalt have no other gods before me. Thou shalt not make unto thee a graven image, nor any likeness of any thing that is in heaven

---

13, 14. (a) Do Jehovah's witnesses salute the flag of any nation, and why your answer? (b) In ancient time what happened to the Israelites who violated God's commandments in this respect?

above, or that is in the earth beneath, or that is
in the water under the earth: thou shalt not bow
down thyself unto them, nor serve them; for I
Jehovah thy God am a jealous God, visiting the
iniquity of the fathers upon the children, upon the
third and upon the fourth generation of them that
hate me, and showing lovingkindness unto thousands of them that love me and keep my commandments."—Exodus 20:2-6, *AS*.

[14] Because the nation of Israel willfully violated
this command in turning to worship idols, images
or symbols, Jehovah punished them, for they were
in a covenant with him to remain faithful to him.
—Exodus 32:1-8, 30-35.

[15] Many national flags bear likenesses of things
in heaven, such as stars, sun, etc. Others bear
likenesses of things of earth or of its waters, such
as eagle, lion, serpent, fish, etc. All such likenesses
are embraced by Exodus 20:2-6, quoted above.
Any national flag is a symbol or image of the
sovereign power of its nation. The flag of each
nation is commonly regarded by it and its people who give allegiance to it as being sacred. (*The
Encyclopedia Americana*, Volume 11, page 316)
Regardless of whether all people look on the flag-
salute ceremony as religious or sacred, it is just
the same a political ceremony whereby the symbol, the flag, is saluted or bowed down to religiously.

[16] This is an act that ascribes salvation to the
national emblem and to the nation for which it
stands. Through the salute the saluter impliedly

---

15. (a) Of what are national flags symbols? (b) What
is the attitude of the people toward the flag of a nation,
and what kind of ceremony proves this?
16. (a) What does this act imply? (b) Why can no witness of Jehovah ascribe salvation to any national symbol?

declares that his salvation comes from the thing for which the flag stands, namely, the nation symbolized by the flag. Let patriots do what they want; Jehovah's witnesses will not interfere. But true ambassadors for Christ and ministers of God have sworn their unbreakable allegiance to the true God and Savior for all time. They cannot ascribe salvation or deliverance from evils and foes to any other sovereign or a worldly power. Their salvation is from the ever-living Supreme Sovereign, Jehovah, and his Son, Jesus Christ. Hence no witness of Jehovah, who ascribes salvation only to Him, may salute any national emblem without violating Jehovah's commandment against idolatry as stated in his Word.—1 John 5:21.

[17] This is not the result of private misinterpretation of the Scriptures. It is no warping of the commandment of God. The conclusion reached by Jehovah's witnesses is one that has been dictated by Him, and he reveals the meaning of his commandments to all people dedicated to him. This conclusion is also supported by cases recorded in the Bible where other faithful servants of Jehovah refused to salute or bow down to symbols or images, whether man-made things or men. Since God expressed approval of the course taken by such faithful worshipers, it provides Jehovah's witnesses of today with precedents to follow, which prove that their conclusion is correct.

[18] Ancient Persia's absolute ruler by decree re-

17. Is their refusal to salute a flag the result of private interpretation, warping the Scriptures? Why your answer?
18, 19. (a) What two outstanding cases in the Bible support the conclusion reached by Jehovah's witnesses as to saluting? (b) By those cases what principle of action has Jehovah shown to his witnesses, and why does the same principle apply to them today?

quired every person in the realm to bow down to his prime minister Haman. Haman was a representative or symbol of the Amalekite persecutors of Israel, and Jehovah had condemned the Amalekites to be exterminated. Mordecai, a faithful Jew under the law covenant with Jehovah, refused to bow. For his defiance preparations were made to hang him and liquidate all the Jews. Because he, together with Esther, was faithful, Jehovah God saved him and the Jews from destruction.—Esther, chapters 3, 4 and 5.

[19] Earlier, before Persia dominated the world, Babylon's emperor made an image. He had it set up and issued a decree that at a given signal all persons assembled should bow to that image of the political state. Three faithful Hebrews refused to comply with the order of the dictatorial ruler. He cast them into a fiery furnace, made seven times as hot as usual. For firmly refusing to disobey him Jehovah delivered them from the fiery furnace, unsinged. By this the Most High God plainly showed that one dedicated to him cannot salute the emblem of any nation. Those experiences of such faithful men were recorded for no idle purpose. As examples, "they were written for a warning to us upon whom the accomplished ends of the systems of things have arrived."—1 Corinthians 10:11, NW.

[20] A witness of Jehovah does respect the good principles represented by the flag of the nation in which he dwells, though he salutes the flag of no nation. He shows his respect by not casting re-

---

20. (a) Do Jehovah's witnesses respect the flag of the nation where they reside, and what is the proof? (b) Why do they comply with all righteous laws of any nation?

proach upon it through misconduct. By willingly obeying all valid laws of the land that do not conflict with God's law he shows respect for both the flag and the nation for which it stands. He complies with all such good laws because it is right and proper to do so as a God-fearing follower of his Master, Jesus Christ. So it is not because the law includes penalties for violators that Jehovah's witnesses obey the law. Courts of the liberal and enlightened governments of many lands have declared that it is not an illegal act nor is it showing disrespect of the flag for Jehovah's witnesses to refuse to salute it.

²¹ Jehovah's witnesses are not against people who salute or desire to salute the flag of any nation. Nor do they oppose the desire of any person to serve in the armed forces of any nation. Nor do they oppose the efforts of any nation to raise an army by conscripting its manpower. If a citizen wants to salute a flag or to enter the armed forces of any nation, it is his right to do so, and Jehovah's witnesses regard it as wrong *for them* to oppose the efforts of such person or to condemn him. They do not attempt to convert the world to a refusal to salute flags or to decline to bear arms. They merely keep their neutrality and their obligations as ambassadors for God's kingdom, and they declare their reasons for refusing to break their allegiance to their God and Savior. Persons not under an agreement to obey him and who do not want to be his witnesses are not urged

21. (a) Why are they not against any other person's desire to salute a flag or to serve in the armed forces? (b) Are they trying to convert the world to their own position on flag saluting and the bearing of arms? And what are their purposes in preaching?

to take such a stand. Even each one of Jehovah's witnesses must decide for himself what stand he will take on such issues, as he will not be interfered with or coerced by any other witness.

LAW–ABIDING, NOT SUBVERSIVE

²² It is wrong for Christians to be subversive and to engage in subversive activities within the nations where they dwell. But they are not seditionists just because they act within such nations as ambassadors for God's kingdom. All enlightened nations guarantee freedom to worship Almighty God. Such worship requires that the true servant of Jehovah be a minister of His government. People of all Christendom have been taught to pray for the coming of God's kingdom to earth. Therefore those who, as ministers, preach that the answer of God to that prayer is now near are not against the government of the nation in which they do such preaching. The activities of the worldly ambassadors of foreign governments do not work against the interests of the countries in which they each, respectively, reside. So also the works of Jehovah's witnesses are not against the government of any land where they reside.

²³ True, they announce the judgment of Jehovah God to destroy all evil systems of this world and to set up his everlasting kingdom of righteousness.

---

22. (a) How can it be proved that Jehovah's witnesses do not engage in subversive activities and are not seditious? (b) In what respect do their activities compare with those of an ambassador sent by one worldly nation to another?

23, 24. (a) Whom do they expect to destroy present evil governments and to set up the kingdom of Jehovah God? (b) So what are they commanded to preach, and what stand to take during conflicts?

But this does not mean Jehovah's witnesses will have a part in executing the judgment of destruction and in setting up that new permanent government. They will have no part in either. They act only as Jehovah's messengers, heralding worldwide his promised kingdom. They are not authorized by him to act as executioners. Only his chief officer, Christ Jesus, acting under Jehovah's direction, will do the act of destruction. (Ezekiel 9:1-7; Revelation 17:14) For any of his witnesses to attempt to take part in destroying a government by use of force or other unlawful violence is contrary to the law of Almighty God.

²⁴ Moreover, the everlasting kingdom of Jehovah will not be set up on this earth by his witnesses. They will perform no overt act in the erecting of such government. Jehovah has already set it up in the heavens by Christ Jesus, its King. (Isaiah 9:6, 7; Daniel 2:44; Psalm 2) So they are commanded at Matthew 24:14 to preach the good news of this established kingdom among all nations before the end of this world comes. Hence they must be neutral amid all the controversies and violent conflicts of the nations. Expressing their neutrality, Jesus said: "They are no part of the world just as I am no part of the world."—John 17:16, *NW*.

²⁵ Religious enemies falsely accuse Jehovah's witnesses of being against this world's governments because of their stand as ambassadors. They contend that Jehovah's witnesses should comply with every command of the political rulers. Such

---

25. (a) What contention do their opponents make about their complying with all commands of worldly rulers? (b) Who are the "higher powers" to whom they submit themselves, and why?

religionists insist that those rulers are the "higher powers" mentioned at Romans 13:1-7, and to which all should submit themselves. But the "higher powers" there mentioned are the principal ruling factors of God's congregation, namely, the invisible governing body of God's kingdom. The apostle did not intend his mention of the higher powers to be applied to men visible to human eyes who are rulers of this evil world run by Satan. So the "higher powers" the apostle mentioned are Jehovah God and Christ Jesus, and Christ Jesus is Jehovah's great Minister.

²⁶ Persons who importune them to break their agreement with God contend that Jehovah's witnesses must comply with all commands of officials of the governments of this world because Jesus declared: "Pay back Caesar's things to Caesar, but God's things to God." (Mark 12:17, *NW*) Perversely and privately interpreting that saying of Jesus for their own purpose, enemies aim at having Jehovah's witnesses render to "Caesar" the things that are God's. But, like Christ Jesus, Jehovah's witnesses refuse to render to "Caesar" the things belonging to God. Even Pilate could find no fault with Jesus because of his claiming to be a King and refusing to give allegiance to pagan Caesar. (Luke 23:2-4) So no fault can properly be found with these followers of Christ Jesus, Jehovah's witnesses, who render like allegiance to God. They rightly quote Peter's words: "We must obey God as ruler rather than men."—Acts 5:29, *NW*.

---

26. (a) What interpretation do worldly rulers place upon Jesus' words at Mark 12:17? (b) How does that interpretation compare with the apostolic practice of Jehovah's witnesses today?

CHAPTER XXI

THE END OF THE WORLD

WHAT once sounded fantastic now appears a grim possibility. The people viewed the Scriptural warning of an end to this world thus in 1945 after the second atomic bomb burst over Japan. The appalling loss of property and life caused deep concern to earth's inhabitants as man had at last stumbled on something he might not be able to control and so the end of the human race might result. This is but one of many developments from A.D. 1914 onward which have caused sincere, God-fearing people to wonder if we are not living in the "last days" before the destruction of this world. For proof it will be necessary to turn to God's Word and there search the prophecies relating to such a time and see if events of the day fit them.

² Questions concerning the end first arose in the minds of Jesus' apostles, as shown by their question: "Tell us, when shall these things be? and what shall be the sign of thy coming, and of the end of the world?" (Matthew 24:3) Showing that this expression "the end of the world" does not mean the destruction of our earthly globe, the *New World Translation of the Christian Greek*

1. What question have recent developments caused people to wonder about, and where may the answer be found?
2. Who first asked a similar question, and how did Jesus answer it?

Scriptures renders Matthew 24:3 as follows: "Tell us, When will these things be, and what will be the sign of your presence and of the consummation of the system of things?" The similar question at Mark 13:4 the *New World Translation* renders this way: "Tell us, When will these things be, and what will be the sign when all these things are destined to come to a consummation?" In answer Jesus foretold many things that would mark the time of his invisible presence and the setting up of God's kingdom. The end of the Gentile times or "appointed times of the nations" in 1914 was the time for these to begin appearing.

³ "Jerusalem will be trampled on by the nations, until the appointed times of the nations are fulfilled." (Luke 21:24, *NW*) The "appointed times of the nations" indicated a period in which there would be no representative government of Jehovah on earth, such as the kingdom of Israel was; but the Gentile nations would dominate the earth. Those "times" must have been running in Jesus' day, for that very situation existed. Was not Jerusalem then in bondage to imperial Rome, and, before that, to Greece, to Persia, and to Babylon? Yes. So when did the appointed times begin, and for how long a period would they extend?

⁴ Contrary to common belief, Jehovah has not reigned over the whole earth since man's rebellion in Eden. The divine Record reveals that after the Flood only one nation had God's guidance and provisions, the nation of Israel, and Jehovah used it to form a prophetic moving picture of the gov-

3. (a) What prophecy shows an important time period was involved? (b) By what was the time period characterized?
4. Where was theocratic rule exercised, and when did it end?

ernment which will one day exercise dominion over all the earth, God's kingdom by Christ Jesus. Through unfaithfulness Israel lost her sovereignty and was carried into captivity to Babylon, in the year 607 B.C. The local theocratic rule in the earth ended that way.

⁵ Years after this Babylonian captivity began Jehovah caused a prophetic vision to be dreamed and also to be enacted concerning the times of the nations and the restoration of Jehovah's Theocracy. The prophetic dream disclosed a great tree which grew from the earth and reached to heaven and furnished food and shelter to all creatures. Suddenly a holy one from heaven commanded: "Hew down the tree, . . . nevertheless leave the stump of his roots in the earth, even with a band of iron and brass, . . . and let seven times pass over him." Within one year this prophecy began its miniature fulfillment on the dreamer, Nebuchadnezzar. In a fit of boasting he was deprived of his sanity and throne, and browsed about the field like a beast. At the end of seven years he was reinstated. In this drama Jehovah used the king of Babylon to picture a yet greater fulfillment of the prophecy, namely, the cutting down of the unfaithful cherub from his position in Eden and the later reinstatement of theocratic rule over earth. —Daniel, chapter 4; see *"The Truth Shall Make You Free"*, chapter 18.

⁶ "Seven times" meant seven literal years in the case of Nebuchadnezzar, deprived of his throne.

5. (a) What prophecy did Jehovah record foretelling the appointed times of the nations and the restoration of theocratic rule? (b) What two fulfillments were there to the prophecy?
6. How are the "seven times" reckoned, and when do they end?

The seven years were equal to 84 months, or, Scripturally allowing 30 days for each month, 2,520 days. At Revelation 12:6, 14, there are 1,260 days mentioned and described as a "time, and times, and half a time", or 3½ times. Seven times would be twice 1,260 days, or 2,520 days. By his faithful prophet Ezekiel Jehovah said: "I have appointed thee each day for a year." (Ezekiel 4:6) By applying this divine rule the 2,520 days mean 2,520 years. Therefore, since God's typical kingdom with its capital at Jerusalem ceased to exist in the autumn of 607 B.C., then, by counting the appointed times from that date, the 2,520 years extend to the autumn of A.D. 1914.

"APPOINTED TIMES OF THE NATIONS" END

[7] Expiration of the "seven times" marks the time for the symbolic tree stump to be released from its bands. This could not, of course, mean the returning of Satan to power as man's covering cherub, for for thousands of years since the global flood he has continued as the "god of this system of things". Never again could he be in God's favor and be placed in charge of righteous man in the new world. Satan the Devil has been sentenced to destruction, and the sentence will be carried out. Neither could the return of the natural Jews to Palestine and their setting up the democratic state of Israel indicate that God's kingdom had been restored to fleshly Israel, for such Jewish movement is political and social, without a thought for God's theocratic government. No; neither a restoration of Satan to God's organization nor the Jews' re-

---

7. What things were not meant by removal of the "bands" from the prophetic stump, but what did result from this?

patriation was meant by loosing the "bands" about the symbolic tree stump. The time for reinstating Jehovah's Theocracy was meant. What did result was a new sprout from the stump, namely, the Kingdom under Christ Jesus. It is a new theocratic government toward our earth, the New Jerusalem which comes down out of heaven from God. —Revelation 21:2, NW.

8 When Jesus was on earth it was not his Father's due time to set up the Kingdom, although Jesus then qualified as King. After his death on the torture stake and his resurrection from the dead Jesus was exalted to heaven, there to await the ending of the "seven times" before his installation as King. At the end of this period of waiting, in 1914, the prophecy became due: "Jehovah will send forth the rod of thy strength out of Zion: rule thou in the midst of thine enemies." (Psalm 110:1, 2, AS) Such action marked the beginning of the "time of the end" for the old world and the birth of the new theocratic government toward our earth. No longer would Satan's world operate unhindered, for the "appointed times of the nations" had run out. In the last book of the Bible Christ Jesus described these developments under symbols or signs. A son born to a heavenly woman was snatched from the dragon's jaws and enthroned alongside God.

9 War in heaven followed, with God's organization and Satan's in mighty combat. With what result? The thorough cleansing of heaven of Satan and his demon hordes by their banishment to the earth. (Revelation, chapter 12) Of course, these

---

8, 9. How does Revelation 12 describe the events in heaven at the end of the Gentile times, and what did these mean for Satan's world?

spiritual things were unseen by man, but he has been greatly affected by them.

¹⁰ The direct result of the conflict in heaven was another proof that the world had entered its "time of the end", the first visible proof: "For nation will rise against nation and kingdom against kingdom, and there will be food shortages and earthquakes in one place after another." (Matthew 24:7, *NW*) Furious at the successful birth of the theocratic government, Satan determined to destroy all people ere they learned of the newly established kingdom. This was why he plunged the nations into the war of 1914-1918. It was the first time in history that so great a conflict had taken place. Before its end thirty nations were involved, with war being waged in all quarters of the earth. Of a truth, "the nations became wrathful." (Revelation 11:18, *NW*) They fought, not for the righteous cause of Jehovah's kingdom and against Satan, but for selfish world domination. It is conclusive proof that the "appointed times" have ended, Satan's rule is interfered with, and the enthronement of Christ Jesus has taken place.

¹¹ Woe and misery did not end when hostilities ceased. Following World War I food shortages stalked the earth, and Europe in particular. So much was this so that it was necessary to organize relief measures for stricken areas. Pestilence, too, took its toll. From the "Spanish flu" alone twenty million died in a few months, in spite of modern medical science, this being a far greater loss of life than that caused by the four years of war. (Luke

10. What was the first visible proof, and how did it prove the end of the times of the nations?
11. What things made up the "beginning of pangs of distress"?

21:10, 11) Also, since 1914 there have been reported more seismic disturbances than ever before in history, some causing great destruction to both property and life, as, for example, the 1923 earthquake in Japan, which brought death to 99,331 persons. Yet Jesus said: "All these things are a beginning of pangs of distress."—Matthew 24:8, *NW*.

[12] How truly has the history of the past half century borne that prophecy out! The nations had not recovered from World War I when, in 1939, they were again enmeshed in war. This time there were the same sides and the same issue, world domination. But, measured by combatants and equipment, the expenditure of monies, the loss of life and property, and the world-wide effect, World War II far outstripped its predecessor. Pestilence, famine and earthquake and local war have followed in its wake, exacting a further toll in human lives, misery and suffering. Certainly the world is shot through with pangs of distress under the oppressive influence of its invisible demon-god, Satan.

KINGDOM PUBLICITY

[13] The Kingdom's birth has been given wide publicity. Long prior to it, *The Watchtower* as of March, 1880, page 2, said: " 'The Times of the Gentiles' extend to 1914, and the heavenly kingdom will not have full sway till then." During World War I the Kingdom proclamation by Jehovah's witnesses was interrupted, but in 1919 they began to be regathered, reorganized and commis

12. What events since World War I prove the "pangs of distress" have continued?
13. To what important proof did Jesus refer at Matthew 24:14, and to what extent has this been carried out?

sioned to perform a still greater publicity work. (Matthew 24:31) This time it was to announce God's now established kingdom in fulfillment of Jesus' command: "This good news of the kingdom will be preached in all the inhabited earth for the purpose of a witness to all the nations, and then the accomplished end will come." (Matthew 24:14, *NW*) So faithfully have Jehovah's witnesses done this that since World War I closed in 1918 down to 1952 over a half *billion* bound books and booklets on this subject, besides magazines, free tracts, and public lectures, reached the people in over 90 languages. Since World War II ended in 1945 their work has expanded more than ever to reach over 120 lands.

[14] Satan and his worldly subjects would like to put an end to this Kingdom message. However, this they cannot do, as the message is of Jehovah. But they do slander and persecute. Jesus knowingly stated: "If they have persecuted me, they will persecute you also." (John 15:20, *NW*) Such treatment of these Christians has reached a climax in these last days. (Matthew 24:9) World War I was occasion for much persecution, but with the advent of the total state the opposition to the Kingdom has multiplied. As victims of Nazi-Fascist-Vatican aggression, Jehovah's witnesses suffered indescribable torture through twelve long years of Nazi domination. Many sealed their testimony with their lifeblood. Persecution was not restricted to Nazi-Fascist–occupied Europe but was felt throughout the earth; as in Japan, Australia, Canada, and even America, which witnessed hundreds of cases of mob violence. Communist-

---

14. How have religionists and others reacted to the message?

dominated countries and other countries under authoritarian rule have since joined in to intensify the persecution. All this because Jehovah's witnesses announce God's kingdom.

MAN-MADE SUBSTITUTE FOR GOD'S KINGDOM

[15] Without heeding Jesus' warning the leaders of this old world plunge ahead in the forming of a world supergovernment. Little do they care to know that they are taking part in setting up a substitute for God's kingdom by Christ, and so bringing destruction upon themselves. Since the end of the appointed times in 1914 God's kingdom alone is worthy to rule the globe, for it is dedicated wholly to the honor, praise and vindication of the universal Sovereign, Jehovah God. Any substitute for it is blasphemous and is doomed to destruction. Yet the great majority of mankind are placing hope and confidence in such an organization. Ignoring Jesus' words, "My kingdom is no part of this world," many look upon the United Nations organization as the political manifestation of God's kingdom. Was not the old League of Nations so viewed? Early in 1919 the "Council of the Federation of Churches of Christ in America" issued the statement: "The League of Nations is the political expression of the Kingdom of God on earth." Protestantism gave enthusiastic support to the League. The pope was excluded from a seat in the League, and so the Roman Catholic Hierarchy set out to destroy it by Fascism and Nazism. This she accomplished through totalitarian aggressors, and

---

15. (a) To what means of security do worldly rulers resort, and why is it blasphemous? (b) How was the League of Nations viewed, and how did it go into the abyss?

the League bowed from the scene during World War II, into the abyss.

[16] Jesus revealed that this beastly international organization would return from that condition of nonexistence, but this time with "organized religion", including the Roman Catholic Hierarchy, in the saddle. "I caught sight of a woman sitting upon a scarlet-colored wild beast that was full of blasphemous names and that had seven heads and ten horns." As for that many-membered beastly association of nations, "the wild beast that you saw was, but is not [during World War II], and yet is destined to ascend out of the abyss [as the United Nations]." In man's history till A.D. 1914 there had been seven great world powers, the seventh being the Anglo-American empire system. "And the wild beast that was but is not, it is also itself an eighth king [now known as the United Nations], but owes its existence to the seven, and it goes off into destruction." (Revelation 17:3, 8, 11, NW) Note that the prophecy says there was to be an eighth, which owes its existence to the seven previous ones. The conceiving of the former League of Nations was due to the seventh world power, and now the United Nations gets its chief support and backing from the same world power. Even the seat of this eighth world power, the United Nations, is within American territory.

[17] But despite all this, what? It is as Jesus prophesied: "On the earth anguish of nations, not knowing the way out because of the roaring of the sea and its agitation, while men become faint

---

16. How does Revelation, chapter 17, describe the postwar wild beast, and in its order what world power is it? 17. What international condition despite this did Jesus foretell, and what course are the nations induced to take?

out of fear and expectation of the things coming upon the inhabited earth." (Luke 21:25, 26, *NW*) So to many the future seems without hope. "We have reached the crossroads and no one knows the way out," thus a noted modern historian wrote. Fear and uncertainty grip the world as never before. To alleviate the condition the nations turn to collective security arrangements, to regional organizations and to racial and religious blocs, in addition to the United Nations.

[18] How evident it is that the mighty spirit ruler, Satan, is now grouping his forces for the war of Armageddon, and man is merely a pawn in the hands of the ruler of the demons! Worldly conflicts have incorrectly been labeled as Armageddon. Some fear Armageddon will be the eventual conflict between capitalism and communism. Others express concern that some ruthless power may, through the use of atomic energy, destroy both the nations and our earth. But not so! The end of the world will be no burning up of the literal earth. (Ecclesiastes 1:4; Isaiah 45:12, 18) That would not put an end to the spirit demons, though it might to man. The coming war of Armageddon will be Jehovah's fight in which all wickedness will be swept from the universe. Revelation 16:14-16 calls it "the war of the great day of God the Almighty". (*NW*) It will completely destroy the invisible and visible parts of Satan's world, and thus it will spell the accomplished end of this wicked old world. It will be the climax of the tribulation which Jesus predicted, saying: "Then there will be great tribulation such as has not occurred since

18, 19. How do many view Armageddon, but what is it Scripturally?

the world's beginning until now, no, nor will occur again."—Matthew 24:21, *NW*.

[19] Revelation 19:11-21 symbolically describes the King Jesus Christ as riding upon a white horse at the head of Jehovah's vast host of heavenly armies, judging and carrying on war in righteousness. Will men and demons be able to oppose such power? Modern science with its newly found "force of the universe" will pale into nothingness as compared with the mighty forces unleashed by Jehovah and his King in the universal war of Armageddon.

[20] The urgency of the world situation as the complete end draws near cannot be denied. Jesus warned all lovers of truth and righteousness to flee to Jehovah's theocratic system of things, symbolized by the ark of Noah's day. There we may be hid, as Zephaniah 2:3 (*AS*) tells us: "Seek ye Jehovah, all ye meek of the earth, that have kept his ordinances; seek righteousness, seek meekness: it may be ye will be hid in the day of Jehovah's anger." While the world writhes in anguish because of its woes, and while the message of God's kingdom is a sore plague to supporters of Satan's organization, Jehovah's anointed witnesses and their good-will companions are optimistic and rejoice despite the sufferings heaped upon them, for these see that deliverance is near. They do as Jesus said in his prophecy: "As these things start to occur, raise yourselves erect and lift your heads up, because your deliverance is getting near."—Luke 21:28, *NW*.

---

20. In view of the urgency of the world situation, what should people of good will do?

CHAPTER XXII

"A NEW EARTH"

" A NEW earth!" What can it mean? The burning up of our present planet, and its replacement by a new globe? No, not that; for the sure Word of God declares: "The earth abideth for ever." (Ecclesiastes 1:4; Psalms 78:69; 119:90) But that there will be a new earth is made certain by the Creator's own promise: "Behold, I create new heavens and a new earth: and the former shall not be remembered, nor come into mind." (Isaiah 65:17) If, then, not a new earthly sphere, what is the "new earth"? What conditions will prevail in it, and how and when will it come into existence? Doubtless questions like those fill your mind, as you consider the prospect of a new earth.

[2] The term "earth", as used in the Bible, does not always apply to this inanimate globe. In Psalm 96:1 (*AS*), for example, the command is issued: "Sing unto Jehovah, all the earth." Not to the literal planet is this exhortation given, but to intelligent human servants of the Most High, who dwell in the earth. In like manner the expression "a new earth" is used to identify, not the planet itself, but a new human society under new social arrangements. It can rightly be said that God's perfect human son Adam served in Eden as the

---

1. Why does not the "new earth" mean a new planet?
2. In what sense are the words "earth" and "a new earth" used in the Scriptures?

animate "earth" or visible part of the Creator's original righteous world. "The first man is out of the earth and made of dust." (1 Corinthians 15:47, *NW*) Had Adam remained obedient to his Maker, he would undoubtedly have occupied a prophetic position, handing down to his offspring God's perfect law, by virtue of which the paradise of Eden would be spread to the four quarters of the earth. However, disobedience lost for Adam forever the blessed privilege of serving as God's earthly representative.

[3] Nevertheless, God will have on earth righteous, faithful representatives, men of perfect hearts through whom his just decrees and endless blessings will be dispensed to the human race. Not from among sin-laden worldly rulers alive today will these be selected, but from among men who prove faithful servants and witnesses of God. "Incredible!" you may say, "because that would include many men now long dead." That is true: it will include many such men, according to what the Bible reveals. In Hebrews, chapter eleven, are enumerated the names of some members of a great "cloud of witnesses", persons who lived before Jesus' death and resurrection. (Hebrews 11:1 to 12:1) The record preserved of their lives stamps them as being trustworthy, men of faith and devotion, centering their hopes solely in the then future "city [or Kingdom] having real foundations and the builder and creator of which is God". Faithfulness to death earned for them the promise of a "better resurrection", a raising to life, not in heaven, but on earth under a divine government

---

3. What is God's promise respecting the faithful men of old, and why will they be thus rewarded?

under which they need never die again but may attain to human perfection.—Hebrews 11:10, 35, *NW;* Acts 2:34; Matthew 11:11.

⁴ Many of the faithful men of old had the privilege of actually being the forefathers of the man Jesus and are spoken of as "fathers". (Romans 9:5; 15:8; Acts 3:13) Today, however, these "fathers" of Jesus are dead, and also the other faithful witnesses of old like them, whereas Christ Jesus is fully alive. (Hebrews 11:13; Acts 2:29; Revelation 1:18) Can they return to life and be commissioned to serve in a representative capacity in the "new earth"? Yes, but only through the life-restoring power of Jesus, who said: "I am the resurrection, and the life." Thus, those called "fathers" and their fellow faithful ones must become the children of the "everlasting Father", Christ Jesus, through the resurrection. (John 11:25; Isaiah 9:6) Hence God's Word prophetically said to Christ Jesus the King: "Instead of thy fathers shall be thy children." And what is the special position to which these resurrected servants are appointed? The latter part of Psalm 45:16 answers: "Whom thou mayest make princes [*sarim*] in all the earth."

⁵ By an early resurrection many faithful witnesses long dead, from Abel onward, will be made available for a new, visible governing organization created by God's hands. Along with them many faithful witnesses of today, who are the Right Shepherd's "other sheep", will be made "princes", even surviving the war of Armageddon into the

---

4. How do Jesus' "fathers" become children, and what position is in store for them?
5. How will the "new earth" differ from the present "earth", and when will it be established?

new earth. (John 10:16) What a contrast with the
Devilish wicked earth of today the "new earth"
will be! Justice, goodness and uprightness will
mark every move of its "princes", as they work
in perfect accord with their King-Father, Christ
Jesus. (Isaiah 66:22; 2 Peter 3:10, 13; Psalm
85:11) And when may we expect the setting up
of the "new earth"? After Armageddon, although
now a "great crowd" of those who will become a
part of that "new earth" is being gathered.—Revelation 7:9-17, NW.

"OTHER SHEEP"

⁶ Yes, even now the King of the new world is
being hailed by a "great crowd" of persons, "out of
all nations and tribes and peoples and tongues".
These are persons now living who diligently study
God's Word, in their desire to acquire right knowledge. They are lovers of righteousness, who during
this interval of God's patience come out of the
great tribulation inflicted upon this world and dedicate their lives wholly to the continual service of
their God and his Lamb Christ Jesus. (Revelation
7:9, 10, 14, 15, NW) By him these meek persons
of good will have been named his "other sheep",
for they are not of the heavenly "little flock".
(Luke 12:32) Their hope of future life lies in a
paradise earth. In this day they delight to share
in the obligation resting on every Christian, that
of preaching this good news of God's kingdom.
Gladly they go, from house to house, on the streets,
and in public-meeting places, making known to
righteously disposed Catholics, Protestants, Jews,

---

6. Who are the "great crowd", and how are they distinguished from the rest of mankind?

and those professing other religious beliefs, or none at all, God's way to life.—Matthew 24:14; Revelation 22:17.

[7] Unbelievable as it may sound, many of these "other sheep" may never die. They were foreshadowed by Noah's sons and daughters-in-law, who, because of their faith and righteous works in the midst of a corrupt world, passed alive through the flood with Noah. As in Noah's day, so today, wickedness overruns the earth. Millions forget God and seek to perpetuate this old world. The "other sheep", however, remember their Creator, hold fast their faith, and break clean away from the satanic elements that now reign. Zealously they preach of Armageddon's approach and of the Kingdom blessings to follow. Continuing faithful till Armageddon, the other sheep who seek righteousness and meekness will, like the flood survivors of Noah's day, be hid in the antitypical ark, Jehovah's theocratic system of things, and come through into an earth cleansed of evil. (Genesis 6:5, 11, 18, 22; 7:1; Matthew 24:37; 25:31-46; Zephaniah 2:1-3; Isaiah 26:20) Those of the other sheep who die now rest assured of a "resurrection of life", with full enjoyment of the many earthly blessings promised, even the opportunity to be some of the "princes in all the earth". Cast now your eye to the future and glimpse some of the new world blessings in store.

NEW EARTH CONDITIONS

[8] The clearing out of the wicked rule paves the

---

7. Why is it that many of the "other sheep" may never die?

8. What will be one of the first privileges enjoyed by the "great crowd" in the "new earth"?

way for new visible rule of the "new earth" in which righteousness is to dwell. Then in all quarters of the globe the worshipful survivors of Armageddon will carry forward the new world society on the cleansed earth. "What shall we now do?" the other sheep may ask, as they then seek divine guidance through God's princely visible representatives. If any old-world war tanks, cannon and other murderous weapons are then to be found, the divine command will apply: 'Beat them into plowshares and pruninghooks'; for all weapons of destruction must be turned into implements of construction. In the new world this planet will never again be subjected to the ravages of international war, with its wanton flow of blood, its heartless brutality, and its tragic aftermath, for "nation shall not lift up sword against nation, neither shall they learn war any more".—Isaiah 2:4; Micah 4:3.

[9] Why should there ever be another international war? Those members of the "new earth" are not divided into opposing factions by bitter racial or national or religious differences. All such barriers to lasting peace and unity will have been stamped out. One worship remains: the clean, pure and right worship of the true God of the universe, Jehovah. It is this united worship of their Creator that binds together unbreakably the post-Armageddon o c c u p a n t s of our globe.—Isaiah 66:23; Zechariah 14:16.

[10] Then, with the end of worldly warfare, freedom in the full sense of the word sets in. Freedom

9. Why will the new world experience no international war?
10. Why will there be no cause for fear in the "new earth"?

from fear will be there, for no more will atomic or hydrogen bombs or the devilish demonic heavens hang like a threatening cloud over the people. Gone will be the need for armed troops to 'preserve international peace', or even a local police force, to subdue crime and maintain order. Lawlessness and vice, together with casualty-producing accidents, fires and floods, will be things of the old-world past. Neither will there then be millions of unemployed or displaced persons wandering aimlessly from one city to another, for Jehovah's promise is: "They shall sit every man under his vine and under his fig tree; and none shall make them afraid."—Isaiah 11:9; Micah 4:4.

[11] Famine and drought, together with rationing and black marketing, will cease for all time, as freedom from want makes itself felt. Jehovah's assurance is that "then shall the earth yield her increase". The terrestrial globe, free of those who ruin the earth, takes on a new appearance, developing into a place of Edenic grandeur and beauty such as the human mind cannot now visualize. (Psalm 67:6; Revelation 11:18; Psalm 96:11, 12; Genesis 2:8, 9) Righteous man will again be authorized to "subdue" the earth and "have dominion" over the lower animal creation, for then even the beasts of the field will be at peace with one another and their guardian, man.—Genesis 1:28; Isaiah 11:6-9; 65:25.

[12] The visible part of the new world will be a disease-less "new earth", for the curative power of the divine Physician will be turned toward mankind. Aches and pains will die out, as radiant

11. What changes may be expected with the literal earth, and with what result to man?
12. What will happen to sickness, old age, and death?

health, unmarred by cancer, influenza, or even a
toothache, implants itself in every soul. (Matthew
4:23; Psalm 103:2, 3; Revelation 21:4) This means
the vanishing of old age, with its wrinkled skin,
its gray hair, its feebleness. It means that vigor-
ous, energetic youth, so fleeting today, will be the
eternal lot of every faithful human. To enjoy these
blessings perpetually necessitates the removal of
man's long-time enemy, death. And this Jehovah,
the Fountain of life, has promised to bring about.
(Psalm 36:9; 1 Corinthians 15:26) Describing this
sublime new world state, his recorded Word fore-
tells: "I saw a new heaven and a new earth."
"Look! the tent of God is with humankind, and
he will reside with them, and they will be his peoples. And God himself will be with them. And he
will wipe out every tear from their eyes, and death
will be no more, neither will mourning nor outcry
nor pain be any more. The former things have
passed away." (Revelation 21:1-4, *NW*) No dream
is this, nor propaganda scheme to solicit support
for a man-made "better world", but it is the truth.
Such conditions are certain to come, for Jehovah
added to the above words this command: "Write,
because these words are trustworthy and true."

[13] But that is not all, for the Armageddon survivors will enjoy also the grand privilege of fulfilling a divine mandate to procreate. This earth was
created, not to be destroyed, but to be inhabited
forever by righteous, perfect men and women.
(Isaiah 45:12, 18; Proverbs 10:30) To this end
God commanded the perfect pair in Eden: "Be
fruitful and multiply and fill the earth." (Genesis
1:28, *Ro; Dy*) Sadly, through sin Adam and Eve

---

13. What mandate will Armageddon survivors be privileged to fulfill, and when was suchlike first issued?

became unrighteous and forfeited the privilege of bringing forth a righteous race. But God's purpose never fails; his mandate to have righteous creatures bring forth offspring of their kind will be carried out. (Isaiah 14:24, 27; 55:11) But when, and how?

¹⁴ Following the deluge of Noah's day, Jehovah repeated to the flood-survivors his mandate: "Be fruitful and multiply and fill the earth." Although counted righteous by reason of their faith, the family of Noah could not, in reality, fulfill this mandate. (Genesis 9:1, *Ro;* Hebrews 11:7) But why? Because Jesus had not yet come, to relieve men of inherent sin and condemnation. (Romans 5:12; 1 John 1:7) The reissuing of the mandate to fill the earth following the flood was, therefore, but a small-scale pattern of the real fulfillment by those whom Noah's sons and daughters-in-law pictured, namely, the "great crowd" of Armageddon survivors. In the purified earth, free from evil satanic influence, and with the sin-canceling merit of Christ's sacrifice operating toward them, the Armageddon survivors under the direction of the King and his visible princes will marry and bring forth children in righteousness, to the glory of God. (Matthew 24:37-39) At birth their offspring will be born in the way of life. Hence infant-death with its overwhelming grief will be unknown. Every child, reared in the "discipline and authoritative advice of Jehovah", will have full opportunity for life through Christ the King. Any not desiring to serve Jehovah will be executed, rightly. —Isaiah 65:20, 23; 38:19; Ephesians 6:4, *NW;* Psalm 145:20.

---

14. Under what conditions and with what results will they fulfill that mandate?

RETURN OF THE DEAD

[15] The carrying out of the mandate to fill the earth will not proceed to the extent of making it inconvenient and impossible to accommodate the resurrection of those dead in the memorial tombs. Filling the earth will include transforming it into a paradise like Eden and will not require the full thousand years of Christ's reign. During that time the Devil and his demons are in the abyss into which they have been hurled bound, and his death-dealing organization will be out of existence. An extensive educational work will therefore be necessary in the course of the thousand-year reign when millions of "unrighteous" dead, needing instruction in God's law, are scheduled to arise from their tombs. At the very end of this period the abyssed Devil and his demons will be released. His mental attitude unchanged, he will again seek to usurp Jehovah's position of universal sovereignty and endeavor to turn all perfected mankind against God. Some will be misled, like Adam in Eden, while those who keep integrity in this concluding test of faith will share in the final vindication of Jehovah's sovereignty. Those supporting Satan will, with the Devil himself, be cast into the "lake of fire and sulphur". "This means the second death, the lake of fire." They are drowned in everlasting destruction, and for them there is no resurrection.—Revelation 20:1-15; 21:8, NW.

[16] Then, in the righteous world, the Almighty

---

15. What will the thousand-year reign do for those in the graves, and what test will mark the end of that reign?

16. With what conditions and how long will the new world last?

by means of his kingdom will shower down upon earth's billions of perfect, loyal inhabitants an overflow of divine blessings that will fill their hearts with everlasting gladness. Here will be a world without Adamic death, illness, sorrow, tears, or religious confusion. A secure world it will be, worshiping Jehovah and filled with love and joy and all things desirable. It will remain, not for a thousand, or a million, or even a thousand-million years, but forever.—Psalm 72:5-7.

[17] This is the world everlasting. Would you enjoy living in it? If yes, then become one of the "other sheep" now, share in giving out the heart-cheering proclamation of the Kingdom, and be assured of God's blessing, guidance and protection, as your steps lead you into full realization of the glorious prospect of life ahead.—Psalms 148:12, 13; 145:10-13, 21.

---

17. What must you do to gain life in the world everlasting?

CHAPTER XXIII

RESURRECTION

FROM the time that the first mortal man fell in death till this very hour countless millions have gone to untimely graves. Disease and pestilence have gnawed at the vitals of those of humankind. By means of violence in war, accident, fire, flood and kindred calamities men have hastened to the realms of the enemy, death. Facing these grim realities, many yearning persons ask: "Are we destined to live only a few troubled years on this earth, then to enter the grave never to return? Is there hope that those who have entered the tomb can ever live again?"

[2] In seeking a satisfying answer the levelheaded person wisely looks to a truthful source, God's Word. There he finds words of comfort and light. He sees that men of old, such as Abraham, Job and Isaiah, had kindled within them the hope of living again on earth amid more happy conditions. Concerning a faithful friend of God it is written: "By faith Abraham . . . reckoned that God was able to raise [his son Isaac] up even from the dead." (Hebrews 11:17-19, NW) Job in his distress testified that a release would come and that God would call and he would answer him from the grave. He

---

1. What unhappy conditions have hastened humankind into the realms of death, and so what questions are often asked?

2. Where does a levelheaded person look for the answer, and what words of comfort are found regarding the hope for the dead?

said: "Oh that thou wouldest hide me in Sheol, that thou wouldest keep me secret, until thy wrath be past, that thou wouldest appoint me a set time, and remember me! If a man die, shall he live again? All the days of my warfare would I wait, till my release should come. Thou wouldest call, and I would answer thee: thou wouldest have a desire to the work of thy hands." (Job 14:13-15, *AS*) Isaiah too voiced his faith in God's power, saying: "He hath swallowed up death for ever; and the Lord Jehovah will wipe away tears from off all faces."—Isaiah 25:8, *AS;* see also Luke 20:37, 38.

³ That the trust and confidence of these and of others having kindred faith are certain to bear fruit in due time, we have this consoling assurance by the "firstborn from the dead", even Jesus: "Do not marvel at this, because the hour is coming in which all those in the memorial tombs will hear his voice and come out, those who did good things to a resurrection of life, those who practiced vile things to a resurrection of judgment." Paul, too, at Athens declared: "God . . . has furnished a guarantee to all men in that he has resurrected him from the dead." (Acts 17:30, 31 and John 5:28, 29, *NW*) So the raising of Jesus was a basis of faith or a guarantee given to men that they may confidently rely upon God's promises to raise the dead.

⁴ The resurrection of Jesus is no illusion or imagined thing, even though religious leaders of that day tried unsuccessfully by their puny efforts

---

3. What assurance did Jesus and Paul give regarding the dead?
4. What proof does Paul bring forward to show that the resurrection of Jesus was no illusion or imagined thing?

to thwart the Son of God's coming forth from the grave. (Matthew 27:62-66) Paul was able to testify so confidently to this important fact of the resurrection because he had seen the glory of the risen Lord, while en route to Damascus. Not only that, but he recalls for us the witnesses who saw Jesus after he was raised from the dead: "He appeared to Cephas, then to the twelve. After that he appeared to upward of five hundred brothers at one time, . . . After that he appeared to James, then to all the apostles; but last of all he appeared also to me as if to one born prematurely."—1 Corinthians 15:5-8, *NW;* see also Acts 13:29-37 and Matthew 28:5-9, 16.

⁵ Satan and the demons, after failing to destroy the faith of Jehovah's people in the resurrection, then sought to obscure the true meaning of this doctrine. They caused wrong beliefs about it to be fostered and taught by apostates. "These very men have deviated from the truth, saying that the resurrection has already occurred, and they are subverting the faith of some." (2 Timothy 2:18, *NW*) Arguing and teaching that the resurrection was only in a spiritual sense and so was in the past for Christians and that it was out of date, this led others into error and thus into a course that made them unfit for life. Later the pagan doctrine of the "inherent immortality of human souls" was introduced and adopted into the apostate "Christian" organization. Belief in that teaching wrecked man's true Christian faith, because it set at nought the Scriptural truth that at death the human soul goes to the grave where "there is

5. Failing to destroy Christian faith in the resurrection, what further schemes did Satan pursue and with what results?

no work, nor device, nor knowledge, nor wisdom". (Ecclesiastes 9:10) It confused the fact that the dead must remain in the grave or condition of death until God's time to bring them forth, after he established his kingdom.

[6] None of the loyal, faithful men of old were resurrected before Jesus came to this earth, nor did they believe in inherent immortality of the soul. Rather the Scriptural accounts about them show they died and that in death they were unconscious as being asleep, but from this death sleep they will be awakened in Jehovah's due time. To Moses he said: "Behold, thou shalt sleep with thy fathers." David also knew that he must sleep in death, for God had told him: "When thy days be fulfilled, . . . thou shalt sleep with thy fathers." (Deuteronomy 31:16; 2 Samuel 7:12) Later, at Pentecost, Peter said to the Jews: "Brothers, it is allowable to speak with freeness of speech to you concerning the family head David, that he both deceased and was buried and his tomb is among us to this day. Actually David did not ascend to the heavens." (Acts 2:14, 29, 34, *NW*) Although they were still dead in Peter's day, yet the time must come when they would stand again in life. However, before their resurrection comes, others must first rise from the dead. There is a proper order in coming forth from the graves.

"FIRST RESURRECTION"

[7] Jesus was the first one to rise from death to

6. (a) How is the dead condition of men of old described? (b) What shows they did not go to heaven?
7. Who was the firstborn from the dead, and what testimony is there in proof of whether he was raised a human or spirit?

perfect life. Hence he is spoken of as "the first-born from the dead", "the firstfruits of those who have fallen asleep in death." This firstborn from the dead was raised from the grave, not a human creature, but a spirit. Hence he was the firstfruits, too, of those who would have a heavenly resurrection, "he being put to death in the flesh, but being made alive in the spirit."—Colossians 1:18; 1 Corinthians 15:20 and 1 Peter 3:18, *NW*.

[8] It was God's purpose, though, that Jesus should not be alone in his heavenly resurrection, but that others should be joined with him. (John 14:3) Regarding those who share with Christ Jesus not only in his sufferings but also in his resurrection Romans 8:29 says: "Those whom he gave his first recognition he also foreordained to be patterned after the image of his Son, that he might be the firstborn among many brothers." (*NW*) Thus a new way and a new hope were opened up for followers of the Son of God, those who would be Christ's brothers. This hope was that they might partake of the heavenly life on their resurrection from the dead. "For if we have become united with him in the likeness of his death, we shall certainly also be united with him in the likeness of his resurrection." (Romans 6:5, *NW*) The "likeness of his resurrection" is a heavenly resurrection such as Jesus had; and like him those partaking of it must die faithful to death.

[9] Paul expressed his hope to fellow Christians that he would be raised out of death to life in heaven: "knowing that he who raised Jesus up will raise us up also together with Jesus and will

---

8, 9. (a) Was Jesus to be alone in his heavenly resurrection? (b) What is the likeness of his resurrection, and how many share it?

present us together with you." (2 Corinthians 4:14, *NW*) This resurrection is the first as to time and importance; and "happy and holy is anyone having part in the first resurrection". (Revelation 20:6, *NW*) The Scriptures also indicate that the number of those who participate in this first resurrection is not great, but is a "little flock" and is limited to the Lord Jesus and the 144,000 members of the "body of the Christ".—Luke 12:32; Revelation 7:4; 14:1, 3.

¹⁰ Here the question arises: When do these come forth from the death condition? Paul, when nearing the end of his life on earth, wrote to Timothy and shed light on this matter. He said he had fought the right fight and had run his course to the finish and had observed the faith; and, because he had faith in a heavenly resurrection in that day of the Lord's appearing, "from this time on there is reserved for me the crown of righteousness, which the Lord, the righteous judge, will give me as a reward in that day, yet not only to me, but also to all those who have loved his manifestation." (2 Timothy 4:8, *NW*) Paul knew that not only he but also all those who have loved his manifestation must sleep in death until the second presence of the Lord. Therefore it is definitely fixed that none of Jesus' apostles or others like them were raised out of death until at least the second coming of Christ. "That day" to which they looked forward is the day of judgment which began with the Lord Jesus' coming to the temple in 1918.

¹¹ Paul exhorted his fellow Christians not to

---

10. How did Paul's expression of his hope show when these would come forth from the death condition?
11, 12. What is the meaning of 1 Thessalonians 4:13-15?

sorrow about those sleeping ones. They should have hope in God, because he had promised them a resurrection even as he had assured Jesus that He would not leave Jesus' soul in the grave. Read his words of comfort and hope at 1 Thessalonians 4:13-15 (NW): "We do not want you to be ignorant concerning those who are sleeping in death, that you may not sorrow just as the rest also do who have no hope. For if our faith is that Jesus died and rose again, so, too, those who have fallen asleep in death through Jesus God will bring with him. For this is what we tell you by Jehovah's word, that we the living who survive to the presence of the Lord shall in no way precede those who have fallen asleep in death."

¹² Clearly this means that the first resurrection is certain for those faithful followers who have fallen asleep in death through Jesus and that it will take place at the "presence of the Lord". It further means that when such resurrection occurs there would be some of that heavenly class alive here on earth. They would be busy at the work of gospel-preaching at the time he comes to judge, and they would then declare his judgment message. It also means that these will not "precede those who have fallen asleep in death". The glorious prospect which had been set before those asleep through Jesus will then be realized: "because the Lord himself will descend from heaven with a commanding call, with an archangel's voice and with God's trumpet, and those who are dead in union with Christ will rise first." (1 Thessalonians 4:16, NW) It being a spiritual resurrection, their rising first will be invisible to human eyes, as Jesus' resurrection was. It is quite fully described at 1 Corinthians 15:42-54.

¹³ What, now, about those who will at last be in heaven but who are of the remnant that survives to the Lord's invisible presence? When they finish their earthly ministry in death, must they sleep in death like those who died before the Lord's coming to the spiritual temple? The inspired record at 1 Corinthians 15:51, 52 (*NW*) answers: "Look! I tell you a sacred secret: We shall not all fall asleep in death, but we shall all be changed, in a moment, in the twinkling of an eye, during the last trumpet. For the trumpet will sound, and the dead will be raised up incorruptible, and we shall be changed." Hence those of that heavenly class who die in this day of the Lord's invisible presence have an instantaneous change, "in the twinkling of an eye." They do not sleep in death, but they are at once changed at death. They are also resurrected in the spirit.

EARTHLY RESURRECTION

¹⁴ Since the Scriptures plainly say that, besides Jesus Christ, the 144,000 are the only ones that have part in the heavenly resurrection, does this not argue that there will be no others who will come forth from the tomb? No; there will be an earthly resurrection. The greater mass of humankind will find life here on earth amid paradise conditions. Jesus' words are true: "All those in the memorial tombs will hear his voice and come out, those who did good things to a resurrection of life, those who practiced vile things to a resur-

---

13. What is the resurrection prospect of the heavenly class that survive on earth until Christ's second presence?
14, 15. (a) What others are raised from the dead, and where will they live? (b) Who are those who "did good things" and those who "practiced vile things"?

rection of judgment." (John 5:27-29, *NW;* Psalm 72:6-8; Isaiah 2:4) Those who "did good things" include such ones as Abraham, David, Daniel, and others, who "stopped the mouths of lions, stayed the force of fire, escaped the edge of the sword, . . . but other men were tortured because they would not accept release by some ransom, in order that they might attain a better resurrection". (Hebrews 11:33-35, *NW*) They will be made "princes in all the earth". In view of this future office they will be raised early. This occurring under God's kingdom of righteousness and of life, it will be a better resurrection.—Psalm 45:16.

¹⁵ Those who "did good things" would also include those of the "other sheep" class who may die now before the war of Armageddon in devotion to God and his kingdom. It appears that they will be brought forth early after Armageddon is past. On the other hand, "those who practiced vile things" are those who have had no faith and knowledge of God and who have done wrong because of being ignorant and being conceived in sin and shaped in iniquity. They have part in the resurrection of the rest of those of mankind to whom Christ's ransom sacrifice extends benefits. After being raised from the tombs they do not participate in bringing forth any children, but Jesus' words at Luke 20:34-36 show their opportunities.

¹⁶ A vision of the earthly resurrection appears at Revelation 20:12-15 (*NW*): "I saw the dead, the great and the small, standing before the throne,

16. How does Revelation 20:12-15 describe their resurrection, and how long is the day for this?

and scrolls were opened. . . . And the dead were judged out of those things written in the scrolls according to their deeds. And the sea gave up those dead in it, and death and Ha'des gave up those dead in them, and they were judged individually according to their deeds. And death and Ha'des were hurled into the lake of fire." The great and the small must await the appointed day for their coming out of the graves or Ha'des and the sea. All will be judged according to their future deeds on earth under God's kingdom. No crooked work will be permitted, "because he has set a day in which he purposes to judge the inhabited earth in righteousness by a man whom he has appointed." (Acts 17:31, *NW*) That judgment day is not twenty-four hours long. "One day is with Jehovah as a thousand years and a thousand years as one day."—2 Peter 3:7, 8, *NW*.

[17] This "day" will be long enough, and plenty of opportunity will be afforded, for all those who come forth from the graves to be judged "according to their deeds". The principle is re-emphasized, that "he that exercises faith in the Son has everlasting life; he that disobeys the Son will not see life, but the wrath of God remains upon him". (John 3:36, *NW*) So the disobedient one is judged adversely. It would be unreasonable and unscriptural to argue that everlasting life must be given to all persons, even to those who spurn with contempt God's loving provisions. Those who now continue willfully wicked and unreformable will doubtless be among those who will "sleep a perpetual sleep, and not wake, saith Jehovah".—Jeremiah 51:39, *AS*.

17, 18. Why will some not gain, and others gain, eternal life?

¹⁸ On the other hand, those who exercise faith will be saved. (Romans 10:9, 10) During Christ's millennial reign they will return from the realms of the enemy and will ultimately, if obedient, see the promise fulfilled, "As the last enemy, death is to be destroyed." (1 Corinthians 15:26, *NW*) At the end of Christ's reign, after successfully passing the final judgment test, these will attain to their justification to the right to life from Jehovah God, and that is why we read: "The rest of the dead did not come to life until the thousand years were ended." (Revelation 20:5, *NW*) So then their coming to perfect human life will be completed. Songs of praise will go up to Jehovah God, who will have given obedient mankind the victory over death through our Lord Jesus Christ.—1 Corinthians 15:57.

¹⁹ Belief in the resurrection, therefore, fills the believer with a glorious hope. He knows the time will come when hell or Ha'des, mankind's common grave, will be emptied and death traceable to Adam "will be no more, neither will mourning nor outcry nor pain be any more". (Revelation 21:4, *NW*) Those believers especially whom God has begotten to a hope of the "first resurrection" set us an example in laying aside all entangling things that may hinder them in obtaining life. Like Paul, they say: "I consider them as a lot of refuse, that . . . I may by any means attain to the earlier resurrection from the dead."—Philippians 3:8-11, *NW*.

---

19. What will believers in resurrection now do?

CHAPTER XXIV

THE JUDGMENT DAY

THERE are few subjects upon which the adversary has confused and blinded the people more than upon that of the "judgment day". Many well-meaning and sincere persons look ahead to the judgment day with a great deal of fear and mental anguish, because of what they feel will happen to them or their loved ones when that day arrives. This, despite the fact that the Scriptures refer to it as a very joyous occasion. Listen to the psalmist's prayer of thanksgiving as he contemplated that glad event: "Say among the nations, Jehovah reigneth: the world also is established that it cannot be moved: he will judge the peoples with equity. Let the heavens be glad, and let the earth rejoice; let the sea roar, and the fulness thereof; let the field exult, and all that is therein; then shall all the trees of the wood sing for joy before Jehovah; for he cometh, for he cometh to judge the earth: he will judge the world with righteousness, and the peoples with his truth." —Psalm 96:10-13, AS.

² According to this the judgment day is an event over which all creation, animate and inanimate, rejoice. The psalmist manifested no mental anguish

1. (a) What effect has the confusion that generally exists about the judgment day had upon well-meaning persons? (b) As what kind of occasion do the Scriptures refer to that day?
2. So will persons of good will fear the judgment day?

as he considered this glorious event. Neither has any other person who is of good will toward God any cause to fear His judgment day.

[3] The thousand-year judgment day mentioned in the Scriptures does not include all the judgments of Jehovah as these relate to mankind. This particular day refers to only one of these judgments. So, for one thing, it has no reference to the present judgment of the members of the "body of the Christ" referred to in 1 John 4:17 (NW), which says: "This is how love has been made perfect with us, that we may have freeness of speech in the day of judgment, because, just as that one is, so are we ourselves in this world."

[4] Nor does it refer to the present judgment of the nations which Zephaniah 3:8 (AS) describes: "Therefore wait ye for me, saith Jehovah, until the day that I rise up to the prey; for my determination is to gather the nations, that I may assemble the kingdoms, to pour upon them mine indignation, even all my fierce anger; for all the earth shall be devoured with the fire of my jealousy." This occurs before the thousand years of Christ's uninterrupted reign begins.

[5] Seeing that the millennial judgment day has reference to only one specific judgment of Jehovah, it is important for us to ascertain what judgment this is, to whom it applies. Then, to ascertain who the judge will be, we must consider his qualifications, how he will execute the judgment, and what the result will be when completed. It is only

3. Does this thousand-year judgment day include all of Jehovah's judgments relating to the human family?
4. Does this judgment day relate to the judgment of the nations?
5. What pertinent questions must we understand in order to appreciate the judgment day?

after we have answered these questions to our own satisfaction and in harmony with the Scriptures that we are in position really to appreciate Jehovah's judgment day.

⁶ Up to this point we have simply considered what the judgment day is not. Now, to find out what it is. In Acts 17:30, 31 (*NW*) the apostle Paul calls our attention to it in these words: "God has overlooked the times of such ignorance, yet now he is telling mankind that they should all everywhere repent. Because he has set a day in which he purposes to judge the inhabited earth in righteousness by a man whom he has appointed, and he has furnished a guarantee to all men in that he has resurrected him from the dead."

⁷ Five points stand out in this text as it relates to the judgment day. (1) Jehovah God himself set this day. (2) The object is to judge the inhabited earth in righteousness. (3) Jehovah has selected and appointed the judge. (4) That judge is Christ Jesus. (5) Jehovah has furnished his guarantee of this judgment day by resurrecting Christ Jesus. The fact of the judgment day is therefore established beyond the possibility of doubt.

⁸ The only point that may not be quite clear is the "inhabited earth" which is going to be judged. Is it not the present "inhabited earth" of which Satan the Devil is the ruler? (2 Corinthians 4:4; John 14:30; 1 John 5:19) Because of continuing in unbelief the present inhabitants of the earth are judged and condemned already. Hence the present earthly society or social arrangement will be de-

6. What did Paul tell the Athenians about the judgment day and its certainty?
7. What five outstanding points do we find in Paul's words?
8. What "inhabited earth" is to be judged, and why?

stroyed. As 2 Peter 3:7 says: "By the same word
the heavens and the earth that are now are stored
up for fire and are being reserved to the day of
judgment and of destruction of the ungodly men."
(*NW*) The inhabited earth in question, then,
where the righteous judgment of Jehovah will
take place, must be the "inhabited earth to come"
after Armageddon, to which Paul refers in Hebrews 2:5 (*NW*), where he says: "It is not to
angels that he has subjected the inhabited earth
to come, about which we are speaking."

⁹ Thus we see that this particular judgment day
refers to a period of time in which Jehovah God
sits to judge all earth's inhabitants in the new
world of righteousness by his own appointed
Judge, Christ Jesus. It is the first thousand years
of the new world, and not a 24-hour day; for "one
day is with Jehovah as a thousand years and a
thousand years as one day". At 2 Peter 3:7, 8 (*NW*)
we are warned not to let this time feature escape
our notice. Hence anyone not inhabiting the earth
in the new world will not be involved in this particular judgment. All creatures who want to reap
its benefits must be in the new world.

WHY THEN, AND UPON SUCH

¹⁰ Now to the question, When does the judgment
day of mankind take place? It must be after the
judgment of the nations, for, at Psalm 110:1, 2
(*AS*), we read: "Jehovah saith unto my Lord, Sit
thou at my right hand, until I make thine enemies
thy footstool. Jehovah will send forth the rod of
thy strength out of Zion: rule thou in the midst

9. Summarize what we have found as to the judgment
day.
10, 11. After what preliminary execution of various of
God's judgments does the judgment day begin?

of thine enemies." Here Jehovah is telling us that for a period after his anointed King or Judge Christ Jesus ascended to heaven he would remain inactive as to setting up the Kingdom; but when Jehovah's due time would arrive he would be commissioned to go into action and rule. Verse 6 says: "He will judge among the nations, he will fill the places with dead bodies." This indicates he executes judgment on the nations at Armageddon, and destroys the wicked inhabitants of earth.

[11] The apostle John refers to when the Lord Jesus Christ begins to rule amidst his enemies, in these words: "The kingdom of the world has become the kingdom of our Lord and of his Christ, and he will rule as king for ever and ever." (Revelation 11:15, *NW*) The physical facts in fulfillment of Jesus' prophecies at Matthew 24, Mark 13 and Luke 21, and numerous other scriptures, clearly establish that Christ Jesus was enthroned as King by Jehovah in 1914. This was forcibly evidenced to us by the outbreak of World War I and the occurring of the other things enumerated in these prophecies. Therefore that date marked the time when Jehovah's King went into action against Satan's organization. In the spring of 1918 he came as Jehovah's Messenger to the temple and began judgment first of the "house of God" and then of the nations of this world. (1 Peter 4:17; Malachi 3:1-5; Matthew 25:31, 32) The executing of judgment against those nations takes place at the battle of Armageddon, where he will "fill the places with dead bodies" and will wound their invisible head, Satan the Devil, abyssing him for a thousand years. Then the new world of righteousness will begin, and with it the thousand-year day of judgment.—Revelation 20:1-3, 11-15.

[12] The question, Where does this judgment take place? must be quite well answered in the mind of everyone who has followed us to this point. It will be at the earth; for there the Judge and King will turn his attention. "He shall judge the poor of the people, he shall save the children of the needy, and shall break in pieces the oppressor. In his days shall the righteous flourish; and abundance of peace so long as the moon endureth. He shall have dominion also from sea to sea, and from the river unto the ends of the earth."—Psalm 72:4, 7, 8.

[13] So, then, to whom does this millennial judgment apply? Quite evidently it applies only to those who are on earth in the new world. The Scriptures clearly show that in the new world there will be on earth, first of all, people who survived Armageddon and who were living at the time of the new world's establishment and who could accept its terms. But many who died and entered their graves prior to its establishment will be raised to life on earth. As a consequence this judgment applies to both the living and the dead. At Acts 10:42 (*NW*) Peter said: "He ordered us to preach to the people and to give a thorough witness that this is the One decreed by God to be judge of the living and the dead." At 2 Timothy 4:1 (*NW*) Paul wrote: "I earnestly beg you before God and Christ Jesus, who is destined to judge the living and the dead, and by his manifestation and his kingdom." At John 5:28, 29 (*NW*) Jesus said: "The hour is coming in which all those in the memorial tombs will hear his voice and come out, those who did good things to a resurrection

---

12. Where does Psalm 72:4, 7, 8 show the judgment will take place?

13. To whom will this millennial judgment apply?

of life, those who practiced vile things to a resurrection of judgment." All this testimony eliminates any doubt about whether the dead as well as the living are included.

¹⁴ Not all persons who have lived and died on the earth during the past six thousand years will come forth to judgment in this judgment day. Adam, for example, had his final judgment in the garden of Eden, where he was sentenced. (Genesis 3:17-19; 1 Timothy 2:14) Others who will not come forth are those religionists who Jesus said could not escape the judgment of Gehenna because of being the seed of the Serpent: "Serpents, offspring of vipers, how are you to flee from the judgment of Gehenna?" (Matthew 23:33, *NW*) The apostle Paul referred to some such when he wrote: "The sins of some men are publicly manifest, leading immediately to judgment, but as for other men their sins also become manifest later."—1 Timothy 5:24, *NW*.

¹⁵ Those who die wicked beyond reform or correction and beyond redemption by Christ's blood will not be brought out of the grave to judgment in the new world. (Numbers 35:31) "Jehovah preserveth all them that love him; but all the wicked will he destroy." (Psalm 145:20, *AS*) Those who have sinned against the holy spirit will be barred: "Every kind of sin and blasphemy will be forgiven men, but the blasphemy against the spirit will not be forgiven. . . . whoever speaks against the holy spirit, it will not be forgiven him, no, not in the present system of things nor in that to come." (Matthew 12:31, 32, *NW*) All this goes to prove

---

14, 15. Will all humans who lived and died on this earth attain to that millennial judgment day, and what is the proof for it?

that this judgment narrows down to the living and the dead humans who can come under the benefit of the ransom sacrifice of Christ Jesus.

[16] In the judgment of the nations which began after Jehovah's Messenger and Judge came to the temple, the individuals of the nations are being divided from one another like sheep and goats. The goatlike persons show no appreciation of God's kingdom but reject the Kingdom message and its bearers and show them no help and kindness. They will be destroyed in the coming battle of Armageddon. The sheeplike hearers of the message rejoice at the Kingdom's coming and do good to the remnant or last members of "Christ's body" on earth and are gathered to the side of the Judge's favor. They will be spared alive during the war of Armageddon, similar to Noah and his family's survival of the flood, and will enter into the new world without dying. (Matthew 25:31-46) Continuing faithful to God and his King of the new world they will be approved throughout that thousand-year judgment day and will at its close gain the judgment of the right to eternal life. Being Armageddon survivors, they will be the "quick" or the "living" whom Christ Jesus judges.

[17] Another favored class due to receive the blessings of the judgment of the new world are those faithful servants of Jehovah God who lived prior to Jesus' death and resurrection. Many of them are mentioned in Hebrews, chapter 11, in which the apostle Paul says at verses 39, 40: "All these, although they had witness borne to them through their faith, did not get the fulfillment of the

16. Who are the "living" whom Christ will then judge?
17. Who of old time will enter into a favorable judgment, and with what privilege?

promise, as God foresaw something better for us, in order that they might not be made perfect apart from us." (*NW*) They could not enter into their reward before the congregation, the "us" class which Paul mentions, began to be glorified. The glorification of the congregation began after the Judge's coming to the temple. Faithful men among the witnesses of ancient time will be honored by being made visible representatives on earth of the heavenly Judge. Jehovah says to his King regarding those men: "Instead of thy fathers shall be thy children, whom thou mayest make princes in all the earth."—Psalm 45:16.

[18] In due time, all conditions on earth being in readiness, the hour will come when the Judge will utter his voice to the other human dead in the graves and then they will come out, "those who practiced vile things to a resurrection of judgment." (John 5:27-29, *NW*) They will include the evildoer to whom Jesus on the torture stake at Calvary said: "Truly I tell you today, You will be with me in Paradise."—Luke 23:43, *NW; Ro; Lamsa.*

[19] Jesus Christ could rightly speak that way because he will be the righteous Judge on judgment day. He himself said: "Just as the Father raises the dead up and makes them alive, so the Son also makes those alive whom he wants to. For the Father judges no one at all, but he has committed all the judging to the Son."—John 5:21, 22, *NW.*

THE JUDGE'S QUALIFICATIONS

[20] Now as to the qualifications of this Judge. The

---

18. In due time what other humans are resurrected?
19. To whom has God committed the judging of them?
20, 21. What are his qualifications for this office?

Scriptures say he served God his Father with a godly fear and learned obedience by the things which he suffered, and that hence those who meet his favorable judgment will be granted everlasting life. But let the Scriptures speak for themselves. Hebrews 5:7-9 (*NW*) says: "In the days of his flesh Christ offered up supplications and also petitions to the one who was able to save him out of death, with strong outcries and tears, and he was favorably heard for his godly fear. Although he was a Son, he learned obedience from the things he suffered, and after he had been made perfect he became responsible for everlasting salvation to all those obeying him."

²¹ Isaiah 11:1-4 (*AS*) foretold: "There shall come forth a shoot out of the stock of Jesse, and a branch out of his roots shall bear fruit. And the spirit of Jehovah shall rest upon him, the spirit of wisdom and understanding, the spirit of counsel and might, the spirit of knowledge and of the fear of Jehovah. And his delight shall be in the fear of Jehovah; and he shall not judge after the sight of his eyes, neither decide after the hearing of his ears; but with righteousness shall he judge the poor, and decide with equity for the meek of the earth." Hence that judgment holds no possibility of being thwarted by human limitations and frailties. The Judge's qualifications assure proper consideration of every circumstance affecting each one on trial.

²² How will the judgment of that great day operate toward the people? Revelation 20:11, 12 tells of the destruction of this old world and the beginning of the thousand-year judgment day, say-

22. According to what will humans then be judged, and when and how will their final test come?

ing: "I saw a great white throne and the one seated on it. From before him the earth and the heaven fled away, and no place was found for them. And I saw the dead, the great and the small, standing before the throne, and scrolls were opened. But another scroll was opened; it is the scroll of life. And the dead were judged out of those things written in the scrolls according to their deeds." (*NW*) They will not be judged by their past deeds, but on the basis of what their deeds will be during the judgment day they will be tried. Those obeying the King and Judge will gradually be lifted up out of their fallen condition to human perfection. All the while they will be learning righteousness from the Judge and through his earthly princes. At the end of the thousand-year day of judgment will come the final test upon all of earth's inhabitants then living, to determine who will be written in the book of those entitled to the right to everlasting life on earth. This final test will come by the loosing of Satan the Devil out of his restraint.—Revelation 20:7-9.

[23] All who then yield to Satan's temptations and misguidance will be judged unworthy and will be consigned to the "second death", symbolized by the "lake of fire". "This means the second death, the lake of fire. Furthermore, whoever was not found written in the book of life was hurled into the lake of fire." (Revelation 20:14, 15, *NW*) Those resisting Satan and abiding faithful in their integrity toward Jehovah God will receive the Judge's approval. Through him they will receive from God the gift of the right to eternal life in human perfection on a paradise earth.—Luke 20:35, 36.

---

23. In what two decisions will the judgment result?

CHAPTER XXV

DEDICATION TO GOD —THE WAY TO LIFE

HOW favored the lot of the first man was! He was perfect, enjoyed the right to life and had communion with his Creator. Being endowed with a measure of wisdom, justice, love and power, he was in the likeness of his Maker. As his visible representative he had dominion over the lower animals. He was given a beautiful home, Paradise, and a lovely helper, Eve, and a divine command or mandate to extend that garden to the earth's limits and to fill it with righteous creatures, all to God's glory. What blessings! What privileges! What a prospect!—Genesis 1:26-28.

[2] Instead of appreciating all that God had given him, man chose to take a selfish course, and so, through disobedience, lost all. Sentenced and unrepentant, he was driven from Paradise into a cursed earth, there to eke out a miserable existence until he returned to the dust. That unhappy lot he passed on to his offspring, even as we read: "Through one man sin entered into the world and death through sin, and thus death spread to all men because they had all sinned." (Genesis 3:17-19; Romans 5:12, *NW*) As a result, today the great majority of the human race are hastening down the broad road that leads to destruction. They even seem content to do so, getting ever

---

1. What blessings and prospects did the first man enjoy?
2. By reason of disobedience what resulted to him and his family?

farther away from the likeness of God and from
the hope of life.—Matthew 7:13.

³ A few honest hearts, however, are out of harmony with these evil conditions. Such sigh and
cry because of the abominations which they see
committed even in Christendom, and they are
weary of toiling and loaded down because of their
own weaknesses and shortcomings. Being honest,
they hunger and thirst for righteousness. Desiring
to come into harmony with their Maker, they seek
God, if they might grope for him and really find
him.—Acts 17:27, *NW*.

⁴ To find God one must first come to Jesus, for
he said: "No one comes to the Father except
through me." But neither can anyone come to
Jesus unless the Father draws him. (John 14:6;
6:44, *NW*) How does God draw such honest-
hearted ones to Jesus? By bringing them into contact with the truth as contained in his Word, the
Bible. Being meek and teachable, such ones repent
upon hearing of the true God and his purposes and
have a change of mind as regards sin and this
wicked world.

⁵ "Faith is not a possession of all people."
(2 Thessalonians 3:2, *NW*) But the honest hearts
exercise faith as they receive this knowledge. "So
faith follows the report. In turn, the report is
through the word about Christ." (Romans 10:17,
NW) And what is faith? "Faith is the assured expectation of things hoped for, the evident demon-
stration of realities though not beheld." (Hebrews
11:1, *NW*) Faith means that by reason of Bible

---

3. How do honest hearts show themselves out of harmony with present evil conditions?
4. How are these led to repent?
5. What does faith mean, and how is it obtained?

knowledge one has a firm assurance that God exists and that he will reward those who earnestly seek him, and that the Bible is his truth and man's sure guide. It further means to accept Jesus not only as a Teacher and Example but also as one's Savior and Ransomer. Such faith causes one to be converted or turned, to change his course of action. —Hebrews 11:6; Matthew 1:21; 20:28; 13:15; Acts 3:19.

[6] Making progress in knowledge and understanding, such one then appreciates Jesus' words: "If anyone wants to come after me, let him disown himself and pick up his torture stake and follow me continually." (Matthew 16:24, NW) That means to give up one's own will and dedicate oneself to do God's will, just as Jesus did. Dedication means a giving of oneself over to God. To be acceptable to him it must be an unconditional surrender. One cannot say: "Jehovah, I will do your will if—." No, for that would be selfish and would indicate a lack of faith. One having faith appreciates that 'it is not in man to direct his steps' and that God with his perfect wisdom, justice, love and power knows best; and that to serve him is not only the one right thing but also the one wise thing to do. So faith is demonstrated by simply agreeing to do God's will, being content with whatever place God may have for one.

[7] Jesus made a public confession of his dedication to do his Father's will. How? By being baptized in water. He instructed his followers to "make disciples of people of all the nations, bap-

---

6. How does one really demonstrate his faith?
7. What public confession of one's dedication should be made, as shown by what example and commandment of Jesus?

tizing them in the name of the Father and of the Son and of the holy spirit". Therefore each one that has agreed to do God's will should be baptized. —Psalm 40:8; Hebrews 10:7; Mark 1:9-11; Matthew 28:19, *NW*.

[8] Perhaps someone will say: "I was baptized when a mere infant, by being sprinkled. Is that not enough?" No, it is not. Why not? Well, the Bible word translated "baptize" in our English versions is the Greek word *baptizein,* and literally means to dip, to immerse, to cover with liquid. For this reason some emphatic modern translations, such as Rotherham's and the *Diaglott,* use the words "dip", "dipper," "immerse," and "immerser", instead of "baptize" and "baptist". Further, when a man dedicates himself to do God's will, he agrees to give up his own preference, becoming, as it were, dead to his own will. Only immersion could be a proper symbol of that. The being dipped under the water pictures the death to one's own will. The being lifted out of it pictures being raised and made alive to the doing of God's will.

[9] Besides, the candidates for baptism are to be baptized "in the name of the Father and of the Son and of the holy spirit". This means they must recognize Jehovah not only as their Life-giver, but also as the Supreme One to whom they owe allegiance and service. They must recognize the part the Son performs in Jehovah's purpose and what he has done for them. They must also recognize the holy spirit as the active force of God which will help them to carry out their dedica-

---

8. What facts show how water baptism is to be performed?

9. In whose name must baptism be done, and what does this mean?

tion and that they are at all times to act in harmony with it. Only one's immersion in recognition of these truths constitutes a proper symbol of dedication. Only such is Scriptural water baptism.

THE WAY TO HEAVENLY GLORY

¹⁰ All who by reason of faith in Jehovah God and in Christ Jesus dedicate themselves to do God's will and then faithfully carry out their dedication will be rewarded with everlasting life. (Romans 6:23) However, that life will not be the same for all. The Bible plainly shows that some of these, that is, 144,000, will share in heavenly glory with Christ Jesus, while the others will enjoy the blessings of life down here on earth. (Revelation 14:1, 3; Micah 4:1-5) God bestows his gifts according to his purposes and as it pleases him to do so. As all his gifts are unmerited favors, it is for his creatures to accept them gratefully.—2 Corinthians 9:15.

¹¹ God having fixed a time for every purpose, his time to give creatures on earth the opportunity to get in line for a heavenly reward has been from A.D. 29 onward and has been called the "day for salvation". (2 Corinthians 6:2, *NW*) It began with Jesus at Jordan and is now rapidly nearing its end. During this time the heavenly hope was made known to those who dedicated themselves to God. But, since "flesh and blood cannot inherit God's kingdom", the dedicated ones would have to be brought forth as God's spiritual sons, begotten by

10. What prospect is set before the one who agrees to do God's will, and what determines the particular prospect?
11. When did the heavenly hope begin to be held out, and what is necessary for those humans who are to realize that hope?

his spirit to a heavenly hope, before God could give them such a glorious reward.—1 Corinthians 15:50, *NW*.

¹² For such to enter on the heavenly way they must undergo the sacrifice of all human life right and hopes, even as Jesus did. (Colossians 3:1-4) But Jesus, being perfect, had access to God and had the right to life as a human creature. However, his followers are imperfect and sinful and so under condemnation. They do not have access to God and have neither the right to life nor a body acceptable to offer as a sacrifice. How, then, is it possible for such to be offered by Jehovah's High Priest Christ Jesus? By being justified or declared righteous; that is, by having righteousness imputed or reckoned to them. How is this accomplished?

¹³ First of all, the creature must exercise faith in God's provision, meaning faith in the shed blood of Christ. This he shows by dedicating himself to God through Christ. Christ Jesus then acts as an advocate, covering the sins of such dedicated one by the merit of his sacrifice. The dedicated one is now in position to be justified or declared righteous by God, and thus he has access to God through Christ Jesus. He has an acceptable body and the right to perfect life on earth, and all this can be presented for sacrifice with Christ Jesus. Thus we see the truth of the scriptures: "We have been declared righteous as a result of faith, . . . we have been declared righteous now by his blood." "God is the One who declares them righteous." —Romans 5:1, 9; 8:33, *NW*.

¹⁴ God now choosing them, he accepts the High

12. What must be imputed to them, and why must it be?
13. What factors enter into their justification?
14. By what steps are they brought forth as spiritual sons?

Priest's sacrifice of the dedicated ones and causes his active force or holy spirit to act upon them so as to bring them forth as spiritual sons with the hope of life in the heavens and he acknowledges them as his sons. God's holy spirit does not operate toward these apart from his Word of truth, and therefore such are spoken of as being "born from water [truth] and spirit". So to them it is said: "Because he willed it, he brought us forth by the word of truth." (John 3:5 and James 1:18, *NW*) As Jesus' anointing at Jordan marked the beginning of him as a spiritual son, so Pentecost after his ascension to heaven marked the beginning of spiritual sonship for his followers, they there being baptized by the holy spirit.—Matthew 3:17; Acts 1:5; 2:3, 4, 17.

[15] This making of them new by the holy spirit is a call, putting them in line for heavenly glory with Christ Jesus. (Titus 3:3-5; 2 Thessalonians 2:13, 14) They now have new hopes, new aims, new relationships. "If anyone is in union with Christ, he is a new creation; the old things passed away, look! new things have come into existence." (2 Corinthians 5:17, *NW*) Christ Jesus being the Anointed Head, such new creatures by becoming members of his body receive of his anointing. "You have an anointing from the holy one; all of you have knowledge." Thus for them there is a baptism into "Christ's body". "For truly by one spirit we were all baptized into one body." (1 John 2:20, 27 and 1 Corinthians 12:12, 13, *NW*) The holy spirit with which they are thus sealed is a token in advance or a pledge guaranteeing them their heavenly inheritance. "Beloved ones, now we

15. To what are they then called, and how are they then baptized?

are children of God, but as yet it has not been made manifest what we shall be. We do know that whenever he is made manifest we shall be like him, because we shall see him just as he is." —Ephesians 1:13, 14 and 1 John 3:2, *NW*.

SANCTIFICATION

[16] Before such members of Christ's body can receive their heavenly inheritance they must be set apart more and more from this world and to the holy service of Jehovah God, demonstrating their dependability by carrying out their dedication faithfully until death. This work of setting them apart the Scriptures speak of as "sanctification": "For this is what God wills, the sanctifying of you." (1 Thessalonians 4:3, *NW*) Both the Creator and the dedicated ones have a part in this, as indicated at Leviticus 20:7, 8 (*AS*): "Sanctify yourselves . . . I am Jehovah who sanctifieth you." God furnishes the truth that sanctifies: "Sanctify them by means of the truth; your word is truth." (John 17:17, *NW*) His holy spirit or active force is an aid in this respect. On the other hand, the sanctified one must earnestly study God's Word so as to discern His will. He must seek to apply the things that he learns and must not resist or grieve God's holy spirit, but must seek at all times to be led by it.—Matthew 7:21; Romans 8:14; Ephesians 4:30.

[17] Having been called to be "saints" or "holy ones", they must be holy even as God is holy. "In accord with the holy one who called you, do you also become holy yourselves in all your conduct."

16. What is sanctification, and how is it accomplished?
17. What admonitions must the ones being sanctified heed?

(Romans 1:7 and 1 Peter 1:15, *NW*) That means
they must be entirely devoted to God and righteousness. They must keep their minds fixed on the
things above, and deaden their fallen cravings.
(Colossians 3:2, 5) They must do as Proverbs 4:23
says: "Keep thy heart with all diligence; for out
of it are the issues of life." Living up to their dedication is a serious matter. They are therefore further admonished: "Keep working out your own
salvation with fear and trembling."—Philippians
2:12, *NW*.

¹⁸ Being anointed followers of Christ Jesus, they
too must preach the good news of the Kingdom
and comfort all who mourn and must honor Jehovah's name. (Matthew 4:17; Luke 4:17-21; John
17:4, 6) By doing so they will, of course, incur
the hatred of Satan and his world just as Jesus
did. "In fact, all those desiring to live with godly
devotion in association with Christ Jesus will also
be persecuted." (John 15:19; 2 Timothy 3:12,
NW) If they resist Satan and his world and maintain integrity until death, they are assured of the
"crown of life", immortality, divine nature.—Revelation 2:10; 1 Corinthians 15:53, 54; 2 Peter 1:4.

¹⁹ Wanting to do what is right, desiring life, loving Jehovah for what he is and for all he has done
for them, longing to see him and his Son Jesus
Christ, and, above all, desiring to have part in
vindicating Jehovah's sovereignty, those dedicated
ones have no alternative. They must carry out
their agreement. To turn back would mark them
as agreement-breakers, worthy of death, annihila-

18. What work must they do as anointed followers of
Christ, and under what test must they remain faithful?
For what reward?
19. From what dare they not turn back, and why not?

tion. (Proverbs 27:11; Romans 1:31, 32; Hebrews 10:38, 39) God consecrates the faithful ones to his service.

²⁰ Today, consecrated Christians who have these heavenly hopes and who are faithful to their commission to preach the good news are the ones God is using to direct his work in the earth of proclaiming his name and kingdom. As compared with the entire body of the Christ they are only a remnant and their number is daily decreasing as one by one they finish their course in death. This remnant of them is known as the "faithful and discreet slave" collectively. (Revelation 7:4-8; 12:17; Matthew 24:45-47, NW) However, the preaching work is ever increasing. Why? Because earthly hopes are now extended to an increasing number of righteously disposed persons, and these are joining with the remnant and having an ever greater share in the work. Jesus called these his "other sheep", as distinguished from his sheep who have heavenly hopes and whom he calls a "little flock". All these also he must bring in order that at last there may be one flock under one Shepherd.—John 10:16, NW; Luke 12:32.

²¹ For these other sheep to receive their reward of everlasting life on earth and blessings under the Kingdom, they too must make a dedication to God through Christ. They too must carry out their dedication faithfully, conforming to the best of their ability to God's standard of righteousness. Surviving Armageddon, they need "never see death" in the flesh.—John 8:51.

---

20. What work are a remnant of these now directing in the earth, and who are joining them in ever-increasing numbers?
21. What is required of these other sheep, and with what reward?

CHAPTER XXVI

LIFE TRANSFORMED
BY MAKING THE MIND OVER

BY TURNING from traditions and philosophies of worldly men and by taking God's Word and thus 'letting God be found true', we have come to appreciate more the comparison he makes between himself and shortsighted, low-minded man, saying: "My thoughts are not your thoughts, neither are your ways my ways, saith Jehovah. For as the heavens are higher than the earth, so are my ways higher than your ways, and my thoughts than your thoughts." We are convinced that his word is true because he upholds it and makes it come true, for he adds: "As the rain cometh down and the snow from heaven, and returneth not thither, but watereth the earth, and maketh it bring forth and bud, and giveth seed to the sower and bread to the eater; so shall my word be that goeth forth out of my mouth: it shall not return unto me void, but it shall accomplish that which I please, and it shall prosper in the thing whereto I sent it." (Isaiah 55:8-11, AS) The loftiness of his thoughts and ways is uplifting to us. The infallibility of his word makes it true knowledge and safe guidance for us.

1. Why is it that God's thoughts and ways are uplifting to us, and what makes his Word true knowledge and safe guidance for us?

² The righteous new world is immediately before us. Jehovah God will be its Creator. So it will be according to his thoughts and will operate according to his will and ways. It is therefore high time for us to find out what God's true thoughts are and what his ways are. Only by taking this course shall we be able to begin living for the new world, preparing to live in it. True, that will mean a revolution in our lives, that is, if we have been living our lives in harmony with the religions, the philosophies and the manners of this world. But to escape destruction in the oncoming war of Armageddon we simply have to make such a thoroughgoing change in our lives now. Such a life transformation must begin with our minds. The apostle Paul makes this point sharp and clear when he says to Christians living amid this worldly system of things: "Quit being fashioned after this system of things, but be transformed by making your mind over, that you may prove to yourselves the good and acceptable and complete will of God." Paul appeals to the mercies or compassions which God has shown as an inducement for us to undertake this life transformation.—Romans 12:1, 2, *NW*.

³ Our brain is a marvelous creation of God. Just how it functions excites the wonder and admiration of even materialistic scientists of this world. In giving us brains our Creator endowed us with mind. The mind is a most vital part of our makeup, for with it our thought originates. It is that

---

2. What will living now for the new world mean in our lives, why is it imperative, and with what part of us does it begin?

3. What is mind, and what will result from conforming the law of our mind to this world?

faculty of our consciousness with which we assemble information, then exercise reason and reach conclusions which we think are justified. You can establish a rule of action or law for your mind. It is advisable to establish a good rule for mental health, for the mind operates according to a mental rule. If you turn your mind to evil, it will follow that rule of operation in the evil direction and will move ever farther that way. Not only do your inborn sinful tendencies incline your mind to evil, but the world or system of things about you tends to make your mind gravitate toward base things. More than that, the "god of this system of things", Satan the Devil, together with all his invisible demons, tries to cast an unseen power over us and to control our ways of thinking, so as to debase them and turn them away from the "God of truth". For this reason you can never change this world over to a good one, but it can change you according to its likeness if you let it. To be conformed to this world means your at last being destroyed, and that shortly. Almighty God will not change this world but shortly will destroy it and all who conform to it.

[4] Our Creator, who constructed our intricate brain and gifted us with mind, understands its mechanism and operation better than any college psychologist or psychoanalyst of this so-called "brain age". Instantly he detects any bent of man's mind and knows what it will surely lead to. So he encourages good leanings and warns us of the fatal consequences that follow an evil bent. He can best help us make our minds over so as to

4. Why and how can God best help us to make our minds over so as to transform our lives in expectation of the new world?

transform our lives in expectation of the approaching new world. How? Why, by giving us his Holy Word in writing; by giving us his spirit or active force to make that Word clear to us; and by providing us his theocratic organization, his "faithful and discreet slave", to help us to understand that Word. As the mind is that faculty of our consciousness with which we gather information, then for us to be transformed with the new world in view we cannot afford to submit ourselves to the psychologists and philosophers of this world. We cannot afford to let them determine our thinking for us. We must gather information from a source higher, purer, more enduring than this world, namely, from God through his Word, for he is the Creator of the everlasting new world of righteousness.

⁵ In his sacred Word God discloses to us what his ways and thoughts are. His Word makes known to us the glorious purpose which he has formed for his creatures here on earth. By his Word he informs us what his will toward us is that we may harmonize our lives with it and gain his approval. So it is by means of his Word that we get acquainted with him. By it we learn to love and adore him, yes, learn to want to do his will. His Word is no dead letter. It is highly charged with power to alter our personality and our lives for true righteousness. Those who let his Word have sway in their minds know the truth of what Paul said: "The word of God is alive and exerts power and is sharper than any two-edged sword and pierces even to the dividing of the soul and spirit, and of the joints and their marrow, and

---

5. By his Word what does God disclose to us, and why is his Word no dead letter?

is able to discern the thoughts and intentions of the heart." (Hebrews 4:12, *NW*) It probes into us and shows us just what sinners we are. It also proves itself true in the light of prophecies fulfilled in the past and prophecies now fulfilling. So God's Word carries conviction to us.

6 With God's Word in our heads, we have a new force to dictate the law of our mind and to correct our thinking and our way of life. We now see how futile all the plans and schemes of this world are and that they are faced with absolute frustration, and how empty all its philosophies, ways and glory are. We no longer care to conform to this world and its false god. No, we want to be Christlike in personality. This is as it should be, according to Paul's words: "You should put away the old personality which conforms to your former course of conduct and which is being corrupted according to his deceptive desires; but . . . you should be made new in the force actuating your mind, and should put on the new personality which was created according to God's will in true righteousness and lovingkindness." (Ephesians 4:22-24, *NW*) Because it is created according to God's Word and by the power of his Word and spirit, our new personality is indeed created according to God's will.

7 We cannot afford to relapse and fall back into imitating this world and submitting ourselves to its false, unrighteous standards. With each fresh revelation of God's truth and purpose, our lives must undergo further transformation in harmony

6. In what way does God's Word in us act as a new mental force, and in what way is personality created according to God's will?

7. How may we avoid a relapse into worldliness, and how may we love God with our whole mind?

with it. By continual, progressive study and practice of God's Word we must train our minds in right ways of thinking. We must view things as God views them. We must arrange our affairs in keeping with his revealed purpose. We must keep our minds fixed on him and his will. Only in that way shall we be able to keep loving him above all. His greatest commandment according to Jesus' estimate is this: "You must love Jehovah your God with your whole heart and with your whole soul and with your whole mind. This is the greatest and first commandment." (Matthew 22:37, 38, *NW*) Ah, yes, love Jehovah the true God with our whole mind. But we cannot do this if we let this wicked world which God condemns to destruction shape our minds and fill us with its ideas and aims. We must gather God's thoughts from his Word and lovingly meditate on these.

[8] When we transform our minds by making them over according to the knowledge we get from the Bible by which God speaks to us, then we prove to ourselves the "good and acceptable and complete will of God". The will of debased, imperfect man falls so short of righteousness, but God's will is only good, perfectly good. It is never best for us to do our own selfish will nor that of any other creature, for such will is not acceptable to God. Only what He has willed is acceptable to him, for his will can never fail or lead to disappointment. It leaves nothing out of consideration. It has provided for everything that is necessary to his own rightful vindication and to our eternal salvation. It is therefore a complete will. By doing it we prove we love him. If we do not want to pass away

---

8. What do we thus prove God's will to be, and what does doing it mean for us?

forever with this doomed world, we must prove to ourselves what God's will is and faithfully do it. "The world is passing away and so is its desire, but he that does the will of God remains forever." (1 John 2:17, *NW*) That means life forever.

[9] Why ever look back at the things of this world which is now nearly passed away with any desire for them? Let us look forward with the new mental vision which God's Word gives us. The Bible is the most forward-looking Book in the world. Under its instruction let us plan for life in the righteous new world which it so lovelily describes. With made-over minds trained in God's way of thinking let us fix our desires and hopes upon the things that the new world holds out for us. Let us uphold God's kingdom which will govern that new world through Christ. Let us keep our minds new by talking to others the things we have learned from God's Word and thereby exalt him and his kingdom and thus help those who listen to us toward salvation. Then, whether we die before the universal war of Armageddon or whether we survive it under divine protection; whether we come up in the resurrection of the dead or we live through this old world's complete end, we shall enter into the new world with a mind made over according to God's will and joyfully in tune with the glorious new world. What a grand start that will be of life evermore under a new system of things, and all this because now we studied and learned God's Word and obeyed it that thus we might "let God be found true".

---

9. To what progressive course of thinking and acting are we exhorted, and what grand start in life in the new world will this assure for us?

SUBJECT INDEX

NOTE: Numbers refer to pages; Roman numerals, to paragraphs on the page, independent of the numbering of the paragraphs within each chapter.

A

Ambassadors, 234, II; 236, II; 237, I; 246, I
Armageddon, 143, II; 201, I; 205, I; 208, II; 219, II; 259, I; 260, I; 287, I; 290, I; 305, I; 310, I

B

Baptism, immersion in water, 297, I
  into Christ's body, 300, I
  into name of Father, Son, holy spirit, 297, I
  of Jesus, 37, II; 136, I; 296, II
  symbolizes, 37, II; 296, II-297, II
Bible, Apocrypha no part of; reasons why, 50, II
  basis for faith, 121, I; 158, I; 295, III
  basis of this book, 9, II; 18, II; 67, I; 102, III; 284, III
  endures forever, 17, II
  interpreted by God, 18, II
  no dead letter, 307, I
  preservation of, 51, I; 54, I
  proves men, Devil liars, 11, I; 13, I; 14, II
  "Septuagint" translation of, 50, II; 51, I
  translation of, 51, I; 52, I, II
  true according to Jesus, 13, I-14, II
  true science confirms, 84, II
  truth in, 8, I; 9, II; 14, II; 272, II; 301, I; 307, I
  unchangeableness of families shown by, 84, II
  writing of, 42, I-46, II

C

Christ Jesus, Advocate, 299, II
  anointed as King, 37, I, II; 39, I; 136, I
  ascension of, 34, I; 40, I
  baptized, 37, II; 56, I; 136, I; 296, II
  birth as a man, 35, II; 36, I
  commission of, 130, II
  death on stake, 34, II; 39, I
  exalted, 31, II; 40, II; 118, II
  Executioner, 205, I; 246, III
  Head of the congregation, 104, I; 126, I; 180, I
  Head under Jehovah, 40, II
  Judge, 203, I, III; 204, I; 285, II; 291, II, III
  Mediator, 151, I; 159, I
  names of, 31, I; 33, I
  not equal to God, 32, I; 33, I; 34, II; 40, II; 104, I; 105, I; 110, I
  only-begotten Son, 32, I
  ousts Satan from heaven, 253, II
  prehuman existence of, 31, II; 33, I; 34, I; 40, II; 106, I; 107, I
  Priest, 40, I; 118, II; 190, II, III; 299, II
  resurrection of, 40, I, II; 92, III; 94, I; 110, I; 138, I; 273, II; 275, II

secondary purpose of coming to earth, 38, I
  the ransom, 38, I; 40, I; 71, I; 110, II; 112, I; 114, II; 116, I; 118, II; 121, I; 159, I; 190, II; 191, I
  witnessed to truth, 37, I; 130, II
  Word or Logos, 33, I
Christ's 1,000-year reign, after Satan bound, 179, II
  earthly children during, 163, I
  educational work during, 270, I
  follows Armageddon, 177, III
  preliminaries to, 206, II; 284, II
  the antitypical sabbath, 179, II-180, II
  the judgment day, 284, I; 287, I; 292, II
"Congregation of God," apostles foundation stones, 127, I
  Christ Head of, 104, I; 126, I; 180, I
  Christ Jesus Cornerstone of, 127, I
  commission of, 130, II-132, I
  conflicting claims on, 122, I, II
  defined, 125, I; 130, I
  faithful until death, 129, I; 131, II; 301, I; 302, I, II
  founded on Christ, 125, II
  growth of, 128, I-III
  is heavenly, 128, I; 129, I
  members chosen, placed by God, 128, I
  members preachers, 128, II; 131, I; 132, I; 133, I; 224, I; 230, II; 302, I
  no visible earthly head, 126, I
  number comprising, 130, I; 136, II; 231, I; 279, II; 298, I
  only one true, 125, I
  purpose, responsibility of, 132, I; 133, I
  remnant yet on earth, 129, I; 303, I
  sacrifice human life-rights, 299, I, III
  spirit-begotten, 126, I; 131, I, III; 137, I; 298, II; 299, III
  time of selection of, 298, II
  See Jehovah's Witnesses; Kingdom
Consecration, by holy spirit, 37, II
Covering cherub, 57, I-59, I
  fell, 58, I
  manifested selfishness, 58, II
Creation, Genesis account proved true, 84, II

D

Dead Sea Scroll of Isaiah, 48, II
Dedication, fulfilled, 301, I; 302, II; 303, II
  Jesus made, 38, I; 296, II
  meaning of, 296, I; 297, I
  "other sheep" make, 303, II
  symbolized by baptism, 296, II-297, II
Devil, abyssed, 63, II; 93, I; 179, II; 206, II; 270, I; 287, I
  cause of woe, 62, II; 141, I
  destroyed forever, 58, III; 64, II, III; 94, II; 233, I; 270, I
  existence of; doubted, 63, I
  not created by Jehovah, 26, I; 33, I

311

INDEX TO SCRIPTURES CITED

BIBLE STUDY AIDS

"Let God Be True" Anyone desiring additional copies of this book may obtain them for 50c per copy, postpaid.

"This Means Everlasting Life" A 320-page book on unsectarian education. Read the Scriptural requirements for Christian living today. Postpaid, 50c per copy.

What Has Religion Done for Mankind? The major religions, from the start of human creation down to this very day, are here brought to view and carefully analyzed. It has 352 pages, 50c.

New World Translation of the Christian Greek Scriptures ("New Testament" only) A remarkable translation in modern speech made from the most ancient manuscripts. Has large, clear type, and many helpful study features. Contains 800 pages, $1.50.

For ordering above see addresses on last page.

Chief Office and Official Address of
WATCHTOWER BIBLE AND TRACT SOCIETY
WATCHTOWER BIBLE AND TRACT SOCIETY, INC.
INTERNATIONAL BIBLE STUDENTS ASSOCIATION
is

124 Columbia Heights, Brooklyn 1, New York, U. S. A.

Addresses of Branch offices:

America (U.S.), 117 Adams St., Brooklyn 1, N.Y. ****Australia,** 11 Beresford Road, Strathfield, N.S.W. ****Austria,** Liechtensteinstr. 24, Vienna IX. ****Bahamas,** Box 1247, Nassau, N.P. ****Belgium,** 28 Ave. Gen. Eisenhower, Schaerbeek-Brussels. ****Bolivia,** Casilla No. 1440, La Paz. ****Brazil,** Rua Licínio Cardoso 330, Rio de Janeiro. ****British Guiana,** 50 Brickdam, Georgetown. ****British Honduras,** Box 257, Belize. ****Burma,** P.O. Box 62, Rangoon. ****Canada,** 150 Bridgeland Ave., Toronto 10, Ontario. ****Ceylon,** 35 Beach Rd., Mount Lavinia. ****Chile,** Moneda 1710, Santiago. ****Colombia,** Apartado Nacional 147, Barranquilla. ****Costa Rica,** Apartado 2043, San José. ****Cuba,** Avenida 15 No. 4608, Almendares, Marianao, Havana. ****Cyprus,** Box 196, Famagusta. ****Denmark,** Sondre Fasanvej 54, Copenhagen-Valby. ****Ecuador,** Casilla 4512, Guayaquil. ****Egypt,** Post Box 387, Cairo. ****Eire,** 86 Lindsay Rd., Glasnevin, Dublin. ****El Salvador,** Apartado 401, San Salvador. ****England,** 34 Craven Terrace, London W. 2. ****Ethiopia,** Box 1781, Addis Ababa. ****Fiji,** Box 23, Suva. ****Finland,** Vainamoisenkatu 27, Helsinki. ****France,** 3 Villa Guibert, Paris 16e. ****Germany (Western),** Am Kohlheck, (16) Wiesbaden-Dotzheim. ****Gold Coast, B.W.A.,** Box 760, Accra. ****Greece,** No. 6 Kartali St., Athens 6. ****Guadeloupe,** B.P. 239, Pointe-à-Pitre. ****Guatemala,** 11 Avenida 5-67, Guatemala 1. ****Haiti,** Post Box 185, Port-au-Prince. ****Hawaii,** 1228 Pensacola St., Honolulu 14. ****Honduras,** Apartado 147, Tegucigalpa. ****Hong Kong,** 232 Tai Po Rd., 2d Floor, Kowloon. ****Iceland,** P.O. Box 251, Reykjavik. ****India,** 167 Love Lane, Bombay 27. ****Indonesia,** Postbox 2105, Djakarta. ****Israel,** 44 Herzl St., Haifa. ****Italy,** Via Monte Maloia 32, Monte Sacro, Rome 742. ****Jamaica,** P.O. Box 18, 151 King St., Kingston. ****Japan,** 1 Toyooka-Cho, Shiba-Mita, Minato-Ku, Tokyo. ****Korea,** P.O. Box 7, Sodaemun-ku P.O., Seoul. ****Lebanon,** P.O. Box 1122, Beirut. ****Leeward Islands,** Box 119, St. John's, Antigua, B.W.I. ****Liberia,** P.O Box 171, Monrovia. ****Luxembourg,** rue Antoine Meyer 14, G.D. Luxembourg. ****Mauritius,** 2 Arnaud St., Beau Bassin, Indian Ocean. ****Mexico,** Calzada Melchor Ocampo 71, México 4, D.F. ****Netherlands,** Koningslaan 1, Amsterdam-Z. ****Netherlands West Indies,** Breedestraat 12, Otrabanda, Curaçao. ****Newfoundland, Canada,** 239 Pennywell Rd., St. John's. ****New Zealand,** G.P.O. Box 30, Wellington, C. 1. ****Nicaragua,** Apartado 183, Managua, D.N. ****Nigeria, West Africa,** P.O. Box 194, Yaba, Lagos. ****Northern Rhodesia,** 84 King George Ave., Luanshya. ****Norway,** Inkognitogaten 28 B., Oslo. ****Nyasaland,** Box 83, Blantyre. ****Pakistan,** 8-E Habibullah Rd., Lahore. ****Panama,** Box 274, Ancon, C.Z. ****Paraguay,** Ayolas 394, Asunción. ****Peru,** Pasaje Velarde 165, Lima ****Philippine Republic,** 186 Roosevelt Rd., San Francisco del Monte, Quezon City. ****Puerto Rico,** 704 Calle Lafayette, Pda. 21, Urb. Hip., Santurce 34. ****Sierra Leone,** Box 136, Freetown. ****Singapore 15,** 33 Poole Road. ****South Africa,** Private Bag, P.O. Elandsfontein, Transvaal. ****Southern Rhodesia,** P.O. Box 1462, Salisbury. ****Surinam,** Box 49, Weidestraat 82 B, Paramaribo. ****Sweden,** Jakobsberg. ****Switzerland,** Allmendstrasse 39, Berne 22. ****Thailand,** Box 67, Bangkok. ****Trinidad,** 21 Taylor St., Woodbrook, Port of Spain, B.W.I. ****Uruguay,** Joaquín de Salterain 1264, Montevideo. ****Venezuela,** Avda. Honduras, Quinta Luz, Urb. Las Acacias, Caracas, D.F.